STROKES
OF GENIUS

Books by Thomas Boswell

HOW LIFE IMITATES THE WORLD SERIES

WHY TIME BEGINS ON OPENING DAY

THOMAS BOSWELL

STROKES OF GENIUS

PHOTOGRAPHS BY RICHARD DARCEY

Doubleday

New York London Toronto Sydney Auckland

Published by Doubleday, a division of
Bantam Doubleday Dell Publishing Group, Inc.,
666 Fifth Avenue, New York, New York 10103

Doubleday and the portrayal of an anchor with a dolphin
are trademarks of Doubleday, a division of
Bantam Doubleday Dell Publishing Group, Inc.

Articles and photographs appearing herein have previously appeared in the Washington *Post* and
Golf Magazine.

Library of Congress Cataloging-in-Publication Data
Boswell, Thomas, 1948–
Strokes of genius.
1. Golf.   2. Golf—Tournaments.   3. Golfers
I. Title
GV965.B589   1987   796.352′7   86-19697
ISBN: 0-385-19968-6

BG

3   5   7   9   10   8   6   4

Fore,
      Russell Taylor Boswell

CONTENTS

INTRODUCTION

Golf may be the last civilized professional sport in America. What other game still embodies so many of the values that first bonded our myth-making minds to sports?

When Jack Nicklaus wins the Masters, with his son for a caddie, we feel far more than just nostalgia; an ache of recognition rises in us for qualities that seem endangered. When Arnold Palmer makes a hole-in-one on the same hole two days in a row—a ten-million-to-one shot—it's not just cranky bile that makes us wonder if they still make 'em like they used to.

Human nature doesn't change much, but institutions do. And institutions affect what the people within them can do and be. Our games are just such defining and delimiting containers. That is why golf, an old vessel that's had the luck to remain intact, seems so valuable now. It's still user-friendly. Our other games aren't rotten, but they've suffered spoilage. The 1980s especially have impinged on the archetypal field of play. Where we once looked for the outlines of eternal themes, we're now more likely to face the temporal topics of a particular period. Players' strike, indeed.

Once we glimpsed man against man, man against his limits, man against aging—a slice of lyric poetry. That still happens, but less frequently. We will always have individuals who are so unique, so peculiar, that they seem immune to the institutions of which they are a part. What is the NBA to Larry Bird? His work—made more powerfully mysterious and serious by its speechlessness—has reference to little but himself. However, such cases are becoming rarer. Too often, where we once had heroes, we've learned to settle for (trash word) stars.

When we want to recall what games used to be at their best, golf is one place we can go. The old Scottish ritual has remained in its age of innocence, while attaining a golden age, too.

Before seeing what golf has, let's look at all it does not have. Plastic grass and domed parks. Owners and unions. Agents and free agents. Strikes and arbitration. Trade and incentive clauses. Bonuses for not being fat and guaranteed multimillion-dollar pay.

Much of what fills sports pages these days golf lacks entirely—proof that addition by subtraction works. Golf has no salaries, just week-to-week checks for performance. Nobody gets fired. Backroom politics don't exist. Billion-dollar lawsuits or court cases are unknown. Boorish manners, tantrums and gamesmanship are replaced by an honor code. One that works.

Like much that's best, golf is trend-resistant. True, it's got few natural fibers or pleats—a small price to pay for order. Golf also has no violence or maiming injury. No painkillers, blood doping or steroids. No fixes, recruiting scandals, mobsters or point spreads. No crowd riots, suicides or overdoses. Not even one drug bust. No wonder golf is never on "Nightline." Golf doesn't even have retirement or sob stories about destitute old-timers. You can play the Senior Tour. In a cart.

Tom Watson explains that golf's TV ratings are modest because "We have almost no controversy. Maybe I should get in a fistfight with Jack Nicklaus on the eighteenth green." Nicklaus is not upset at all by golf's lack of mass market success. "Golf is just golf. It doesn't appeal to everybody. So what?"

That "So what?" runs deep in the game and does it great credit. Golf grew as an aristocratic pastime; now, while it's come within Everyman's budget (and is cheap, next to skiing or boating), it has kept its elitist code of conduct. Fore on the tee. You're away. Quiet, please. Penalize yourself. Tend the flag. Repair ball marks. Rake the trap. Rub of the green. Things you'd certainly never want to teach children.

Golf has always been limited—and will always be protected—by the fact that it is more a game of head and heart than of guts and muscles. Golf tales at the nineteenth hole rival golf shots on the other eighteen. The sport's best medium is not television, radio or the eye. Even more than baseball, it's the sport of words.

No American game is so rigorous in weeding out its audience. Its charm is technical, intellectual and aesthetic as much as athletic. Three focuses hold our attention—the course, the player and the game itself. That is all. No teams, leagues, trades or playoffs. Even head-to-head match play—an impure, slightly sensationalized version of the medal game—is rarely seen. Golfers find it a bit tacky that a poor shot, once played, should ever be forgotten.

Golf is deliberately exclusive, in that it appeals most to those who

Arnold Palmer inspired a generation of golfers.

play it (even poorly) and love it. Only those who know the devilish un-
naturalness of the thing, the way it deceives, torments and misrepresents
—proceeding by paradox—are allowed full pleasure as fans. Golfers aren't
bonded. They're soldered. Know a man as you know him in a sand trap
and you know him pretty cold. Who would be so shallow as to talk much
about anything other than golf while on the course? No group of fans
understand the pros in their favorite sport half so well as golfers know
their Normans and Peetes. The players respect it, too. Outside every gallery rope, there are people who understand the sand game better than
Nicklaus (who has never mastered it). And he knows it.

Conversely, golf fans appreciate and respect their heroes in greater
depth and at more levels than other fans. The gap between the Open
champion and the bogey shooter is tiny compared to the chasm between
the World Series MVP and the Sunday softball player. So most fans sense
that to play competitive golf, you cannot be drastically out of kilter, either
emotionally, athletically, technically or karmically. You must be determined, yet resigned. You must have practiced to the nth degree, yet never
try to guide the ball overmuch or "make things happen." You can create a
par, but a birdie must fall upon you. If you don't master technique, you
will never understand or correct flaws. But if you do not have faith in
subconscious gyroscopes beyond any control, you will never discover the
radar of a master.

It's no accident that the trends that have attacked other sports in the
last twenty years, demolishing much of our sense of innocence and escape,
have missed golf. That's because the game is an hermetically sealed world
of devotees who cherish and understand their sport—and, thus, defend it.
Or, rather, refuse to tolerate damage.

Arnold Palmer popularized golf in the fifties and sixties. But he did
not make it gross. The converts to the game, even Arnie's Army, became,
in some sense, golfers. They liked his hairy forearms and the way he
walked, but they came to accept the values of his game, too.

Thanks to Palmer, a generation of kids got golf clubs for Christmas.
Twenty years later, the world had more quality golfers than ever before.
Growth was inevitable; important new events—the Tournament Players
Championship, the Memorial and the World Series of Golf—joined the
traditional four majors. The LPGA was established and the Senior Tour
was born. Black golfers moved to the top of the Tours: Calvin Peete, Jim
Thorpe, Lee Elder and Charlie Owens. More would be welcome, but it's
still progress.

Just as the sport has de-emphasized country club snobbishness, it has
also been invigorated by international stars. Gary Player led the way; the

Isao Aoki is one of the foremost members of golf's international brigade.

Graham, Ballesteros, Aoki, Norman and Lyle brigade followed. Now golf is not only one of the few games left for the person of average size, it's also one of the more accessible to all classes and nations.

The game does not care who you are, what you have, who you know, what you look like, what you believe or how you act away from the course. You just have to be able to get the ball in the hole. Nobody cares how, just how many.

In the light of all this, the reader may wonder why golf has something of a reputation for dullness. At risk of too personal a note, let me say that golf is, luckily, somewhat mediaproof. There is little news except the game itself and the game hasn't changed in half a century. No headlines here or prizes. Ambitious reporters seldom touch golf; it's considered a career dead end. When I requested the golf assignment at the Washington *Post* a decade ago, my peers teased me, asking why I didn't just cover duckpin bowling and waste my time entirely. My choice was tolerated as a quirk in an otherwise sane fellow.

Golf gets cursory coverage. Any baseball writer in any season spends more time talking to players than most golf writers do in a career. Basically, pro golfers come off as "clones" because the media does not have a clue who they are. All strangers are dull.

In the last seventeen years, I've covered almost every sport going. Super Bowls, World Series, Olympics, Wimbledon, the Indy 500, NBA and NHL, the Orange and Rose Bowls, the Final Four and everything else down to 5 A.M. bike races, riflery in a swamp at the Pan-Am games and boomerang contests around the Washington Monument. From baseball in Havana to cricket test matches in London to World Cup soccer in Montreal to Shoemaker in the jocks room at Santa Anita, I've been exposed to just about every dog-and-pony show in sports. I kind of liked a high-stakes, back-room invitation-only shootout at Weenie Beenie's Pool Hall with King James Rempe and Machine Gun Butera playing one-pocket for their own cash at 3 A.M.

All these sports and athletes have their points and their personalities. But, as a group, I'd rather talk to pro golfers than any of them, except maybe baseball players. Write me off as hopeless.

There was one other reason I wanted to write about golf: to catch Jack Nicklaus's act before it was too late. He may be the greatest world athlete of the last quarter century; at the least, he's the person in sport most worthy of study if the subject that fascinates you most is the source of excellence.

To be plainspoken, Nicklaus is a hero. He tests himself in opposition not to any one man, but to everyone in his game simultaneously. He

---

Jack Nicklaus—perhaps the greatest world athlete of the past quarter century.

measures himself by only one standard—the attempt to be the best golfer who has ever lived and the best who ever will live. He confronts his own limits and flaws with less desire to blink or turn away than any man I've ever met. Only reality interests him, not self-delusion. When thwarted by bad luck or injury, poor performance or better foes, he suffers, accepts, regroups and then relentlessly returns.

By craft and canniness, he has discovered a succession of temporary stays against age and self-doubt—almost against mortality itself. And, repeatedly, he has prevailed. With dignity. With easy good grace. With many of those qualities that seem to lose their substance unless some special person can live them out, embody them on his own terms.

In this era, golf and golfers have really measured themselves against only one yardstick: What would Nicklaus think?

That, as much as anything, is why golf has remained a civilizing game.

THE
OLDEN BEAR

Jacksonville, Fla., March 21, 1979–Eleven days ago at the Inverrary golf tournament, Jack Nicklaus awoke before dawn. By first light, he hit warmup balls. At 8 a.m. that Saturday, he approached the first tee and saw before him a dewy, untouched fairway. This is the PGA world the way the humble see it. The golfers with the tournament's worst score tee off first. Leaders go last. That morning, a dozen of Nicklaus's fellow pros were waiting for him at the first tee—smirking. A red ribbon was stretched across the fairway. As he stepped up, Nicklaus was handed a pair of ceremonial scissors. No one could remember the last time Sir Jack had been the ignominious "dew sweeper"—the first player on the course. Nicklaus smiled between gritted teeth and snipped.

But last Saturday at the Doral Open, Nicklaus was not smiling. Once more, he had set the alarm for 6 a.m. to be the first player on the course. No ribbon and scissors awaited him. Only silence and considerable elbow room. Everyone knows that the Golden Bear likes to sleep. On the eighteenth hole that day, Nicklaus plunked his approach in the Blue Monster lake and took double bogey for 75. Next day, same thing. Nicklaus smashed his offending club into the ground, flipped it at his caddie and stalked off the course. For the tenth consecutive round, Nicklaus had failed to break par. For the worst of pros, that's a slump. For Nicklaus, it's a disaster.

As usual, Nicklaus's worst enemy is his own past performance. Others play against the course or the field. Nicklaus has a tougher opponent: his own ghost. Last year at this moment, Nicklaus was in the midst of the most flamboyant Florida rampage of his career. At Inverrary, he birdied the last five holes—including two chip-ins—to win by a shot. At Doral, he closed with another 65—including eagles on wedge shots of fifty-six and

His eagle eyes and confident smile embody the charisma of Jack Nicklaus—and the game of golf.

fifty-seven yards—to grab second place. When Nicklaus won his third Tournament Players Championship, he had finished second, first, second, first in four straight events. A tough act to follow. "I'll be the last one to fool myself about my own game," says Nicklaus now. "That's what's confusing. I think I'm hitting the ball solidly and, believe it or not, I'm even rolling [putting] the ball solidly. I just can't get anything to go into the hole."

When bad feels like good, that can mean two things. Either good is just around the corner, or there aren't any more corners.

MIAMI, March 15, 1980–Grumblings that have mounted like an ugly thunderstorm the past two years still continue—mutterings that coincided exactly with the Nicklaus Slump. "Pro golf is dull," charges old Tommy Bolt. "It's a chorus line of blond towheads you can't even tell apart."

Amid the PGA's firestorm of flack about drab stars, poor TV ratings and general creeping malaise, Nicklaus has unequivocally announced an imminent comeback. "I'm sick of playing lousy. I've just been going through the motions for two years," says Nicklaus, seventy-first on the money list in 1979 and currently stuck at seventy-first again in 1980. "First, it irritates you, then it really bothers you, until finally you get so damn blasted mad at yourself that you decide to do something about it. I've decided to do something. And I will. Or I'll quit."

Nicklaus has changed his swing, changed his attitude, even changed his practice habits. Who knows to what avail? For years, he's dealt out his enthusiasm in small dollops as though it were honey—playing a minuscule schedule that was tantamount to a thirty-five-week-a-year vacation so that he could avoid the career-shortening nemesis of staleness. The result: He got stale. Now, Nicklaus has taken out the whole honey pot. All the enthusiasm hoarded for so long is being poured out at once in what he obviously feels is Jack's Last Stand—or, perhaps, the first of several last stands.

"I'm fresh. I'm excited. I want to win. I feel like I did when I was a kid," he said. "I realized last month that I haven't been working hard enough at trying to make fundamental improvement. I was just tinkering."

After working with veteran pro Phil Rodgers, Nicklaus has come up with an altered grip, a flatter swing plane and a long-carrying flight pattern that gives him almost Fat Jack distance. Whether it makes an iota of difference is moot. But it's got Nicklaus excited, which, he is convinced, is half the battle.

Is golf's greatest champion whistling in the dark? Is this simply the first symptom of golf's ultimate wearing down of the skills of every player who's ever swung a club? "These are interesting times," says Nicklaus.

"The game is most fun when you are experimenting. One day you're great, the next day scatterload. But you're learning. No, that's not right. I probably have forgotten more about golf than I will ever learn. What you do is remember some of the things you thought you'd never forget."

Nicklaus knows the pitfall that the British call "baffling oneself with science" and that Americans call "paralysis through analysis." "I hope I can start to play golf soon and stop making changes. I'm getting tired of it. It's time to stop thinking, stop talking and start playing.

"For years, I never felt that I needed a short game. Finally, I just decided to do something about it. I'm not as long as I used to be. I need to get up and down from tough spots on the par-fives for my birdies. So I went to Phil. He's the best. For the last couple of weeks, Phil has been staying at my house and we've been practicing in the evenings."

As Leonard Thompson walked off the eighteenth hole of the Blue Monster this afternoon, he saw a line of five red Nicklaus birdies on the leader board. "I think I hear the Bear growling out there," he said with delight. "Jack's been my idol since I was five," interjected Bruce Lietzke. "He's blowing his own horn these days and letting us know he's here. He's worked hard. We've seen more of him. This may not be Jack's Last Stand, but we've been warned."

Obviously, a Nicklaus resurgence—and it is hard to believe that so great a career could end without at least one—cannot come a day too soon to suit the PGA. The Tour is a sitting duck and anybody with an opinion is carrying a shotgun. "Tom Watson's a great golfer, but that's all," cranked Bolt. "Larry Nelson, a nice guy but so absolutely colorless you'd think he'd at least wear some bright clothes. Lon Hinkle, forget it. Ben Crenshaw's Texas drawl is his charisma. Bill Rogers, nothing. Hale Irwin ought to be a banker. Most of these guys don't even drink. Only bullfighting and the waterhole are left as vestigial evidence of what bloody savages men used to be."

Ironically, such outbursts are exactly the sort of intense feeling and candor that the golf tour seldom seems to generate. In most sports, athletes have managers, general managers and owners primed to discipline them for the slightest excursion into honesty. Golfers, by contrast, are autonomous one-man corporations. They don't have to answer to anybody except the golf ball. What other pro sport offers such possibilities for individuality? And what other athletes muzzle themselves so voluntarily? Their problem is not that they are spiritless, meekly obedient sons or country club clones. Rather, golf has ingrained in them a fierce restraint, a low-flame moderation, a constant acceptance of failure that is almost a religious vow. Golf is the humbling game and none know it better than the best.

What is most estimable, yet least appealing, about the Tour was on display here this week when three old Texas buddies—Crenshaw, Thompson and Lietzke—came off the course jubilantly after shooting a trio of 68s that would have, hypothetically, given them a best-ball of 59. "I wish I could have a pairing like this every week," said Lietzke. "We're old friends who are compatible. You start making birdies and it's contagious. We talked about Leonard's little boy and old Texas golfers like Billy Maxwell and Billy Joe Patton. Nobody had to watch what they said or worry about the other guy's feelings. That frame of mind and all the encouragement helps you fight that mean golf course. Just call us the Birdie Brigade—Lenny, Brucey and Benny."

Thompson cringed with embarrassment at what, by some unspoken standard, was too open a show of comradeship. "Why not Huey, Dewey and Louie?" he needled Lietzke. "It's ironic, but golf encourages this sort of atmosphere of everybody pulling for each other," Crenshaw said. "We're all going to try for the rest of our lives to beat the game and we're never going to. We all have our hot streaks and we all have our pitfalls. You have to pull for each other out here and most guys do."

At one level, that speaks well both for the game and its players. But, as Thompson said, "That's not exactly the relationship you find between Mean Joe Greene and Bob Griese." Or, for that matter, between Nicklaus and that world of ordinary golfers whom he has never had the slightest compunction about grinding into dust. Crenshaw, Lietzke and Thompson symbolize the new breed of well-bred, talented, self-deprecating golfers who dominate the Tour. They'd make great friends. But are they the stuff of champions?

Nobody is Nicklaus's protégé, or his buddy. "I couldn't care less who I'm paired with," he said after hearing about the Birdie Brigade. "There's nobody that I've ever played better or worse with, thank goodness. You don't want any factor to be outside your control. What if Arnie's Army had bothered me? What if I'd said, 'Oh geez, I'm paired with Palmer.' I'd never have beaten him. I've never had favorite pairings . . . but there *are* guys that maybe you don't like and you tell yourself, 'I'm not going to let that guy beat me.' "

Is the difference between champion and contender clear enough?

The great mass of pros hope to catch a hot streak, or a favorite course, or a trick-swing thought. They'd just as soon be lucky as great. They need a shoulder to cry on. Golf is a nasty game and they forgive themselves when it wins. Nicklaus allows the game no quarter and gives it no more respect or awe than it deserves. "When you lip out several putts in a row, you should never think that means that you're putting well and that 'your share' are about to start falling. The difference between 'in' and 'almost' is all in here," Nicklaus said, tapping his head. "If you think the game is just a matter of getting it close and letting the law of averages do your work for you, you'll find a different way to miss every time. Your frame of reference must be exactly the width of the cup, not the general vicinity. When you're putting well, the only question is what part of the hole it's going to fall in, not if it's going in."

It's hard to think that this man—trim and youthful at forty—cannot summon himself to the task at least once more. As for the entire state of his sport—the one that is supposed to be in such deep water—Nicklaus puts the matter in perspective with trenchant common sense.

"Golf is just as dull as it ever was or just as exciting, depending on your feeling for the game. Too much is being made of the small fluctuations in TV ratings or whatever. Golf is a nice game, but that's it. It's never been an exciting game to watch on TV. It's not a circus and never will be one. The audience for golf is not going to change significantly. It's always going to be the people who play it, and understand it, and love it.

"You have to have personalities to make the public at large more cognizant of the game, especially now when the public is spoiled. You have all kinds of sports on TV so much that you get tired of them. Your appetite for any game can get worn out. People talk about Tom Watson not having any personality, but he's one hell of a golfer. He's beating all our brains out. If it matters, he's also a nice guy. As for having more stars with personalities, yes, it's important, but it's not critical."

For all these industry-wide problems, Nicklaus has the simplest sort of cure—move your right hand more on top of the club. That is, if the hand in question happens to belong to Nicklaus. At the grimly technical level, Nicklaus thinks that, over a period of years, his right-hand position became too strong. "It was a good idea when I started doing it. But what is good in small doses is bad when it gets big. It's just a bad habit that crept up on me." To compensate for the hook grip, Nicklaus began looping the club a bit at the top, using one error to correct another—absolutely the most common unconscious problem in golf. "Every cure is temporary," said the man who, last year, went without a victory for the first time since joining the Tour in 1962. "But it's nice while it lasts."

Above all Nicklaus's qualities, the most appealing, perhaps, is one the camera never catches. In his personal contact with everybody, from highest to lowest, he is always there—living calmly and intently in the moment. Other stars of other sports seem distracted or self-important or preoccupied. Nicklaus goes slowly, looks everyone quietly in the eye, is fascinated by sizing people up and really talking with them. He has, in reality, the common touch that Palmer projected to a camera.

A friend, talking with Nicklaus today, said, "Gee, Jack, it's good to see Johnny Miller win again. Just like when Gary Player won the Masters at forty-three or Lee Trevino came back after being hit by lightning."

Nicklaus looked the fellow in the eye, a trace of merriment lurking in his face, then grabbed the man by both shoulders. "Yes, it's almost as nice," said Nicklaus, giving the thick-witted fellow a firm shake, "as this year when Nicklaus made his great comeback."

SPRINGFIELD, N.J., June 12, 1980–The U.S. Open began today with the trumpet blast of a hole-in-one by Tom Watson, then built to an evening crescendo as Jack Nicklaus and Tom Weiskopf, amid a drumroll of birdies, equaled the lowest score in Open history with a pair of 63s.

No day in Open annals has ever seen such a sacrilegious deluge of low scores as the blitz that befell rain-softened, defenseless Lower Baltusrol in this windless first round. Both Nicklaus and Weiskopf had superb chances to shoot 62 and break Johnny Miller's mark of 63 set at Oakmont in 1973 as they stepped to the easy 542-yard par-five eighteenth hole. However, Weiskopf drove into woods. Nicklaus appeared to have capped the lowest-scoring major tournament round of his pro career with a proper glory when he had a mere three-foot birdie putt at the eighteenth for sole possession of the Open record. But he missed.

"It's hard to imagine shooting a 63 to start the Open, yet feeling disappointed as you walk off the last green," said Nicklaus. "But that's how I feel. I really wanted that 62 and I thought I had it."

For both Nicklaus and Weiskopf—who have suffered through the worst years of their careers in 1979 and 1980—those explosive seven-under-par rounds were like an eruption of long-pent-up psychic frustration. In a glorious afternoon duel the number one and number four money winners in golf history answered each other with birdie roars from two holes apart. If their cards were combined, the fellows from Ohio State would have had a better-ball score of 57.

Only one day ago, Nicklaus and Weiskopf were so in need of commiseration that they played a Wednesday practice round together to critique each other on the eve of the prestigious tournament. "The only record we were thinking about breaking then was the broken record we've both been hearing for the last couple of years," punned Nicklaus. "Jack and I hadn't played together in two years," said Weiskopf. "I wanted to see for myself what was wrong with the Ohio strongboy." What Weiskopf saw was a Nicklaus ready to break loose. "I never saw him play so well . . . so confident in his procedure of play," said Weiskopf. "I knew he was ready." When Nicklaus arrived at the practice putting green today, Weiskopf had left a terse inspirational message with Nicklaus's caddie: "Tell Jack he's playing well."

Weiskopf already had his own pep talk well in mind. "Tommy Bolt came over and told me two sentences," said Weiskopf. "He said, 'This is the Open, Tom. It's a game of patience.' Can you imagine two calm individuals like Bolt and me talking about patience?" Both Nicklaus and Weis-

Jack's gallery is as intent on his ball's direction as he and one of his caddie sons.

kopf needed patience this afternoon. Weiskopf opened with a bogey, while Nicklaus began with two wild drives and was one-over after two holes. Neither could have guessed what was to follow: eight birdies for each, and a half-dozen near misses apiece.

Nicklaus has been one-upping Weiskopf all their lives. "By the time I got to the thirteenth hole, I was aware of Tom. Angelo said, 'Come on, answer him.' And it seemed like I did every time. Sometimes it helps you hold a round together if you 'play off' another guy's hot round instead of thinking too much about your own. . . .

"The last time I putted this well might have been the last time I was here [winning the 1967 Open with a course record 65]," said a laughing Nicklaus, whose birdies came at holes three, five, six, eleven, twelve, thirteen, fifteen and seventeen on putts of three, thirty-five, ten, twenty, thirteen, one, eight and thirteen feet.

Just hours before one of the great afternoons of his career, Nicklaus had been almost pensive. "I miss the pressure. It's been so long since I was in position to win that there's no pressure on me. I'm just wasting time finishing back in the pack. Once a time is past, it's past. I'll never be 215 pounds, hit it so far or have my hair so short again as I did when I was here in 1967. You can never return. I've lost the sixties and seventies. We all have. I'm not the same. I have to look to the future. I have to see what skills I have now. I have to find out what is in store for Jack Nicklaus in the eighties. I can't look backwards, because that man doesn't exist anymore."

The old Nicklaus was never prouder of himself than the new forty-year-old Nicklaus of today. "To shoot 63 in the Open is somethin' else, but to do it after the way I've played . . . I can't tell you how I feel."

For Weiskopf, too, this day was a sort of redemption. When last seen in a major tournament, he was taking a thirteen on the twelfth hole at the Masters two months ago, then coming back the following day to make a seven on the little par-three. This was a day when he could smile, show his good-time face. "I think my gallery outcheered Jack's." Even in their hour of equal excellence, Nicklaus had the instinctive knack for the competitive edge. "I don't think Tom's gallery outyelled mine," he said with a wink. "Tom was just closer to his than I was."

Nicklaus, back where he is most happy—in the midst of the pressure that he calls fun—laughed at his joke. "Did you recapture some of the old magic today?" he was asked. "Nah," grinned Nicklaus. "That was all new stuff today."

SPRINGFIELD, N.J., June 13, 1980–Children wearing "Jack Is Back" T-shirts climbed onto tree limbs today to glimpse Jack Nicklaus teeing off beneath them. Adults waited where they guessed Nicklaus would pass to pat his shoulder and say, "Welcome back."

To scoreboard watchers and casual idolaters at this 80th U.S. Open, Nicklaus's surge to a two-stroke lead—and a thirty-six-hole Open record of 63–71—134—may have seemed a simple and inevitable return to form by the Golden Bear. What could be more natural than seeing that familiar name atop the list of four mortals who are tied for second place: Lon Hinkle, Mike Reid, Keith Fergus and Isao Aoki?

If Nicklaus now seems in a golden position to become the fourth man to win four Open titles, then it is partly an illusion. Those who followed every Nicklaus step today—watching the flawed man, not the legend—saw a proud champion fighting with every reserve of willpower and experience to keep from self-destructing. Golf is a four-letter word. Both Nicklaus and Weiskopf relearned that lesson today. In the dew this morning, they both came unraveled. Only Nicklaus could reweave his game. By the sixth hole, he led the field by five shots. By the twelfth—after two bogeys and a double bogey—he had fallen into a three-way tie for the lead. But, after a birdie and a spectacular save of par on the two closing par-fives, Nicklaus had put himself back on top. Weiskopf just kept sliding—shooting 75, finishing bogey, bogey, bogey.

Of all the tasks in Nicklaus's career, none may prove tougher for him than managing a steady finish here. His confidence and spirits, seldom higher than they were just a day ago, are teetering once more. In this round, five of his shots hit the hole and spun or hopped out. "I thought one was going to come right back at me," he said. Four other putts "nearly dropped." Nicklaus spent much of his day scowling at noisy airplanes, muttering "Damn" and "Oh God" and staring disbelievingly at the sky after three consecutive tee shots found brutally unlucky lies.

"Today all the putts that I made yesterday stayed on the edge. I had some mid-round problems that could have become very serious. But I salvaged the round. I'm not going to sneeze at 134 in the Open." And then, his nose full of summer pollen, Nicklaus sneezed. "Now, honest"—he laughed—"I didn't do that on purpose."

What Nicklaus knows is that he had a chance to sneeze at the entire field. For the first five holes, he was a magnificent animal of attack, knocking down the pin at the 465-yard first and 438-yard third holes for tap-in birdies that put him nine-under-par. At that juncture, Nicklaus had played a streak of twenty-one holes in ten-under-par. "I had a chance to leave the field behind." "I thought," said partner Aoki, "that Mr. Nicklaus would shoot 65, at that point." But then an airplane passed overhead as Nicklaus hunched over a three-foot par putt. He backed off. He walked around. He lipped it out. He gave a little curse. The charm was broken.

Golf magic deserts a man a bit at a time. First, it is the birdie putts that won't drop, like the inviting uphill fifteen- and ten-footers at the eighth and ninth that Nicklaus dearly wanted but couldn't get. Then, slowly, the metabolism changes. At the eleventh, Nicklaus drove dead right into an oblivion of trees and traps. Stymied, he had to chip back to the fairway and take bogey. At the 193-yard twelfth, Nicklaus's four-iron shot needed to fly six more inches to clear a trap and bounce at the pin. Instead, it buried itself under the front lip. A feeble blast, an ugly too-hot chip out of the fringe and a badly missed ten-foot putt later, Nicklaus had his first double bogey of the Open and his wheels were off.

"Don't blow your cool now, Jack!" wailed a fan. But Nicklaus was in a beauty of a blue funk. At the thirteenth, he tried to hit a high fade and, instead, snap-hooked a drive through a trap into a hideous downhill, side-hill lie that might easily have been unplayable. "I was starting to feel unlucky." By pure good luck, he had a merciful lie and gouged an iron onto the green. But he babied a twenty-five-foot putt and left himself a terrifying ten-foot downhill snake for par. His round had reached the crisis point. "I was disgusted with myself. If I hadn't made that putt to save par, I honestly don't know what I might have shot."

Even for Nicklaus, the game is that dicey. But he made the putt and from there to the clubhouse, he never hit a bad shot. At the 630-yard seventeenth, he clubbed two woods 580 yards, then flipped a wedge to tap-in a length for a birdie to regain the lead alone. Finally, at the eighteenth, bad luck more than bad management conspired to give Nicklaus one last chance to immolate himself. His third shot bounded over the green and under a TV camera. "I was faced with the sort of little soft flip wedge that I never learned how to hit until this year." His perfect touch shot trickled to six inches to save par.

This Open is approaching the point where its central drama may be the internal battle between Nicklaus and himself. "When I stepped to the first tee today, I took out the driver instead of the three-wood. I told myself, 'Be aggressive. You've got a chance to run away and hide from everybody.' Tomorrow when I get to the first tee, I'll have exactly the same opportunity again."

The reason he still has that chance is because on a Friday the thirteenth when he could have cursed his luck and folded, Nicklaus once more decided to determine his own fate.

SPRINGFIELD, N.J., June 14, 1980–The screws of the mind game tightened at the U.S. Open today as Jack Nicklaus stumbled back into a tie for the lead with Japan's Isao Aoki after three rounds of golf's most elegant form of torture. The stage is set for a final Sunday of frayed nerves, and perhaps some tacky gamesmanship, as four others—including Tom Watson—are bunched within two shots of Nicklaus and Aoki's record-setting three-day Open total of six-under-par 204.

"I'd love to have made this a very dull tournament, and I had the chance," said Nicklaus, who shot 70, but held a three-shot lead before playing the easy final six holes in an undistinguished two-over-par. "But, instead, I gave back all the lead I had," said an almost-depressed Nicklaus who three-putted the eighteenth green for a final hangdog par. "If I'd played the last six holes two-under-par, instead of two-over, which isn't an unreasonable expectation, I'd have a four-shot lead."

As a perfect final fillip, Nicklaus and Watson, who will be in the last and next-to-last twosomes, are on the brink of a spat. Seldom have two champions been as hungry for a prize as Nicklaus and Watson are now. Nicklaus wants to join Bobby Jones and Ben Hogan as the only modern players with four Open titles, while Watson is sick to his heart about never winning golf's highest prize. "If Jack won tomorrow, I think he might retire from golf," said Watson. "He's probably thinking about that now. That's why there's probably a lot more pressure on Jack Nicklaus now than there is on Tom Watson." Watson said this with his best Huck Finn nonchalance, but they were irritating words and blatant gamesmanship. "I don't see how Jack could help but think about retiring on such a high note."

"I'll let you know about that on Sunday—if I win," said Nicklaus with a glare. "I'll let Watson know, too." Then, shaking his head, Nicklaus said, "That's a ridiculous thing for him to say. Why would he volunteer that?"

"Was it Watson's place to bring up such a subject at such a time?" Nicklaus was asked. "That's the first thing that crossed my mind," said Nicklaus. "Particularly when I haven't talked to him about it. It's a very strange subject for him to bring up. I have no intention of missing out on this kind of fun as long as I can be in the thick of it. . . . Maybe I have more pressure on me, but maybe it will be easier to win because I've done it before."

Nicklaus himself is not above a bit of one-upmanship when it comes to the fellow with whom he will be paired, the enormously rich, six-foot, thirty-seven-year-old putting wizard Aoki. "Would I be stunned to see Aoki win? Gee, that's a hard question. He hasn't won much outside Japan, has he? Really, the World Match Play in England [1978] is the only thing he's won."

What Aoki can do is score. "He's one of the three best players in the world from inside 100 yards," said Watson. "Maybe the best." "Aoki plays a style with which I am not personally familiar," said a laughing Nicklaus, who has watched the perennial Asian money-winning leader go around in twenty-seven, twenty-three and thirty-one putts. "His putting stroke is so smooth, so utterly confident that I'd expect lightning to strike if he ever three-putted. We've played together all three days and he hasn't even come close to three-putting." Billy Casper's total of only 113 putts in the 1959 Open is the record. Aoki has a mere 81 so far. "I've been counting," said Nicklaus, "but he's watched a few of mine go down, too. He's said, 'Nice putt' to me a few times."

When Aoki is prodded about being matched with a "big name" like Nicklaus, he enlarges his calm, merry eyes and says, "I am big name, too."

Pressure has claimed many. Tom Weiskopf continued his disintegration with a 76 to tack on to his bizarre 63–75 progression. Andy Bean, after missing the cut, was asked for an autograph by a child. Instead, Bean insisted that the boy take his miserable putter as a gift. Already those near the lead have begun their long night of thinking and dreaming—figuring up what an Open crown means. "On Father's Day, I'd like to win the Open for my father, who taught me the game," said Watson. "He's told me to take it easy before this Open and not get too excited for it." Yet, even as he talked about relaxing, Watson, who almost never smokes in public, was sucking on a cigarette.

"The final round of the Open," said Nicklaus, "is not so much a test of golf as a test of judgment."

SPRINGFIELD, N.J., June 15, 1980–At sundown today, the clouds above Watchung Mountain finally burst and shed their rain on Baltusrol Golf Club. That downpour at dusk was like the bursting of an emotional dam that had borne ever more weight here for four days as Jack Nicklaus struggled with himself to win his fourth U.S. Open championship. This Open was a rack straining the nerves and tormenting the sentiments of thousands of Golden Bear fanciers, some of whom hung from trees and howled to the heavens here, pleading with their long-slumping hero to reclaim his golf majesty. Finally, on the final nine holes, Nicklaus released that tension with an explosion of some of the most nearly perfect golf of his unmatched career. With a grand birdie, birdie finale, Nicklaus shot 35–33—68 to set an Open scoring record by three strokes with 63–71–70–68—272.

In any other Open in history, Isao Aoki would have taken first prize with his 68–68–68–70—274. All he got, after four rounds of head-to-head dueling, was second place by two shots over Tom Watson—and what he called "the great lesson of playing with the greatest golfer in history."

At his victory ceremony, Nicklaus was at a befitting loss for words. "I don't know where to start," he told the crowd that now adores him as much as it resisted him when he won the Open from Arnold Palmer when it was last played here in 1967. "If you don't mind, I'm just going to stand here and enjoy this." And he did. Nicklaus stood so still for so long, simply gazing out at the crowd and the mountain in silence with a beatific smile on his face, that the throng spontaneously broke into applause.

Nicklaus was eloquent with more than his silence, with more than his golf clubs. "I have to start with self-doubt. I kept wondering all week when my wheels would come off like they have for the last year and a half," said Nicklaus, who, after driving into the rough at the sixth, seventh and eighth, played flawless golf the last ten holes. "But they never came off. When I needed a crucial putt, or needed to call on myself for a good shot, I did it. And those are the things I have expected from myself for twenty years.

"I've wondered for the last year and a half if I should still be playing this silly game," admitted Nicklaus, who now has eighteen major golf championships. "I wondered if by playing I was being fair to the game, to my family or even to myself. If I wanted to go out with all the dramatics, I'd probably say good-bye to golf today. But I'm not going to retire. Maybe I should, but I don't have that much sense. I'm serious when I say that maybe I should. But I still think this old body has a few more wins in it."

Nicklaus's most bitter disappointment was the haunting notion that he had, in some deep inner sense, lost contact with himself. "You see guys who have been winners who get to the point where they ought to get out of their game. They are the last to know. They make themselves seem pathetic. It hurts to think that that is you."

All around Nicklaus, the young and strong were falling apart. Watson drove wildly off the first tee, made a bogey and never got close to threatening position. In fact, only four players finished this Open under-par—that is to say, fewer than eight shots behind Nicklaus. Only Aoki proved to have the staying power to push Nicklaus until the very end. He was overly modest, saying, "It's finally finished. It's over. . . . On the front nine, I felt the pressure of the U.S. Open. It kind of worked on me. I just wanted to hang on to Nicklaus more than I wanted to win. I never really offered him a challenge."

Only half-true. Aoki did look exhausted early in the round. And he did back out of his third-round tie for the lead with Nicklaus by bogeying four of the first nine holes. His putter, which set an Open record of 112 strokes in seventy-two holes, betrayed him completely in that stretch. He looked woebegone and beaten. After his only three-putt performance of the Open at the second hole, Aoki missed six consecutive makable putts of four to twelve feet on the front nine as Nicklaus took that two-stroke lead. To Aoki's credit, when Nicklaus became inspired on the final nine, so did the Oriental Wizard, turning in an identical card for the back with birdies at ten, seventeen and eighteen.

This Open lacked one moment—one shot—of crunching drama.

However, two situations on the back nine will remain in Nicklaus's mind —once when he resisted the possibility of letting those wheels come off, and once when he rose to a great occasion.

At the tenth, Nicklaus slammed a seven-iron shot a yard from the hole on the 454-yard par-four for a seemingly certain birdie. Aoki was in the fringe with a tough chip. "You know," Nicklaus said to his caddie, "I bet he holes this." Aoki did, for a stunning birdie that cut Nicklaus's lead to one shot. As Nicklaus prepared to putt, a boozy voice from fifty feet away, beyond the circle of the green, bellowed out. "Aaaeeeee, Kami- kaze!"

A Nicklaus fan yelled back, "Jack's the best!"

The anonymous voice cut through the green-side silence again with an obscenity. An even deeper nervous silence fell. Nicklaus badly needed the three-foot birdie putt. His wheels had wobbled at numbers six, seven and eight on those wild drives. Twice he saved par and once took bogey. And he was worried. After the last of the erratic tee balls, he moaned to his caddie, "Angelo, I can't find the fairway." Now, at the tenth, Nicklaus took the putter head back. And just at mid-stroke the idiotic voice cut through the air at full volume, screaming, "Aaaeeeee, Kamikaze!" The voice was that of an American and the face that went with it, too. Likely not an Aoki fan, but another of those Nicklaus haters that this man thought he had left behind with his fat and his short hair and Arnie's Army.

Somehow Nicklaus backed off in mid-putt. The crowd was ready for an impromptu lynching. "That's all right," Nicklaus said firmly to the crowd, putting up his hand in a gesture of peacemaking. But Nicklaus was rattled. As he stepped away, he fumbled his putter to the ground, bent over and muttered to himself, "I guess."

On Friday, when he had a five-shot lead, Nicklaus backed off a three- footer after hearing a helicopter. He missed. His concentration was lost for the rest of the day (three-over thereafter) and his lead evaporated. This time he sank the putt. His lead was two shots. And that's where it stayed all the way to the clubhouse.

"I played as good a nine holes on the back as I ever have in my life. But I didn't think I had won until I made birdie at the seventeenth." At that point Aoki, the specialist at match play, was, in a sense, "closed out" since he trailed by three shots. Aoki then ran home a ten-footer for his birdie at seventeen, and following Nicklaus's birdie on the final hole, tapped in a three-footer there for another. No one will ever know if he could have made those final birdies if the stakes heretofore on the table had not been in Nicklaus's hip pocket.

That final seventy-second hole was a triumphal march for Nicklaus, similar to his walk up the last fairway at St. Andrews in 1978 when he won his only other major since 1975. The crowd's surge was so wild, with shouts of "Jack is back!" and "Take it on home, Jack!" and the like, that few in the crowd of 27,029 noticed that Aoki's sixty-yard wedge into the last green burned the edge of the cup for what would have been an eagle—thereby making Nicklaus's last ten-foot birdie putt a necessity to avoid a tie, rather than a mere touch of dramatic window dressing. "You can believe that I saw it," said Nicklaus.

That final mob scene, alien to golf but totally indigenous to American sports fans when they are moved by a seminal event in a great hero's career, was properly emotional and on the very edge of control. "Isao and I were just trying to get off the last green with our lives. But I'd never complain about that. These were the most vocal galleries I've ever heard and the warmest reception I've ever gotten anywhere." Jack Nicklaus, who has won all his Opens on Father's Day and who now joins premodern Willie Anderson, Bobby Jones and Ben Hogan as the only four-time winners, understated it nicely. "I think that a lot of nongolfers enjoyed what happened today."

July 10, 1980–Within the last month, Bjorn Borg, Jack Nicklaus and Muhammad Ali—each of whom may, in time, be seen as "The Greatest" in the history of his individual sport—have brought themselves again to center stage. Borg says quietly, "I want to be the greatest ever." Ali desperately yells, "I am still the greatest!" And Nicklaus says nothing, certain that others will. These larger-than-life world athletes, all uniquely in sync with the psychic needs of their games, encourage us to rethink their place in the century-long history of their sports. And, since they have so thoroughly dominated their own arenas, to compare them with their only equals: each other.

Beneath all their dissimilarities, this trio has a large link in common. Just a month ago, all three were—in very different ways—on a tightrope. Each knew that what he did in the near future might determine his final place in the pantheon of his sport. Nicklaus told friends all spring how dearly he would love one "great comeback"—a romantic, almost sentimental victory—to crown a career of crushingly efficient wins. Ali, fixated on becoming "quadruple" or "quintuple" heavyweight champion (or whatever it is), thinks he has spotted another overhyped mountebank he can puncture to his greater glory—this time his former sparring partner Larry Holmes. After making a career of seeing the faint heart or the feeble mind behind Sonny Liston's scowl, George Foreman's physique or Leon Spinks's dumb courage, Ali can perhaps be forgiven for smelling easy millions behind Holmes's please-don't-hit-me-in-my-face jab.

Even the young Borg, who now has five consecutive Wimbledon titles, knows he must play with a sense of no-time-to-lose urgency. Tennis history is full of ephemeral short-lived champions whose fall from being world-beaters to also-rans was sudden, total and unexpected. Ashe and Connors all carry a similar message: Once you slip, the climb up the ladder of the "greats" may well be over. In his short reign since 1976 as King Bjorn I, the Swede may have reached, and even passed, the high plateau of Budge and Kramer. Perhaps he is now at the high cold-tree line with Gonzales and Laver, with the peak called Tilden finally in sight. Rank them how you will, one thing is apparent about tennis greats: They each have their well-defined eras, their periods when they define and even change the game, whether it be Kramer's serve-and-volley or Borg's backcourt topspin ground strokes. Tilden won six U.S. championships in a row (1920–25) and two Wimbledons in the same period. Gonzales was pro champion eight years in a row (1954–61). Eat everybody while you can, because the next young fuzzy-ball shark—trained from adolescence just to defeat your style of game—will come soon enough.

So, despite their different ages, Borg, Ali and Nicklaus must all operate on the same assumption: Don't save anything for tomorrow, since there may not be one.

Of the three, Nicklaus has taken the most dramatic and perhaps conclusive step on his quest. His record-setting victory at Baltusrol may have pushed the Nicklaus legend past that of Bobby Jones and Ben Hogan, those other modern four-time Open winners. A mere compilation of wins might not have been enough, sometime in the twenty-first century, to place Nicklaus's tempered power, his middle-brow stability, ahead of Jones's elitist, intellectual, simon-pure-amateur snob appeal. Now, like Hogan after his return from a car wreck in the 1950 Open, Nicklaus seems more human, more appealing, thanks to his new fallibility. Even eighteen major championships spread over four decades, stretching back to the U.S. Amateur of 1959, can use a dash of schmaltz.

Where tennis greatness is usually proven by one sustained stretch of dominance in a player's prime, golf supremacy is a series of intermittent battles and temporary victories over the game itself, rather than a particular foe. The best tennis player of the day wins with far greater frequency than the best golfer. A five-set, four-hour Wimbledon match is a bit like watching two NBA guards play one-on-one to 500 baskets. You're going to see the same "moves" ad infinitum. But you're also going to find out who's better. Golf is far more indeterminate. The accomplishments of Borg and Nicklaus are of similar stature, yet incomparable. Nicklaus couldn't win the U.S. Open five years running, as Borg did at Wimbledon. It's not in the nature of the game. And Borg almost certainly won't win at Wimbledon in three different decades—eighteen years apart—as Nicklaus won the Open in 1962, 1967, 1972 and 1980. That's not in the nature of his game.

Perhaps, to come full circle, that is the source of the morbid fascination of watching Muhammad Ali, so determined to prove that none of the normal standards of sport apply to him. Perhaps a golfer can win the Open in 1962 and 1980, as Nicklaus did. But can a boxer win the heavyweight title in those same years, which is what Ali keeps saying he is going to do? At the Leonard–Duran brawl in Montreal, Ali created the impression that he was a muttering, punch-drunk shell of himself. Few public figures have operated so long, and so lucratively, on the assumption that you can never underestimate the public's taste. Whatever the true state of Ali's mind and motives, he has paid a bitter price in order not to lose the aura that surrounds those few athletes who really can dominate an entire sport.

Today Borg and Nicklaus seem like the finest of champions—poised, self-possessed and cloaked in their latest regal robes. Time, and the public's judgment, will be kind to them. Ali, if he continues to try to trick the public instead of trust their memory of him, may not be so lucky.

SANDWICH, ENGLAND, July 16, 1981–Maybe nobody in sports handles the bad times the way Jack Nicklaus does. That's probably why he has so many good times. Today was one of the worst.

Nicklaus teed off in the British Open, knowing that, the day before, his eighteen-year-old son Steve had been charged with drunk driving after flipping and wrecking the Nicklaus family station wagon while driving on Jack Nicklaus Freeway in Columbus, Ohio. Maybe you don't think that bothers Jack Nicklaus. Maybe you don't think his five children mean more to him than his nineteen major golf championships. And maybe you think it was just a coincidence that today he shot the worst golf score of his twenty years as a pro: an 83.

As Nicklaus walked off the eighteenth at Royal St. George's, the Royal and Ancient press officer asked if he would answer a few questions for the media. "No," snapped Nicklaus. "Ask me about today tomorrow. I don't wanna talk about it 'cause I'll probably say something I'll be sorry for." And Nicklaus shouldered his way into the crowd, just like all the other bores in sport who eat up the fame but can't face the blame. That's when the autograph hounds attacked him, notebooks and papers actually smacking him in the face as he walked to the clubhouse. Instead of being angry, he was thinking. He walked more and more slowly. He signed everything.

Nicklaus's jaw was still clenched, but he started talking, a phrase at a time. "Need another pen, don'tcha?" he asked a kid with a dead pen, making the child's day. The boy shoved a new jacket into Nicklaus's hand. "Jacket, huh?" said Nicklaus. "You really wanna ruin this with my name, huh? A year ago, I'd have been happy to sign this. Now I probably can't even sign my name right."

Finally, Nicklaus got to the clubhouse door, his head still down. What he didn't know was that nearly every person for whom he had signed over the 100-yard walk had continued to follow him, all of them nonplussed at his poise and generosity. As he opened the door to the clubhouse, every scrap of paper signed, the crowd broke into a spontaneous ovation. "You're the greatest," said a middle-aged man. "The rest of 'em don't even know what it's about."

Inside the door, Nicklaus realized he was faced with hounds more aggressive than any autograph seekers: newshounds. "You guys are persistent," he said almost genially to the half-dozen who hadn't taken several "no's" for an answer.

As Nicklaus walked toward the locker room, he looked over his shoulder at his entourage of pests and said, with a sudden snicker, "Oh come on." Jack Nicklaus, you see, always talks. About everything.

Nicklaus sardonically went through his round—shot by shot—just as though it had been the 63 he shot in the U.S. Open the year before. Even so, Nicklaus knew the question that wasn't being asked but would be. Nicklaus could have ducked the issue of having a son charged with drunk driving on the road that his hometown named for him. It's tough enough being famous, or being the son of someone famous, without having your family life lived in public. But Nicklaus doesn't think that way. He thinks you just face things and take your chances.

"No, Steve's accident had nothing to do with today," said Nicklaus. (You thought maybe he'd blame his own child for shooting a bad score?) "He just fell asleep [at the wheel]," said Nicklaus. His face broke into a little smile as he added, "He had a couple of beers and then fell asleep. . . .

"Yes, I talked to him last night. . . . He just has a scratch on his leg. . . . He was lucky no one was with him and he didn't hit anybody else. The car was totaled but he's fine."

Nicklaus paused. He didn't want to take it too lightly. Those who know Nicklaus best say that nothing makes him blow his composure and get upset like the scrapes his active and sometimes mischievous children get into. "I don't really get enthusiastic about something like this happening," said Nicklaus, twisting the words so it was clear that Father had been extremely unhappy and had said so. "But Steve's no different than any other college kid. He took his date home. He was tired. And he fell asleep. . . . Yeah, on my road."

Nicklaus let out a little snort of chagrined laughter at that. You can't get around him. You can't make him strike a false note. The man just doesn't have it in him to be a fraud. When Steve Nicklaus goes to Florida State as a freshman this fall on a full football scholarship as a flanker, there won't be a prouder father in the stands than Jack Nicklaus.

The power in those legs, arms and eyes seems perfectly harmonized.

Nicklaus sat back and stretched, scratching the sand trap sand from his hair. "I don't know what's wrong with me," he said. "Nothing more than has been wrong all year. Yeah, I've still got that diarrhea [now in its fifth month]. But that's nothing that should affect my game. . . . Today I shouldn't even have turned in a card. It would have helped my stroke average. . . . That about it, guys?" asked Nicklaus. "I didn't mean to avoid you. Sometimes I need three or four minutes to get hold of myself."

It's true that Nicklaus is so intelligent that he is capable of considerable calculation. He can manage the media as he must manage many people in his life. But it is also true that he is one of those men who carries with him an inalienable sense of due north on his personal compass. For Nicklaus, it only takes a quick three- or four-minute check to get himself aligned.

Nicklaus walked to his car and prepared to drive away. Before he left, however, one more person needed to be cheered up. Nicklaus slapped his caddie on the back. "Okay, pal," he said to the old Scotsman, "see you tomorrow."

• • •

The next day, Nicklaus shot 66.

He eventually came back from last place to finish tenth in the 1981 British Open.

• • •

MIAMI, March 1985–Little by little, greatness drips away from them all. But nobody, none of the kings and princes of our games, clings to his glory with the tenacity, the style and the gracefully loosening grip of Jack Nicklaus. Whatever it is that youth possesses and middle age has lost has been taken from him by now. Whatever time could steal is gone. Yet he's still here. The Golden Bear's gone forever, but the Olden Bear's still around. And, to both his and our delighted surprise, he might be around a long time.

Yes, the golf season can begin again. The first Bear of spring's been sighted; the Franchise is back. For the sixth straight year, Nicklaus—now forty-five—has used the Florida chunk of the PGA Tour to reassert himself. On Sunday at Doral's Blue Monster, Nicklaus's name was atop the leader board for hours. He finished third and could have won with more luck. Since 1980, we've welcomed Nicklaus back each season like a staggering warrior who's on his last legs. Yet, every year he's finished between twelfth and sixteenth on the money list, had a marvelous Vardon stroke average and been a contender in most of the major championships. Maybe it's time to reassess.

Just because Arnold Palmer only won one Tour title after age forty-one doesn't mean Nicklaus must pack his cue, too. Palmer never cracked the top twenty-five in money after forty-one; Nicklaus hasn't been worse than sixteenth since turning forty. From 1962 through 1978, Nicklaus had seventeen uniformly great seasons; in 1979, he hit the wall and faced jock mid-life. The magnitude of the adjustment he has made—in every corner of his game—still is coming into focus. His next level of athletic erosion probably is five years away, or, who knows, maybe ten, if he stays as fit as Sam Snead. The magic's gone, but the craft and competitiveness remain. Is it possible this Olden Bear, perhaps winning a tournament a year and finishing on the top ten leader board every other time he tees it up, will stick around as long as the Golden Bear? Will we see a Masters win in 1988 and an Open title past age fifty? Don't laugh. All Nicklaus has left to prove is that he's the best old athlete ever. And he's working on it. At forty-four, he won his own prestigious Memorial Tournament and was second in stroke average on Tour despite playing the toughest courses.

Lest we romanticize, let's emphasize that Nicklaus can't hit overdrive on command any more. Sputterings down the stretch are his norm now. Luck and circumstance must attend him. Which, of course, makes him all the more beloved. Nicklaus is color-blind, nearsighted and has legs of different lengths. His back can lock up at times and a virus once dogged him a whole season. His course building and the rest of his mammoth business empire might sap him. Despite this, if any athlete is entitled to wishes for longevity, it's Nicklaus. He defines and protects what is best in his sport, and in sportsmanship. If golf has the most gentlemanly tone of any game and the highest level of intelligence among its stars, doesn't some credit go to Nicklaus? When Fuzzy Zoeller waved his towel to Greg Norman at the 1984 Open, and Norman waved back the next day, wasn't there some of Nicklaus's generosity to Tom Watson (and others) in the gesture?

Nothing in golf—and not much in sports—approaches the excitement that's sparked when Nicklaus gathers his game and his glare one more time. When the wind blows or the rough is high or the greens are so bumpy that nobody can make anything—when the game of golf comes down to ball-striking and shot-making, experience and composure, ball management and self-management, Nicklaus can still win.

Fortunately, Nicklaus brings far more with him than victory. With the sports pages full of stars in detox centers and coaches throwing chairs, he seems to show that—damn it—somebody can do it all. Be the greatest player his game ever saw. Start out as a pharmacist's son and build an empire worth hundreds of millions of dollars. Stay married to one good woman and raise a bunch of devilish but decent kids. Lose forty pounds after age thirty, keep it off and discover, to his amusement, that he was more movie star than fatso. Find a way to fade out of his game so gradually that the long, slow going becomes as much a pleasure as the years at the peak. And, above all, *be there.* Be just another man who looks you in the eye, remembers everybody's name, enjoys a joke and puts his foot up after he's lost, sticks a pen behind his ear and says, "Had enough of me yet? I don't even know what to call myself anymore."

No, we haven't had enough of him yet. And he shouldn't worry about what we'll call him. He's still the original Jack Nicklaus and probably will be for longer than we ever dreamed.

AUGUSTA, GA., April 13, 1986–As Jack Nicklaus walked up the eighteenth fairway this evening, the sun was going down on Augusta National Golf Club, just as it is surely going down on Nicklaus's career. The slanting light through the Georgia pine woods lit up his yellow shirt and his receding blond hair. As he and his twenty-four-year-old son Jack Jr., his caddie, approached the green, Nicklaus slowly raised his left hand, then his right, his left and his right again, to acknowledge the waves of joyous ovation rolling from the crowd. In tens of thousands of minds, a camera shutter was clicking. This, among all the photos in the Nicklaus family album of our minds, would be the frontispiece.

First, he was Ohio Fats, then the Golden Bear and now—finally, most unexpectedly, most sweetly of all—he is the Olden Bear, glorious one last time, walking off the final green into legend with his son's arm around him.

Jack Nicklaus won the Masters today.

• For the sixth time. The others were 1963, 1965, 1966, 1972 and 1975.

• For his twentieth major title.

• With a final round of seven-under-par 65 that culminated a week of relentless recovery from the rear: 74–71–69–65—279.

• With a back nine score on Sunday of 30, tying the course record.

• With six birdies and an eagle on the last ten holes. "That was as fine a round as I've ever played, especially the last ten holes," Nicklaus said.

He won by one desperate, slender stroke over Greg Norman (70), who bogeyed the final hole to fall out of a tie, and Tom Kite (68), who'd already missed a ten-foot birdie putt on the last hole that would have forced a playoff.

Nicklaus, forty-six, who first competed here in 1959, won by coming from ninth place, four strokes behind to start the day. In fifty Masters

Jack and his son like what they see.

since 1934, only one last-day charge is in the same class—Gary Player's 64 in 1978 to erase seven shots of handicap.

For glorious spice, Nicklaus won by storming past almost every famous young golfer of this period: not only Norman and Kite, but Seve Ballesteros (70—281, fourth), Tom Watson (71) and defending champion Bernhard Langer (75). They all started ahead of him by two, three or four shots. Except for Norman, who birdied the fourteenth, fifteenth, sixteenth and seventeenth holes, all these stars faded while Nicklaus rolled through the Amen Corner and the bud-swept banks of Rae's Creek like a demigod.

Nicklaus won with 300-yard drives such as the one that set up an eagle at the fifteenth hole. A winter fat attack—he weighs 190—accidentally "got me hitting the ball an awful long way." He won with cover-the-flag iron shots that his eyes were too weak to see land. "I'm missing the pleasure of seeing my ball finish." You can bet he'll enjoy the replays of the five-iron fade he hit at the sixteenth hole. On the heels of his eagle at fifteen, the ball trickled past the cup—missing a hole-in-one by perhaps an inch—and stopped a yard away. Had he followed eagle with ace, the sport of golf might have been discontinued, since no further developments in the game could realistically be expected.

And Nicklaus won with putts that tracked the center of the cup until they disappeared, time after time after time, at the ninth, tenth, eleventh, thirteenth, fifteenth, sixteenth and seventeenth holes. The first three birdies—on three of the hardest consecutive par-fours anywhere—awoke his gallery. The next birdie revived him after a bogey at the twelfth when his par putt hit a spike mark and lipped out. His eagle at fifteen "really got me going." And his birdie at sixteen so unnerved Ballesteros that the leader immediately snap-hooked into Rae's Creek at the fifteenth and unraveled fast. Finally, Nicklaus's birdie at number seventeen put him in front alone and, though Norman caught him briefly, proved to be the final margin of miracle.

His biggest enemy was not his forty-six years, although only one older man—Julius Boros at forty-eight—had ever won a major golf championship. Perhaps no middle-aged man in twentieth-century sport has done anything more remarkable—not Pete Rose or George Blanda or anyone. All week, Nicklaus was in a suppressed fury about countless comments that he should retire; that he would never win again; that, with only two tournament victories and no major titles since 1980, he was deluding himself to stay in the game. Nicklaus even had one of those "Jack Should Quit" newspaper stories pasted on his refrigerator throughout the tournament. "I kept saying to myself, 'Done, washed up, finished.' I was trying to make myself mad, but it didn't really work too well because I thought it might be true."

His biggest enemies were not that roused and ravenous Great White

Shark from Australia, nor the Small Gray Kite from Texas who hung on like a terrier for yet another Masters disappointment. From the moment that Ballesteros snap-hooked an iron shot into the water to the left of the fifteenth—making bogey to fall back to eight-under-par, rather than getting a birdie to reach ten-under—Nicklaus was at the top of the leader board, sometimes tied, but never again headed.

Nicklaus's biggest problem was a surprise even to him. It was the tears in his eyes. From the fourteenth hole on, the vast crowds would not stop their worship, and "four or five times" he started to cry and had to lecture himself, "We have to play golf. This isn't over. . . . I was so pumped up by the crowds that all I knew was, I was hittin' it on the greens and makin' birdies and I was goin' to keep doin' it. . . .

"What I really don't understand is how I could keep making putts in the state I was in. I was so excited I shouldn't have been able to pull it back at all, much less pull it back like I wanted to. But I did. One perfect stroke after another. When I don't get nervous, I don't make anything. Maybe I've been doing it backwards."

After Nicklaus's fifteen-foot birdie dropped at the seventeenth hole—completing a birdie, birdie, birdie, bogey, birdie, par, eagle, birdie, birdie streak in which he'd cashed putts of ten, twenty-five, twenty, one, eighteen, three and fifteen feet—the crowd knew it was part of perhaps the most exciting and memorable day in the history of the sport. What, since Bobby Jones's Grand Slam in 1930, would come close? Hogan's comeback, perhaps. Nicklaus's own victory in the 1980 U.S. Open at Baltusrol is now just a runner-up on the goose-pimple meter.

"You're the man, Bear," bellowed one good-old-boy who, turning to his neighbors, laughed and said, "And he sure is, ain't he?"

Kite, who has finished in the top six here in nine of the last eleven years, was stunned that his final ten-foot putt at the eighteenth curled around the cup. "How that putt did what it did. . . . At least this time I did everything I could to win. I felt like I lost the tournament the other time [finishing second to Ben Crenshaw in 1984]. . . . This one I almost won." Then Kite murmured, "He was as close to being out of the golf tournament as you can be and still have any chance at all."

Norman was so proud of his four straight birdies to tie Nicklaus that he seemed not to recall his sins. He double-bogeyed the tenth hole—for the second time in the tournament—with two snap-hooks. Far worse, he spun off his four-iron approach to the eighteenth from the center of the fairway when he seemed to have a playoff safely in hand. "When we got to the fourteenth hole, there were only about fifty people left in our gallery," said Norman. "They were all up with Nicklaus. . . . The noise they made today makes the 1984 U.S. Open at Winged Foot feel like playing through a graveyard. . . . I told Nick [Price], 'Let's wake these people up and show them we're still here.' And we did."

By the time Norman had sunk birdie putts of twelve, twenty-five, two and twelve feet to draw even with Nicklaus, the whole tenth fairway was lined ten deep with fans awaiting a playoff. Perhaps they'd forgotten how Norman, on the seventy-second hole of the 1984 Open, had spun off a mid-iron shot and fanned it fifty yards dead right. That time he sank a miraculous forty-foot putt for par to force a playoff with Fuzzy Zoeller. Remember Fuzzy's waving towel? This time, Norman hit the same gruesome fall-back and spin-out atrocity—100 feet wild to the right. But this time he couldn't come close on the final 15-foot par putt.

"I was sitting watching on TV as Norman kept making birdies," said Nicklaus. "So when he came to that last putt, I said, 'Maybe I'll stand up.' I like to win golf tournaments with my clubs, not on other people's mistakes," said Nicklaus, apologetic that he would root against anyone. "But when you're coming to the finish . . . I'm in the December of my career. . . . Well, somebody did something to me at Pebble Beach, as I remember." Norman also remembered Tom Watson's miraculous wedge shot in that 1982 Open that turned almost certain Nicklaus victory into defeat. "Maybe he deserves it after what Watson did to him," said Norman.

For the past ten months, Nicklaus has been in his most serious period of self-doubt. Last summer, his weight down to 170 pounds, he missed the cut in the U.S. and British Opens. He ended the year forty-third on the money list and winless. This spring, in seven events, he was horrid, missing three cuts, withdrawing once, and winning only $4,404. Everywhere the same thought sprang up like a brush fire: "Jack, retire, please."

"I was in Atlanta last week and people kept asking if I'd retire," said Nicklaus. "I told them, 'I'm not going to quit playing when I'm like this.' I've played too well for too long to let a relatively short period of time be the last time I play golf.

"Now, I know you're expecting me to say, 'I retire.' Well, maybe I should quit right now, but I'm not that smart. . . . I've said a hundred times that I'm not as good as I once was. I just want to be *occasionally* as good as I once was. Today I was."

• • •

AUGUSTA, GA., April 13, 1986–Some things cannot possibly happen, because they are both too improbable and too perfect. The U.S. hockey team cannot beat the Russians in the 1980 Olympics. Jack Nicklaus cannot shoot 65 to win the Masters at age forty-six. Nothing else comes immediately to mind.

Other periods have their Louis–Schmeling memories and the like, events that require only shorthand phrases for a total evocation. For those whose frame of reference begins since World War II, few events in sport will command a higher place—for drama, for sentiment and for value—than what Nicklaus accomplished this evening in the 50th Masters. A golden victory for a Golden Bear.

Now we have a new benchmark for ennobling emotion in games. What Nicklaus achieved, deep in the dogwood, goes beyond mere excellence. His superiority at golf was established long ago. This afternoon was special because Nicklaus called on reserves of poise, of strength, of judgment under enormous pressure, which go to the heart of human dignity. When the youngest and strongest of athletes would have given up, five shots behind the leaders with just ten holes to play, Nicklaus said to caddie Jack Jr., "If I'm going to do anything, I better start doing it."

Even rarer than his golf shot-making, Nicklaus brought, as he has always brought, a regal sense of joy in combat that is the core of great sportsmanship. Where others suffer in the creation of their athletic deeds, Nicklaus exudes both utter concentration and complete pleasure. Others say their prayers in Amen Corner, Nicklaus sings hallelujah. "I haven't had this much fun in six years." Nicklaus, the mature adult who knows deferred gratification to the bone, will wait and work years for one long vital day of the purest adrenaline-filled life.

Golf is the game of failure. More than any of our other sports, golf incorporates both the capricious and the cruel. Ted Williams once said to Sam Snead: "Golf's not that hard. The ball doesn't move." "No," replied Snead, "but we have to play our foul balls." In the last six years, during which he has won only two tournaments out of nearly a hundred attempts, Nicklaus has had to play many foul balls. Only those who follow his career meticulously know how many crucial short putts he has missed, how many shots that he once depended upon have failed him, how many chances to win he has kicked away. And only those who know him can have seen the pain of self-inflicted mediocrity. Playing tournament golf without sufficient practice is like walking downstairs in pitch darkness. And finding time for golf is often nearly impossible for the man who Chi Chi Rodriguez said "is a legend in his spare time."

Devoting days to his family and five children has been a joy. "To have your own son with you to share an experience like that is so great for him, so great for me. I have great admiration for him. He's done a wonderful job of handling the burden of my name." Typically, Nicklaus's first phone call this morning was from his son Steve, who said, "Whataya think, Pop? 'Bout a 65 wins it?" "That's the number I had in mind," replied the old man. "Then let's go shoot it," said Steve.

Less pleasure to Nicklaus has been the building of a $300-million empire, based on golf course design, club manufacturing, clothing lines and dozens of subsidiary businesses. In the last six months, Nicklaus increased his burdens by becoming his own chief executive officer in the wake of some overseas losses. He put his hands on the machinery every day. But not always on his golf clubs.

To what depths of talent and temperament did Jack Nicklaus reach this warm breeze-swept afternoon on the course that his hero, Bobby Jones, designed? Two weeks ago, he pronounced his game a wreck. One week ago, he said, "I've finally started hitting the ball solidly again." One day ago, he said, "I haven't made a putt all week." Yet, when the moment presented itself, he grasped it, felt its texture, turned it to his advantage, fed off it while others were being devoured. "This is a young man's golf course," he said. "Greens fast as glass. Pins on the knobs. Every putt breaks two feet. It's long and hard to walk. The crowds make for lots of emotion, which drains you."

Nicklaus paused. He had no explanation. Something so improbable and so perfect that it could not possibly happen had actually come to pass. He was the center of it, yet could not fully understand. Brought face-to-face with the mystery of his own personality, he could only fall back on that boyish high-pitched giggle and wry smile.

"Obviously," he said, "I'm just tickled pink."

AUGUSTA, GA., April 14, 1986–So, how on earth *did* Jack Nicklaus win the Masters? The sun has gone down and come up. The tidal waves of purple prose have receded. And the time has come to ask: How does a man go from the worst slump of his life to his greatest victory overnight?

All the talk here about emotion, tears and character is just dandy, but the old man still had to hit the golf ball, didn't he? How could Nicklaus crank out 300-yard drives, nearly hole out iron shots, chip like a demon and make almost every putt he looked at in his 65 on Sunday?

Isn't this the same forty-six-year-old who has had his fellow pros covering their eyes all spring? One week ago, this man was getting clubhouse pity. Even on Saturday night, Tom Kite recalled, "We were talking at dinner and I said I not only thought Jack couldn't win this tournament, I said I didn't think he'd *ever* win another one."

Not much was wrong with the Golden Bear's game. Just his full swing, his short game, his putting, his weight, his attitude and his confidence. So, one by one, in two weeks, he cured them all. That might be tougher than shooting 30 on the final nine holes of Augusta National, which should, henceforward, be known as Jack's Back.

Jack Grout, recovering from heart surgery, was the first comeback catalyst, lecturing Nicklaus, "We're going to solve this [swing] problem." "I was hitting it all over the world, especially with my irons," said Nicklaus. "When I had an eight- or nine-iron, I'd be thinking about birdie and walk off the green with bogey. That's maddening."

Grout found the problem. "I was playing more and more with my hands," said Nicklaus. "When I played well, I was very quiet at the top and very quiet at the finish. I had been too violent with my hands going through the hitting area. . . . You have to play with feel. If you don't, you're wasting your time. When you have to make five or six yards of difference in a club, you have the feel of it." And that old touch started returning.

Once Nicklaus "took his hands out of the swing," he started hitting the ball with full body force. And that was lucky, too, because he had more body—at 190 pounds—than he had allowed himself in years. He had hated that tummy in March, but now it was giving him extra yards. That, in turn, encouraged Nicklaus to think "power"—the style that suits Augusta National so perfectly.

Next, son Jack Jr. came home after some short-game lessons from Chi Chi Rodriguez. "He went from the worst short game I've ever seen to being very, very good," said Nicklaus. "So I had him teach me what Chi Chi had taught him—take the wrists out of the chipping as much as possible. I've chipped beautifully this week."

To try to help stir his competitive nature, Nicklaus asked Jack Jr. to caddie for him in the Masters. "If it wasn't for my kids, I probably wouldn't be playing now. You've got to have a reason for doing things. Last time I won [at the Memorial in 1984], Jackie caddied for me."

Nicklaus started getting a tingle in practice rounds. One night just before the Masters, Nicklaus told his wife Barbara, "I think I found that fellow out there I used to know."

All these factors, however, count for nothing if a golfer can't roll the ball in the hole. As always, Nicklaus approached this problem analytically, having the self-confidence in his own intelligence to dissect and revamp a basic part of his game. Few athletes trust their minds as much as their muscles. Nicklaus trusts his more.

"As I've gotten older, I've fallen into the habit of decelerating the putter head at the moment of impact, instead of accelerating," he said, finding a polite way to say that, as your nerves go, so do your guts. You just can't make yourself *hit* the ball anymore. Instead of railing against one of the facts of life, Nicklaus, the club builder and golf theorist, tried to find a new sort of putter to replace his faithful blade. "I wanted something with the largest possible moment of inertia and the smallest dispersion factor," he said. The man sure has a way with words.

Nicklaus wanted a new critter that looked more like a war club than a putter. Last month he showed off his new putter to Tom Watson, who couldn't contain himself and said, "Looks like you're goin' out to kill something for dinner, Jack."

Gradually, Nicklaus saw putting progress. "I was really rolling the short putts well, though I'm not as good a long putter with this one." He could grind in the six-footers for par, but not the fifteen-footers for birdies.

Each Masters day he hit the ball closer to the hole. Each day he was more frustrated. On Saturday night, Nicklaus said, "If I could make a few putts, I might surprise somebody. Like myself."

Come Sunday, no surprises. Nicklaus immediately missed putts of twenty, eighteen, five, twenty-two and ten feet. By the time he had reached the ninth green, his patience was almost shot.

"What do you see?" Nicklaus asked his caddie son of their ten-foot birdie putt.

"Left edge."

"How about an inch out to the right?" said the disbelieving father.

And they both laughed.

"I figured he saw something I was missing," said Nicklaus, "so we split the difference. We had some fun with it."

And made the putt.

"That got me started."

All the pieces were in sync. Distance, accuracy, touch around the greens and the illusion that no putt was too long to make. The huge crowds took care of providing adrenaline, and twenty-six previous visits to the Masters took care of experience. On his twelve-foot eagle putt at the fifteenth, Nicklaus suddenly remembered he'd had the same exact putt in 1975 and misread it. "It's not what it looks like," he said he told Jackie. Then rolled it in the heart. The noise, trapped back in the woody corner of the course, was so loud it was painful.

With every step, memories came back to Nicklaus. As he stood over the fifteen-foot putt at the seventeenth that might give him his sixth green jacket, Nicklaus told Jackie, "This putt is impossible to read." So he just hit it at the hole. "It wiggled left, wiggled back right and went in the center."

An old coach's insight, a few extra pounds, some chipping lessons from his son, a new goofy-looking putter and a lot of experience at handling pressure in the pines. That, outwardly, is the solution to the riddle.

But there was one more answer. For a quarter of a century, Nicklaus has been distinguished by his ability to accept the fact that golf is an unmasterable game. That knowledge is the key to being a master. Instead of searching for the perfect method, or clinging to what has worked in the past, Nicklaus constantly reworks and remolds his game, enjoying the

Jack and his fans acknowledge each other's constancy.

very same process of perpetual loss and rediscovery that panics and infuri-
ates other players.

Many would like to see Nicklaus retire now in his most heralded
hour. There is, however, a contrary point of view. Isn't it possible that on
Sunday, this master of remastery earned the right to stay on our center
stage—tinkering and persevering and learning about his game—as long as
he chooses?

Cathedral
in the Pines

THE PLACE

I've never been to heaven and, thinkin' back on my life, I probably won't get a chance to go. I guess the Masters is as close as I'm going to get.

Fuzzy Zoeller

AUGUSTA, GA.–Rain spattered torrents on Augusta National this afternoon. It was just as well. These silken April days of Masters preamble are meant for recollection as well as preparation. "You don't come to Augusta to find your game," Gene Sarazen said. "You come here because you've got one." Golfers scampered to the shelter of grill and locker room, veranda and loft. There the young and old of golf spun their tales of what has happened here over the generations—and of those things that almost happened. Masters week is like a stroll through a photo album. A benign atmosphere of unreality embraces everything. Glance anywhere and you will find folks lost in reverie. Under the oaks and bee-clad wisteria, or even reclining under a pine on the course, they seem to drift into a daze.

This place has no present tense. Cathedrals have a similar quality, and the mansions of state. But they don't command 365 acres, nor do they often create such ambience. This is life, buffed and burnished. Even the oldest men, on their canes and last legs, seem quaint, rather than decrepit. Any Masters is every Masters: This is golf's equivalent of suspended animation. Here, nature seems gnarled, yet ever young.

"This is where the golf world gathers—a special place set aside for beauty and springtime. You only see it, and remember it, as it exists in this one most beautiful week of the year," PGA Commissioner Deane Beman says. "Spring was designed like an old set of MacGregor irons—to rejuvenate the soul."

Among professional athletes, perhaps only golfers would be sympathetic to the moments of calm transport that Bobby Jones intended to create here with his eighteen chapels carved out of the Georgia woods. "I get so sentimental and starry-eyed when I get here that I can't play," Ben Crenshaw said, laughing. "Sometimes I wish it all didn't get to me so much."

The Masters defends a carefully arranged illusion of order and civility in a larger world that casually disrespects such things. That, perhaps, is why golfers hold on so tightly to their Augusta memories, as though they were kept in a separate and more exclusive treasure chest of the mind.

"I watched Arnold Palmer win his first Masters in 1958," Beman said. "My brother and I jumped the fence behind the fourth hole and spent the day ducking security guards while we followed him. By the next year, I had been chosen for the U.S. Walker Cup team, drove right up Magnolia Lane as a guest of the club. They said, 'Come right in, Mr. Beman.' And they gave me a room in the Crow's Nest in the cupola above the clubhouse."

The Masters pleases the eye and flatters the ego of the insider while simultaneously teasing the conscience. Few events in sports offer a richer blend of splendor and pretense. For many, the veranda of the Augusta National represents the end of the social rainbow. There, under a live oak draped with Spanish moss, one can see author Alistair Cook trying to work up the courage to introduce himself to Arnie. The throngs here, whether they have inherited their tickets or finagled them, bask in the pure self-satisfaction of being at the Masters. Few rewards match a leisurely, rambling week of sniffing the dogwood, ogling the azaleas, lipping juleps and wandering among the dozen prime vantage points that make this course a unique spectator's heaven.

Nevertheless, always hanging in the background are nagging questions. The shacks along Walton Way near Augusta's downtown, with ragged children and old derelicts in the doorways, are, for many, a condemnation of the pomp along exclusive Magnolia Lane. While silver-haired celebrities sip drinks on the terrace at sundown, an all-black legion stoops to pick up their cigarette butts from the hallowed grass. If Lee Elder needed a crusade to get through the Augusta gates, and if Lee Trevino, the Merry Mex, has felt so uncomfortable here that he has turned down his Masters invitation three times, they are in the minority in more than one sense.

It is far easier to resist the Masters from a distance. At close range the flowers smell sweeter, the golf is richer with risk than at any other course in the world and the pomposities of the club seem like amusing and pathetic anachronisms rather than urgent social dangers. The members in their green jackets are such ludicrous old fuds that it is easy to discount their power. The scent of dogwood in April is an addictive drug, a fantasy potion. Why, you might see anything of a Masters night.

"I'll never forget Sam Snead fishing the night before the tournament in Dwight Eisenhower Pond [on Augusta's adjoining par-three course]," said Dave Stockton, veteran of many Masters. "He caught a ten-pound smallmouth bass, which was close to the world record. Sam couldn't wait to tell everybody. But he also didn't want anybody to know where he caught it, since there might be another one in there even bigger. So Sam sneaks through the trees, not knowing I saw him. Then he breaks into a run and carries the fish right into the Past Champions Dinner. He never changed clothes. And he and that fish never left the formal dinner until there wasn't anybody left to hear the story of how he caught it."

Yes, any Masters is, in the best sense, every Masters. This one week is less a golf tournament than a recurring state of mind, a chance to recapture those moments of peaceful clearsightedness that blossom here under gentle Georgia breezes and spring rains. The Masters bears little relationship to the rest of golf, or, for that matter, to the rest of life. Wisely, it has set itself no higher goal than the annual regeneration of a feast of memories.

THE COURSE

First memories of the Masters tend to blot out all others—even moments of victory, or near victory. "I never wanted to see this course until I could see it as a player," said Andy Bean, reared within driving distance. "I earned my way through those gates." "I start choking as soon as I drive up Magnolia Lane," Gary Player said. To which Lee Trevino retorted, "So do I. But I can never figure out how to stop." "I get too jazzed up," Johnny Miller said, "the first round has killed me for fifteen straight years." Don't doubt it. As a professional in the Masters, Miller has played the first round thirty-nine strokes over-par, while playing the rest of his rounds twelve-under-par. "My putting just can't stand the pressure of the first round. After I miss my first twelve three-footers, I recover from the initial blow. But by then I'm out of the tournament."

Just this sort of Masters coma is at the heart of all Augusta lore. Augusta National was created with one purpose in mind: to mercilessly unravel a psyche under stress. Caprice and almost unbearable ill fortune are built into the course. Once, Byron Nelson hit a near-perfect iron shot

---

Lee Elder was the first black ever to play in the Masters.

into the par-three sixteenth hole, only to see the ball hit the flagstick a foot above the hole and bounce back into the water. "That's nothing," Crenshaw said. "Tony Penna hit that stick two years in a row and both times it trickled all the way back down into the lake."

Over the years, certain holes become personal nemeses to great golfers. "The fourteenth is not a hard hole for anyone except Tom Watson," says Tom Watson. "He always leaves it below the mound in front of the green, then three-putts. When Tom Watson does get it over the mound, then he three-putts from six feet and loses by one shot [in 1978]."

"Everything is designed to mislead you, trick you into making an unwise decision. Then you're twice as mad at yourself. My fondest memory of Augusta is the way old Cliff Roberts met me the first year I arrived and tried to make me feel accepted," said Lee Elder, the first black to break the Masters color line in 1975. "He even followed me around the course once. But it wasn't really Mr. Roberts that I needed. You need the spirit of Bobby Jones beside you on this course."

"Of all the courses in the world," says David Graham, "Augusta National places the most emphasis on strategy and is the best example of what a major is all about. Every shot here offers an option. That's the key. You've always got a safe side of the fairway or the green to aim at, where you know you can find your ball sitting on short grass. But from those safe spots, you are not, by any means, guaranteed par. From the wrong sides of the fairways, you have much tougher approaches and then from the safe sides of the greens, you put enormous pressure on your putter. Caution here is an invitation to make bogeys."

Or, as Andy Bean says, "Put the ball in the preferred positions on these greens and you can be bold. Put it in the 'wrong' spots, where you're going downhill or over knobs, and you're scared to death. As soon as you get to your ball, you know you're out of luck. You're gonna be on that green for a while."

"On almost every shot," Graham explained, "there is also a more dangerous shot available that promises greater rewards. But those shots also invite double bogeys. So every hole can be played cautiously with the probability of making par but the danger of getting jittery and making bogey. Or you can risk real trouble but have a good chance for a birdie."

The problem is not whether to gamble, but where to gamble. And the answer is different for every golfer, depending on the parameters of his game, his nerves and his temperament.

"We play many courses that effectively eliminate thought," Graham snarled. "You have traps on both sides of a flat fairway and traps on all four sides of the green. You step up and aim at the center of an obvious target area every time. You have no options, no room for strategy."

In other words, the game is more a measure of pure athletic ability—

who can hit it straight and long most often. The Tour showcases the depth of raw ability now on the scene, but, in many cases, it is unpolished, untested and rather simplistic talent. The Masters is proud that the average age of its champions is a relatively mature thirty-three—an athletic age that symbolizes the last years of youthful strength and the first years of full maturity, composure and masterly shot-making. "You must accept indifferent shots and expect the intervention of fate in a tournament like this," says prominent teacher Phil Ritson in his thick British accent.

Here, the ability to play the type of shot that the course demands, rather than the one you might prefer, is of paramount importance. The 485-yard tenth hole, the par-four that begins the Amen Corner, is a perfect example. "Gary Player hit an ugly little neck hook down the [proper] left side, and I hit a solid drive down the [improper] right side," relates big-hitter Bean. "Because Gary's ball was on the right line, it rolled fifty extra yards to the flat bottom. I had a 207-yard one-iron from a downhill lie. Player had a 162-yard seven-iron from a level lie. He made birdie. I got bogey."

The problems here, the elaborate tactical discussions, never change. They seem as eternal as the horticulture. And every year, the miseries of golf's hallowed ground are passed along. A rookie asks Watson why he waits so long at the twelfth tee before hitting over Rae's Creek, when his normal pace of play is quick.

"You must wait for the wind, no matter how long," Watson replied. "You decide what shot you'll hit before you get there. Then wait for the [swirling] wind to match the shot. Don't look at the wind, then try to pick your shot. The wind mustn't dictate to you. If you study the flags, the trees, the willows for enough years, you'll learn how to read the wind."

That is the essence of Augusta: reading the winds in the pines, feeling the air on your cheek exactly three seconds before you know it will arrive at Hogan Bridge. Nothing changes. Sarazen has been telling about his double eagle in 1935 since before most of today's pros were born. Like a statue, or an elm in plus-fours, Sarazen, now seventy-eight, stands before the clubhouse, looking out over golf's equivalent of the Elysian Fields. His Homeric retelling of the Masters' greatest story never varies; the embellishments were locked in place decades ago.

"My caddie 'Stovepipe' tried to talk me into hitting a three-wood," Sarazen begins. "But I took out my 'turf-rider' [four-wood] instead. The moment I hit it, I felt something in my bones. Walter Hagen was playing with me and Jones was on the green. Twenty-one people were behind the green. The sun was going down. I wasn't sure it had gone in the hole until I saw all twenty-one people jumping up and down."

To those who arrive here for the first time, no venue in sports could seem so elite, so forbidding, so inhospitable. And for just those reasons, with the passage of years, no place in sports gradually becomes so like a protected home, a fortress that is impregnable to all but those who have proved that they belong.

At most golf tournaments, even major championships, it is almost impossible to sensibly predict the winner. In this, as in most matters, the Masters is different. One of the event's shameless prides is that it does everything possible to help the cream of the sport—the Masters—add another jewel to their crowns. Eighteen times since 1958 the winner has been Jack Nicklaus, Arnold Palmer, Gary Player, Tom Watson or Seve Ballesteros. The kings of golf gather here. This is their joust.

The primary reason is Augusta National itself. The 7,030-yard layout favors long drivers who can draw their tee shots, high-and-soft-iron hitters and slick-green putters with pressure-tested nerves. That does a whole lot of weeding out immediately. Even as great a player as Lee Trevino says, "I'll probably never win here unless they put the pins on the tees and the tees on the greens. Then it would be a fader's course, not a hooker's course. I hit it low and left to right. This course rejects me like a skin transplant."

Also, perhaps no other course rewards experience and longevity as much as Augusta does. Of the four majors, it's the only one on a permanent site. Once a top player has this course wired, he almost never leaves the top five. Palmer ran off a ten-year skein when he finished first, third, first, second, first, ninth, first, second, fourth, fourth. Nicklaus: first, second, first, first, second, first, third, fourth, first, third, second. Watson: first, second, second, twelfth, first, fifth, fourth, second.

"You should play this course better and better the longer you come here," Watson said. "Experience means more here than in any tournament. You should learn some subtlety every round at Augusta."

To this exalted end, no means is too extreme. After years of misclubbing, then stewing in his own juices, Johnny Miller decided it was time to put his mind at ease and appearances be darned. A few Aprils ago, Miller did what he had been daydreaming about for years: He brought a 100-foot tape measure to Augusta and, during his first practice round, measured every inch of the deceiving course. Before Miller had finished nine holes, partner Craig Stadler had stalked off in disgust, leaving Miller to do his boring surveying alone. As the sun set, Miller trudged off the course, exhausted but happy.

"Man, is my right arm tired from winding and unwinding that steel tape," groaned the former U.S. Open champion. "But I finally know the exact distance on every shot. A couple of yards is the difference between a six-foot putt and a twelve-foot putt."

"So, Mr. Miller, how long, for instance, is the twelfth hole?"

"I'm not tellin'," said Miller.

Nowhere else is a man forced to stand in the fairway so long and think so hard about what stick he will wield and how hard he will swing it. Above all, there is no place else where a bad decision is so severely and consistently punished.

"Augusta National is many things, but above all, it's a second-shot placement course—a premier iron golf course," says David Graham. "On most good courses, when you're trying to decide between two clubs, what is at stake is perhaps one shot—if that much," says Deane Beman. "At Augusta, the difference between, say, a six-iron and a seven-iron is often two shots, and sometimes three." John Mahaffey puts in: "Every good course has a couple of holes where everybody talks about the tough decisions to make in club selection. But here, there are thirteen or fourteen holes like that." That's how Jones ensured that his champion would be a thinking gorilla.

"Oh, the two toughest decisions to make out there are definitely the second shots on the two par-fours with the elephants buried in the front of the greens—the fifth and fourteenth," offers Lee Elder. "I don't have the proper shot for either of those holes. On fourteen, I keep hitting a three-iron that hits into the hump, doesn't get to the back tier and I may three-putt. Tonight I'm going to increase the loft on that three-iron to get over that hump. I bet that 25 percent of the players in the field change the loft on some, or all, of their irons to fit the idiosyncracies of this course and the demands of certain holes."

The 205-yard fourth hole, with its voracious front bunker, carries more hidden terror, since fewer players realize that unseen winds, funneling at high altitudes, knock down apparently perfect shots. Few amusements match standing along the fourth tee and watching muscular Masters rookies as they scald their customary 200-yard five-iron, then gape in disbelief as the ball lands short of the front traps, a humiliating fifty yards from the pin.

The most novel approach to club selection in the history of the Masters took place in 1979 when rookie Fuzzy Zoeller won in a playoff. "I never had a thought the whole week," Zoeller related. "I figured my caddie [Jerry Beard] knew the course a lot better than me, so I just put out my hand and played whatever club he put in it. I'd say, 'How hard do I hit it?' He'd tell me and I'd swing. The guys who come down here once a year and try to get smart with Mr. Jones's course are the dumb ones."

Of all Augusta National's tests of nerve and judgment, the most harrowing interlude is the daily passage through Amen Corner. Like all Sirens, the dreadfully beautiful corner has her good days—balmy, breezy afternoons when she lures more Masters wayfarers to their doom than even she could hope. The very leaves seem to rustle with hushed discussions of doom. For half a mile, a tunnel of towering pine, flecked with dogwood, cascades downhill until it spills into an amphitheater of redbud and rhododendron behind Rae's Creek and Hogan Bridge. This Masters meeting place of horticulture and horrors has earned its name because, as Inman says, "As soon as you step to the tenth tee, you start to pray."

Jones conceived of Augusta National as a tamable beast, a dangerous big cat that could claw or purr, depending on how she was stroked. The 485-yard, par-four tenth, the 445-yard, water-guarded eleventh and the demonically treacherous 155-yard twelfth are the crux of the test that Jones considered his monument.

"The tournament is decided at the Corner almost every year," said Inman. "That's where the dramatic swings always seem to be. This is the ultimate psychological course—it demands gambles, then plays with your mind. The Corner is the heart of it. You always come out of there in a dramatically altered frame of mind than when you went in."

One gentle day in 1981, the brash, red-hot Wadkins fired a 32 on the front nine, lowest score of the day. "I never felt so good on the practice tee in my life," said Wadkins. "No words for how good I was hittin' it. After the 32, there's no way I figured I could shoot more than 65. A course record. Well, maybe."

Let's watch Lanny Wadkins get the full treatment. At the tenth, Wadkins's tee ball was long, but right rather than left. His second shot found a trap. Three putts sent him to a double bogey. The wheels were wobbling. At the eleventh, like the rest of humanity, Wadkins stayed right of the menacing pond on the left front that is certain double bogey, since the wedge shot from a drop area is almost impossible. So he missed the green and took bogey. Wadkins at the twelfth tee should have been photographed for posterity. He was a man in a hurry to make an appointment with a car wreck. He couldn't wait to lash angrily at a seven-iron, catch it fat, dump it in Rae's Creek and proceed, like a condemned spirit, to another double bogey. As Wadkins trudged up the thirteenth fairway and out of the Amen Corner's sight, his name and numbers were already being dragged down off the leader board.

"I shot 41 on the back," said Wadkins, "and hit the ball as well as I ever have in my life."

"You can't see all the way back to the thirteenth tee behind the twelfth green," said former U.S. Open champion Ken Venturi. "That's because they got a Delta Airlines counter back there. After you take your triple bogey on the twelfth, you just go back there and say, 'I'd like a one-way ticket back home on Friday night because I just missed the cut.'"

THE PROBLEM

Other golf tournaments require preparation. The Masters demands an elaborate battle plan of psychic self-defense for every minute of every day from the moment a player arrives here. Above all its other cagey weapons, the Masters makes war on the golfer's mind because it is different in every possible detail from all other tournaments in the world. From the moment a player strolls through the tiny, elegant Augusta airport with its exposed-brick walkways amid flower gardens, the golfer—that creature of absolute ritual—is faced with an opulent, yet almost alien transformation of the game he thought was familiar.

The Masters' enormous self-importance is its most fascinating strategic element. Every attempt has been made to make the passing of the green coat seem like the bestowing of a royal robe to end a coronation. Aspirants to that golf throne must not only cope with a 7,000-yard course but with a seven-day ordeal of mounting tension. "If you let it, the Masters will play you, instead of you playing it," says contender Joe Inman. "Augusta National can pamper you right off the bottom of the scoreboard. . . ." Pampered before and after your rounds, but mentally and emotionally pulverized during them—that's the formula.

"When you get on this Augusta course, it's a given fact that you're going to get nailed. The variable is how you accept it," says Inman. "Some players never learn to accept misfortune, especially in the major tournaments. You have to remember that you're not God's only child of misfortune."

Bobby Jones made this aboretum an emotional roller coaster. Half the holes on the course play like par-four-and-a-half. The par-fours are created for bogeys and the par-fives for birdies. "If we had to play Augusta National in one hour, the best athlete would win the Masters," said Inman, laughing. "But as it is, they give us time to hang ourselves. Every swing is a 'thought shot.' So, instead of the best athlete, you end up with the best thinker as the winner.

"The Masters is a perfect example of how the pressure of golf—and the buildup about how important it is—can change you so that you hardly know yourself," said Inman. "If every player out here took a tape recording of himself every year and just talked about what was important to him in his life and what his priorities were, most of us would be shocked when we went back and listened to ourselves."

Inman looked out at the flowering lawns, the chic crowds, the television towers. "I love all of this," he said. "I just wish I were a better player, so that I could be more a part of it. But whenever I see everything that goes on here, it just reminds me that I have only one goal in golf—to leave it with my sanity."

The methods for meeting the Masters are as numberless as they are usually futile. Past Champion Charles Coody goes to bed exactly twelve hours before his tee time—whether that means 9:08 P.M. or 1:40 A.M. Former touring pro Bert Yancey stayed at the home of a family named Masters and built clay scale models of the famous swaybacked Augusta greens so he could learn their "feel."

"I always buy something expensive on Masters week for luck," says Arnold Palmer's wife Winnie.

Like what?

"This year, groceries."

Billy Casper always searched out a Mormon church at which he could give a Sunday morning sermon before trying to win for the glory to the Lord.

By Sunday afternoon, however, the most universal reverence is for the color green, and those shades of the spectrum that go well with it. Nicklaus, for instance, has his ensemble—one that would look suitable with a green blazer—chosen for him by ad executives six months in advance. "They let me pick the socks, but my wife has to do that since I'm color-blind."

"No detail is too small to pay attention to this week," says Inman. "The human mind is the most powerful thing in this world and the scientists say we only use 10 percent of it. Well, I'm sure that's certain in golf. You've got more electrical connections in your head than a whole city. You'll do anything to keep 'em from going blooey on you in the crunch."

Two schools of thought predominate: Treat the thing with the pretense of indifference, or else court the course with infinite attention and special treatment. A growing trend among younger players is to cultivate an air of nonchalance, bordering on disdain. After all, Trevino always has said, "If they renamed it the Hartford Open, everyone would shoot 265. Take away the pressure and all these young bucks would shoot the lights out."

"Bruce Lietzke has a new Trans Am with a 500 engine," Crenshaw once said, snickering. "He says that on Thursday, he's going to do a burnout up Magnolia Lane, go into a full skid and come to a stop at the clubhouse door going backwards. I envy the loose guys like Zoeller and Lietzke."

Crenshaw is more familiar with that sinking, helpless feeling at Augusta. In 1977, going head-to-head with Jack Nicklaus in the final Sunday pairing, Crenshaw watched disaster swallow him. He was a spectator at his own demise. "Whatever I had had for three days just left. I could feel the confidence seeping away—out the wrists. The swing slot was gone, then everything was gone. It was the most silent 76 of my life. To sum it up, I felt quite inadequate."

Players desperately want to bring some extra weaponry to this battle. Any security blanket will do. Ray Floyd's last-second discovery of a pet five-wood helped him shoot a record-tying 271 in 1976. "Whatcha got there?" Ed Sneed teased Ben Crenshaw in the locker room not long ago, eyeing an ancient sand wedge in Crenshaw's hand. "Oh, just something I got in the mail," Crenshaw replied.

Actually, it was a 1957 Wilson wedge that is considered vintage. "See the tiny red arrow on the hozel?" Crenshaw asked with a grin. "That identifies the model. I've been looking for one for years. There are three 'psychological' clubs in your bag, especially for this course. The driver, the putter and the sand wedge. They can make more difference than the rest. You'll see a lot of guys fiddling, trying to find a special club for this week."

When Gene Sarazen played here, after inventing the sand wedge in his workshop in 1932, he carried the new club under his coat, or turned it facedown when other players approached. Unfortunately for so many souls here who are in heavenly torment, such gimmicks and gizmos aren't nearly enough.

THE SOLUTION

The only bruises in golf are to the spirit. The only bones that break are those in the skeleton of the personality. The only blood that flows is from a sort of internal hemorrhaging of self-esteem. Golf tests not so much the muscles as those qualities of stable judgment and emotional courage that reside between the ears. The final round of the Masters, more than any other day in the golfing year, brings this irreducible, unrelenting core of the sport into focus.

The man who is in the lead, on the lead or near the lead on the final day of the first full week in April faces the ultimate punishments, humiliations and pleasures of his game. Whether it's the truth, or the merest jock poppycock, every player here believes that Masters Sunday is not only a test of his golf but a relentless examination of his soul. These men have worked too long, reached too precise and predictable a level of craft to think they're just knocking a ball at a hole in the ground. That they believe it so earnestly, in a sense, makes it so.

"Golf is the 'only-est' sport," said Hale Irwin, twice U.S. Open champion. "You're completely alone with every conceivable opportunity to defeat yourself. Golf brings out your assets and liabilities as a person. The longer you play, the more certain you are that a man's performance is the outward manifestation of who, in his heart, he really thinks he is."

Much of the public talk at any Masters is of strategy. Players exchange their annual monographs on how to achieve the proper confident attitude, or how to escape the Sirens in the Amen Corner, or of the necessity to attack (or be attacked by) a course designed to reward boldness and punish timidity. However, in private moments, they don't talk about the tricky winds that swirl above Rae's Creek nearly as much as they talk about the far more devious winds that blow in their own brains.

"I'm convinced it's all here," said Ben Crenshaw, jabbing his forefingers into his temples. "There's no way to make eighteen consecutive pars here; there's no safe way to play. So the course throws you back on your emotional resources.

"Look at Jack Nicklaus and you know what the final round at Augusta is all about. I think he has more belief in himself, more supreme confidence, than any golfer ever. He thinks he deserves to win and that he's destined to win. So he does win. It's written all over him.

"He can channel his concentration and ignore distractions and annoyances better than anybody who's ever lived."

This game and this course, in particular, were created with humiliation in mind. Yet, those who prosper here are those with such stubborn self-regard that they refuse to be humbled.

What happens to a man when he discovers himself in the lead on Sunday, then self-destructs? The 1978 and 1979 Masters produced two of the most vivid examples in Hubert Green and Ed Sneed, a pair of third-round leaders by three and five shots, respectively. Green, after missing a three-foot putt that would have forced a playoff and saved his dignity, went back out to the eighteenth green at sundown—seventy minutes after his disaster—to stroke his putt again.

"I had to find out if I misread it or mis-hit it."

When it didn't count, Green made it.

"I read it right," the crestfallen Green said. "When the pressure was on, I just didn't hit it straight."

Sneed, who led by three shots with three holes to play, only to finish bogey, bogey, bogey and lose in a playoff, survived a year of the most horrific nightmares. "I blew it. It was mine and I gave it away," Sneed recalled. "After I made birdie at the fifteenth, I thought I had won. Thousands of people started running for the clubhouse like it was all over. I think, subconsciously, that I believed them. I had fought so long to hold it together that something inside me turned off and I couldn't get it started again. That coiled concentration kind of sprung . . . and you can't get it back. I can accept that . . . even learn from it," Sneed said, "but it's been a lot harder on the people around me. It's harder for my wife and the rest of my family to keep answering the questions than it is for me."

In 1979 Craig Stadler erupted in the Amen Corner; on a day when 70 would have netted him a green jacket, he shot 76. Behind the azaleas on the twelfth hole, during a delay in play, Stadler sat down and cried. "Most of us are that way. . . . I'm that way. . . . The game just embarrasses you until you feel inadequate and pathetic," commiserated Crenshaw. "You want to cry like a child."

Stadler's suffering wasn't over. In 1982 he missed a six-foot putt for victory. Such experiences sear the mind for years.

"Half a million dollars would be walkin'-around change compared to what that putt on the eighteenth at the Masters may have cost me," says Hubert Green, recalling 1978.

"The putt I missed at the eighteenth at Augusta? What about the one I missed at the seventeenth? That was even shorter. That's the one that I really remember," says Sneed of 1979.

"Yeess, I remember the expression on my face [in photos] after I missed that putt at eighteen. I'd remember it a lot more if I hadn't won the playoff," muttered Stadler, reliving 1982.

"The two best players I've ever seen at ignoring their own mistakes—and I'm talkin' about some really ugly shots in big pressure spots—are Nicklaus and Watson. They refuse to be embarrassed. In fact, everybody on tour knows that Nicklaus probably hits more unbelievably terrible, almost amateurish shots than any great player who ever lived," says Crenshaw.

"You can talk about strategy all you want, but what really matters is resiliency," Irwin said. "On the last nine holes of the Masters or the Open, there's going to come at least one point when you want to throw yourself in the nearest trash can and disappear. You know you can't hide. It's like you're walking down the fairway naked. The gallery knows what you've done, every other player knows and, worst of all, you know. That's when you find out if you're a competitor."

For young promising players, no gift is more cherished than this mysterious ability to hold the swing, the tempo, the psyche and the soul in one meshed piece when your professional world, your highest dreams, are in peril.

"I watch Nicklaus and I know what his key is. Somehow he feeds off his own emotion, yet also puts himself beyond it," says Peter Jacobsen. "I was thinking about it today as I walked through the Amen Corner. I said to myself, 'This is the epitome of golf. After all these years, I'm finally right here.' But, at the same time, I was trying to put myself beyond it. You can't say, 'I'm so excited I'm going to die.' If you get caught up in all the history, and all your own daydreams, you could choke your brains out. Every guy out here has stood on the practice tee for hours and said, 'Okay, this is my drive at the thirteenth at Augusta . . . gotta draw it around the corner, but not too much. Now I gotta smoke this one-iron over Rae's Creek and stop it on this slick green.'

"Well, today I did it in real life just like the fantasy. I had a ten-foot putt for eagle at the thirteenth," said Jacobsen. "I'm convinced that your subconscious can't tell the difference between reality and dream. So you have to paint a mental picture of your future in detail. All those six-foot putts are made back here," he said, patting the back of his head. "You can't do it unless you've imagined it first.

"I could look at my accomplishments and say, 'Jake, you're a midget. You don't belong here.' But I'm sure Nicklaus never said, 'These guys are too good for me.' You can only move to where and what you deep down believe you are.

"I think players have a fear of finding out their true limits, which is even greater than their fear of failure," Jacobsen added. "You want an excuse. You want to say, 'I'm not playing well,' or 'I just took a bad swing.'

"What if I have two more good rounds? What if I come to the seventy-second hole Sunday and I have a chance to do something? Am I going to have the guts to stand in there and hit the best shot I can and accept the consequences? All those practice shots don't mean a thing. You have to be able to stand on the last hole and say, 'It's due right now.' And then perform.

"When the great player screws up, he says, 'I'm going to work on that and not do it again,' " Jacobsen says. "The bad player says, 'Boy, I screwed up again. I guess I really am a dog.' "

"To play well on the final holes of a major championship, you need a certain arrogance," Irwin said. "You have to have a way to rise above—or drop below—anxiety. You have to find a trance, some kind of self-hypnosis that's almost a state of grace. Everything that goes wrong crashes against that trance.

"I'm not sure that Nicklaus knew the legitimate taste of victory until the 1980 U.S. Open because, in his whole career, he'd never known a lack of success," Irwin said. "I think the rest of us, who have scuffled, had a greater love for what he'd done than he did. I'm not sure he really understood the magnitude of his accomplishment. That one bad year in 1979 was a black mark on Jack's dignity. It hurt his self-esteem. That had never happened. I think that's why he's come back with such a vengeance."

Nicklaus's shadow is so long and encompassing, gathering in his whole era, that, whenever his name rises to the top again, the golf world asks, as Shakespeare's Cassius did, "On what meat doth this our Caesar feed, That he hath grown so great?"

After all, the history of golf runs counter to Nicklaus's example. Johnny Miller, after finishing bogey, bogey at the 1971 Masters to miss a playoff, was asked what happened. "I suddenly realized who I was and where I was" he said. And Trevor Homer, a British amateur of a previous generation, when told that the Masters odds against him were five hundred to one, said, "It should be five thousand to one. For an amateur, standing on the first hole of the Masters is the ultimate laxative."

Nicklaus, of course, going into the final day trailing by a shot or two, has no answer to the question: "What gives you the right to be so good?" It's a birthright that he has never questioned. "I'm a golfer," he said. "I like to win. I'm not afraid to dicker with any part of my game at any time. I'm a fiddler. I enjoy working at the things that let you win."

For those who think they can hear golf's heartbeat on Sunday afternoons at Augusta, the most essential, indefinable quality in Nicklaus is the look in his laser eyes. He carries with him an aura of dignity and self-esteem that refuses to be embarrassed by chance or failure. As he walked the final holes of the 1986 Masters, plucking at his shirt front, disguising behind a genial, practiced smile what is really a fierce trancelike concentration, Nicklaus was an example of the rarest thing in sport—a player who epitomized an entire game. At that moment, Nicklaus was a man who, for a few hours, had achieved a perfect state of grace. In large measure, Bobby Jones built his cathedral in the pines to bring forth and show us that grace.

I AM
THE WALRUZ

Augusta, Ga., April 12, 1982–The most peaceful, silent and secluded corner of the Augusta National Golf Club is the tenth green, sitting as it does at the bottom of 485 yards of cascading foliage and precipitously falling fairway. The green at sunset is dappled with shadows from the sentinel pines. On Easter, it's an ideal place for little silent epiphanies. It's also a most unusual place to find a wounded man.

That's where Craig Stadler—the champion of the 46th Masters—was at dusk, torn and bleeding in spirit from one of the cruelest encounters with golf that a man ever had.

The last time the Walrus had been here on the tenth, more than two hours earlier, he was taking a six-shot lead into the back nine on the final day of the Masters. Then he was feeling proud of himself, measuring himself for that chunky, size-forty-six green blazer. "'This is pretty easy,'" Stadler thought. "It got to the point of wondering 'how many' I'd win by. I caught myself thinking like that, and said, 'What are you doin'? Stop this. We got enough problems.'"

Little did Stadler know how right he was. He could not foresee his bogeys at the twelfth, fourteenth, sixteenth and eighteenth holes—the last on a three-putt green, giving him a back nine of 40 that threw him into a stunning playoff at dusk with Dan Pohl. When Pohl's four-foot putt for a par slid agonizingly past the cup on the first hole of that playoff, Stadler did not move. His empty stare wasn't one of disbelief or joy or even of commiseration for Pohl's embarrassment at a sloppy bogey to Stadler's winning par. Stadler was just too drained of emotion to react, to dance, to throw his putter into the air as Fuzzy Zoeller had in the first sudden-death Masters playoff three years earlier. Slowly, Stadler walked to Pohl and shook his hand. Then Stadler walked a little more, aimlessly. Finally, like a

He is the one and only Walrus!

man who has endured an experience far worse than any game and inexplicably survived, he put his hands over his face.

AUGUSTA, GA., April 8, 1983—In the glass memorabilia case in the men's grill of Augusta National, the famous clubs of the great Masters champions of the past are lovingly enshrined. These golf weapons, dating back almost fifty years, are burnished like sacred heirlooms. The wooden shafts of the thirties clubs still glisten and you can see your reflection in the faces of the mashies and niblicks.

The most recent clubs are the putters of the renowned players who have been champs in the eighties, like Seve Ballesteros, Tom Watson and Craig Stadler. The blades of Watson and Ballesteros are in mint condition. That of Stadler looks like it has been run over several times by a bulldozer. All parts of the putter, including the face, are lined and creased with scars and scrapes, nicks and dents. You stop counting the marks at about forty because you can't even see the back of the club.

"Proves I really used the thing," said Stadler, twitching his rusty walrus mustache. "Left my trademark on it." Stadler has since replaced his weapon with a new Ben Crenshaw Wilson 8813. "It's about the same as mine, except it's got about forty-eight less cart-path grooves on the bottom and twenty less spike marks on the face." In moments of trial and disgust, Stadler beats the earth and the trees upon it with his putter. He whacks his bag so loudly with it that spectators jump and at the slightest pique will kick the infernal thing with his spikes. Strange treatment, considering that the putter is easily Stadler's best, not his worst, club.

Some will never develop a taste for Stadler. In the sedate world of golf, he will always impress them as being too fat, too emotional, too defiantly styleless, too earthy, too working-class, too much a blunt wise guy who loves to see through exactly the sort of pretensions that the Masters in particular—and golf in general—cultivates. Within the golf community, it is considered the height of irony that Stadler would win the Masters, and that his game—long off the tee, high and soft into the greens and deadly on the short grass—is just the sort that may make him a winner a couple of more times.

When Stadler finished his first practice round of 1983, he and his playing partners walked into the grill and ordered lunch. This sounds normal, but at the Masters it isn't. In this class-conscious setting, the grill is for the run-of-the-mill players, agents, relatives, even reporters. Directly above is the Champions Room; through those swinging doors pass only the folks who own green jackets. You can go years without seeing Nicklaus, Palmer, Snead or Watson in the grill. When Stadler ordered his burger and beer, "They looked shocked," Stadler said of his partners. "Well, I played with 'em. I'm not going to go upstairs and eat by myself."

On the general subject of how much time he spends in the Champions Room, Stadler said, "Big as I am, I don't need to climb any more stairs." Stadler knows that the Masters brass was less than ecstatic about a hot-tempered fellow with a pot belly winning their snappy affair. At first, he lost twenty pounds, then decided what the hell and put it all back on. Everybody knows a walrus can't climb stairs; it's hard on the flippers.

Stadler does not disdain the Masters pomp, but he does a nice job of keeping it at arm's length. For instance, ask about the condition of the hallowed course, and Stadler says, "There's more grass on the greens this year. Even the twelfth green, which has never been any good, is fantastic. The fairways are spotty, but plenty good enough."

The twelfth green, the most famous hole at Augusta National, "has never been any good"? The fairways are "spotty." What is this, the Joe Garagiola–Tucson Open?

Asked if it was true that winning the Masters brings a fellow an extra million dollars in outside income, Stadler said, "Who says it does? Arnold? No one came knocking on my door with a check for a million. Over the years, it will have an effect . . . maybe a million dollars, maybe five hundred dollars." Stadler refused to change his post-Masters schedule just to make a buck. The people to whom he'd promised his time got his time, even if they couldn't pay him top dollar. "If I'd taken everything I was offered, I'd have beat myself into the ground. I came close to doing that anyway."

While Stadler likes to take pokes at the Masters mystique ("Strategy? I don't have any strategy."), he also has respect for Augusta National's genuine traditions. "I've very much enjoyed the past year, the recognition. The victory has gotten a lot of my thinking time . . . reliving the thoughts. It's all very enjoyable. . . .

"Somewhere in those first one-to-four weeks that followed [the play-off win], it hit me. I can't remember the exact moment, but I'm sure, when I was layin' in bed, I thought, 'My God, I did win that sucker.'"

The eyes of the Augusta official who heard this remark got slightly larger. "My God, I did win that sucker." Heavens, how uncouth. Not the way Robert T. Jones would have phrased it, perhaps, but good enough for the grill—if that's the sort of place you prefer.

And Stadler definitely does.

In an athletic subculture of self-conscious etiquette and genteel, elitist fashion, Stadler is the defiantly unregenerate average Joe. Despite being consistently in the top ten golfers in the world, Stadler does none of the flashy $10,000-a-pop appearances and exhibitions of other stars, preferring just "eight or ten low-key little things a year that I enjoy doing. . . . Going to Colombia [South America] one week and New Zealand the next for $8,000 or $10,000 or $15,000 isn't in my game plan. . . . I don't ask for it and they don't seem to want me. . . . I haven't cared to run my rear ragged."

The head covers on his woods have walruses on them and the license plates on his van and his jeep say "WALRAS" and "WALRUZ." Somebody else has "WALRUS"—correctly spelled—and won't give it up.

This is the guy who drove Southern California Athletic Director John McKay nuts by wearing jeans and sandals to play college golf matches, prompting offended letters to the athletic department about the chubby slob playing number one for the Trojan linksters. Since Stadler was U.S. Amateur champ in 1973, his wearing loafers on the back nine was tolerated.

On tour, Stadler horrified traditionalists by having a bag bearing the advertisement "Taylor's Steak House." Of course, if Stadler's bag had just flacked for a golf ball conglomerate, instead of trying to help out his best friend's small restaurant in Los Angeles, nobody would have hassled him. "I took it [the Taylor's ad] off the bag for the same reason I put it on," said Stadler. "No reason at all."

For years, Stadler also has refused to hide his emotions on course, tossing clubs and curses as he felt the flow of play merited. Once, playing Walker Cup in England, Stadler so offended his British caddie's sense of decorum that the bag bearer walked off the course in mid-round in a righteous snit. Photos of Stadler carrying his own bag made the English tabloids with the caddie portrayed as a minor national hero.

Even now, when he's established as one of the perennial stars in golf, one memory of Craig Stadler defines his past, hangs over his present and clouds his future. The crowds are leaving the Amen Corner at the Masters, filing up the long thirteenth hole. One player has been left behind, sitting inconspicuously on a small hillside full of azaleas behind the twelfth green. It is Stadler—his head in his hands, tears running down his face, sobbing uncontrollably. "I just died back in that corner that day," he says now.

That moment in 1979, when he needed only a 70 to win the Masters and, instead, threw a wheel on his way to 76, defines Stadler's perhaps insoluble problem. In a sport that rewards a steely face, a cold eye, a willed denial of human emotions, Stadler can't stop being a person first and a golfer second.

"I'm basically an emotional person. I know I'll never reverse it. If I come to the last hole and need a birdie and I leave a five-iron forty feet to the right, I'll always get hot and say, 'Damn it' and fire away the club. But by the time I get to the next shot, I think I'm fine now. But people don't see that. . . . I've watched myself over the years just like everybody else

A typical portrait of the scowling Stadler in private. On the fairway, fans always yell, "Smile, Craig!"—and of course, he won't.

has, and I've seen how it has hurt me. I've worked on it and it's gotten to the point where I think I control it. . . ."

The battle that Stadler is fighting—like Tommy Bolt and Tom Weiskopf and thousands of hackers—is the eternal golfing war between normal, fractious human nature and an extremely unnatural game. More than any other game, perhaps, golf is about self-control, restraint of personality and the mastering of the emotions. To all those old Scots and Puritans who loved to see the passions broken on the rack of the will, this would be the most moral of games. To others, however, pro golf sometimes seems intrinsically perverse, like selling tickets to watch a holy man meditate. As with fighter pilots, the question is always the same: Do these guys have the "right stuff," or have they killed the right stuff?

What we've got in Stadler is a guy who looks like everybody's tough bartender with a sunburned neck and the forearms of a jackhammer jockey. Toss in droopy pants and shaggy hair and you've got a fellow who gets the same fan reaction at nearly every hole: "He sure doesn't look like a golfer." In a sense, he isn't. On a tour of mechanics, some say robots, he is the free spirit. "I haven't had anybody work with me since I was sixteen," he says. "I play by feel. I can feel it when my swing gets in a bad spot. I don't know what it is, but I just do little things to get it back in a comfortable position. I have a lot more touch than I have strength. I've compacted my game a good thirty yards off the tee since I started the Tour. And I'm not hitting twenty-five balls a year out of bounds. My short game, fortunately, has always been very good. When I'm beside the green, not getting up and down, no matter what kind of shot or lie I have, never really enters my mind."

That utter confidence within forty yards of the pin has a simple genesis. "When I was a kid, I just enjoyed practicing. I loved getting out there about five o'clock in the evening with 100 balls and hit 'em to five different spots around the green. Then, I'd chip 'em all into a basket. I probably hit 600 or 700 shots every night. Until it got dark, I was always out there."

Golf demands two separate—yet equal—kinds of patience: practice patience and competitive patience. The first is the patience to hit 700 chip shots every evening for years as the sun goes down. The other is the patience to endure the humiliating, exasperating torments of the devil's game in front of millions of eyes. Stadler always has had that first sort of patience. He finally is acquiring the latter. Whether he does or not, however, is not as important to him as we might think. Stadler loves golf—but not nearly as much as he cares about his family or cares about acting like his own frumpy, grumpy, inwardly affectionate self.

For example, at a regular Tour stop in Washington, Stadler will tee off in the dew, play only nine holes and stop practice before noon, just so he can put first things first. "I'm taking the short one to the zoo," says Stad-

ler, speaking of his young son, Kevin. "That is, if I can find Connecticut Avenue. I usually have a good sense of direction."

"Kevin, where are you?" Stadler quizzes the child.

"In a locker room," whispers the boy.

Stadler scoops up the child, then observes cheerfully, "Ahhh, pants soaked."

Everything will be all right, even the wet bottoms. As usual, Stadler's sense of direction is true. The walruses are waiting; it's time to go to the zoo.

THE ULTIMATE
EXAMINATION

To the purist, the U.S. Open is, and should remain, the only golf tournament. All the others, even the majors, are on a different and perceptibly lower level. Only the Open, at its best, has everything.

Keeping it that way, however, is one of the sport's toughest challenges.

The Masters may have the most blissful venue in golf and the blessings of an April date in Georgia. Also, the Augusta National is the best action golf course in America, with many holes that reward a gamble and penalize cautious play; it's the place for streaks and collapses, for marvelous dramatic fun. Unfortunately, the Masters, thanks to its ingrained elitism, has a small and weak field, diluted by doddering former champions, token foreigners and star-struck amateurs. Of the 100 best golfers in the world, the Masters may have no more than half in its field. Add to this the undisguised biases of the course itself and you have a track where the same dozen names gravitate to the top of the leader board for years, even decades, at a time. Some of the game's best players have no chance to win.

The British Open has tradition, plus the quaint appeal of windy, links-style golf, an anachronistic nineteenth-century game full of weird bounces and improvised bump-and-run shots. If you love the smell of the sea and the sight of oceans of grass, it's lovely in its bleak beauty. On the other hand, the British Open is raw and frequently uncomfortable. If you aren't in love with the links look, the royal courses can seem like hopelessly boring eyesores. If the Masters fields are weak, then the British Open's are not much better. Dozens of top American players, who still constitute the majority of the world's best performers, don't even bother to make the expensive trip.

The PGA also has tradition and the spice of a new venue each year.

Periscopes are a typical sight at the crowded U.S. Open. Golfers are (left to right): Jack Nicklaus, Craig Stadler and Dr. Gil Morgan.

However, the PGA often seems to be just a watered-down, secondhand replay of the Open. The same set of great courses usually host both events with the important distinction that the PGA doesn't have the same courage of cruel conviction that the USGA maintains. When the PGA sets up a historic course, as it did with Oakmont in 1978, the result is a difficult, but not really terrifying, layout. Players freely maintain that there is little resemblance between a fair PGA setup and the sort of USGA chamber of horrors that pros remember with a shiver to their dotage.

Affairs like the Tournament Players Championship and Jack Nicklaus's Memorial Tournament are still just young aspirants in the great tournament category. The Memorial is really Nicklaus's attempt to mimic Bobby Jones and create his own May Masters; the TPC is, by utter contrast, a sort of Anti-Masters. That leaves us, thank goodness, with the U.S. Open, the tournament that players love to hate and fans love to love.

By traveling among all of America's greatest courses, the Open offers a fair chance to every sort of outstanding player during the course of his career. The man whose game isn't suited to Merion or Oakmont only has to wait for Pebble Beach or Winged Foot or Baltusrol to roll around.

The Open has the wisdom to maintain two absolute golfing constants. The USGA makes sure that every Open is a paramount test of a player's ability to use the game's two most definitive clubs—the driver and the putter. The longest, and therefore most difficult swing in golf is the stroke taken with the driver. To hit the ball long and straight is the best test of a player's full swing. By making its rough the most fearsome on earth, the Open introduces a rich dramatic tension on every hole. From the time you put the tee in the ground, you're just a muscle twitch away from disaster.

By ensuring that its greens are the hardest and fastest of any tournament, the Open introduces two more valid, though harsh, tests. Only the most crisply and properly struck iron shots will hold Open greens; thus, the slovenly ball strikers, who can prosper on the soft hold-anything greens of many PGA Tour sites, are exposed as imposters.

Second, the sport's best test of nerves is the ability to endure four days of putting on greens where the tiniest misjudgment or mis-hit can produce a spectacularly ugly and embarrassing result. Hit a bad lag putt at the Doral or Kemper Open, and your ball may stop six feet from the hole. Do the same on Sunday at Oakmont and your dimpled co-conspirator could end up off the green.

Golf only becomes a compelling athletic event—as opposed to an artful game—when the screws of tension are at their tightest and the physical demands for creative shot-making border on the impossible. Only at the Open are great golfers consistently asked to execute shots that lie at the extreme outer limits of their ability.

No player can cope with an Open course for four days. Sooner or later, and often with mounting frequency as Sunday arrives, the mistakes appear, the disappointments and frustrations mount. Thus, the final round of the Open is always about emotional and psychological survival, about facing the next test bravely even though you have just botched the last job badly with your whole world watching. On Sunday, every contending player finds himself standing on his head in a church pew bunker, or discovers his ball has burrowed to the bottom of a shin-deep clump of vegetation, or realizes that he faces an unstoppable twenty-foot putt that will either go in the hole or else trickle ten feet past.

That's what makes the U.S. Open golf's best and, in a sense, only championship. However, fine-tuning a golf course to precisely this proper pitch of perfidy is a chancy proposition. One question haunts the U.S. Open almost every summer and lurks at the edge of every conversation. As Jack Nicklaus points out, a fine line exists between a supremely difficult course that is the best imaginable test of talent, and a tricked-up track where luck and a hot short game outweigh overall ability.

"Our margin for error has been reduced to almost nothing," Hale Irwin said. "The difference between a perfect shot that holds the green next to the flag and a disastrous shot that bounces off into the jungle is no more than a pace or two on some holes. Are holes like that a test of skill or a test of luck?"

At its best, the U.S. Open demands straight drives, crisp iron shots, brilliant chipping and putting and strategic position play. Plus the patience of St. Francis and the will of Patton. At its worst, the Open eradicates the difference in ability between a Tom Purtzer and a Tom Watson and throws both into the same jail of high rough and high-risk shots. This is the disturbing tendency in the Opens of the seventies and eighties, one which worries everybody in golf.

The most damning criticism from touring pros is that the USGA has decided that, come hell or high rough, they are going to construct an Open course that will "protect the integrity of par." "The USGA doesn't want to recognize the fact that today's players are better than ever," Irwin said. "They seem willing to do anything to prevent us from shooting scores that would make us appear better than the great names of the past."

"Why can't the USGA leave the great courses alone and stop worrying about what we shoot?" Watson asked. One old-timer, the great Byron Nelson, readily admits that: "In my day we simply didn't believe that it was possible to play as well as these young fellows do. We thought that strength denied touch and that you could not consistently hit the ball both long and straight. It's been proved that you can."

Open scores should be lower than they were in the thirties, forties and fifties—if course conditions are the same. But the scores remain essentially the same. The reason is undeniable—Open courses have been made harder, and some would say trickier, each year.

When will the line between skill and luck be passed—or has it been already? Since 1969, the U.S. Open has been won by gentlemen named Orville Moody, Tony Jacklin, Lou Graham, Jerry Pate, Andy North, Larry Nelson and—to define the problem—North again in 1985. Runners-up have included John Schlee, Forrest Fezler, J. C. Snead, Dave Barr, T. C. Chen and Dennis Watson. The hard truth is that several modern Open winners accomplished more in one week over a USGA layout than they have in the rest of their careers.

Few more exotic tasks exist than the problem of "setting up" a championship golf course with the multiple problems of growing rough, mowing greens to difficult-but-fair lengths and choosing tee and pin placements. Each Open morning, the USGA, always at the mercy of the latest weather forecast, must decide how much to water the greens, how far back to push the tees, where to stick the flags and whether to mow off another sixty-fourth of an inch of green. It is thankless work. Everyone in both golf and television is convinced that the public loves to see the pros humiliated, hobbling to the seventy-second hole trailing double bogeys. Yet, at times, no one knows if the Open will be high drama or low slapstick. Few players symbolize the problem of the U.S. Open as well as North, who has won only one other PGA tournament in his fourteen years as a pro. "I can always look at that trophy on the mantelpiece at home and see my name up there with Nicklaus, Palmer and Hogan. It's really neat. They can't take it off or erase it, no matter how badly you play. Your name is going to be there for a hundred years."

And, of course, that is the question. Are the proper names finding their way to that old trophy? More years than not, the answer is still yes. The USGA has been battered about the head and ears enough to know its problem. For the time being, the Open's mystique is safe.

Just ask Randy O'Linger. He epitomizes what the word "Open" represents. As O'Linger, the first man scheduled to tee off in the 79th Open, walked off the eighteenth green at Inverness after his last practice round, he had a huge grin on his twenty-four-year-old face. "I'm playing terrible," said the assistant pro from the windswept Ocean City (Md.) Country Club—not fazed in the least. "Every time I hit a smoking duck-hook today, it just left a horrible-lookin' trail of people diving out of the way. I really fear for 'em tomorrow. I think I'm gonna aim at the trees so I don't maim anybody. Let it rattle around up in the branches for a while until all the steam's off it."

While the millionaires balk at the Open's demands, the little folks of the game—the hometown pros and sectional qualifiers like O'Linger—think they have strolled through the pearly gates of golf on a pass and are playing in a hellish heaven. "The course is just the way it should be," said the blond, stocky O'Linger. "It's downright impossible. I'd have been disappointed if it was easy enough so I could play it. The first day here, I knocked in every putt on the practice greens. I said, 'Is that all there is to Open greens?' Then I played the first time and that fixed that. What was the difference? I was on the golf course. Those greens are faster than glass."

No other sport offers the delightful incongruity of a man like O'Linger—talented, dedicated, but essentially just the easygoing guy down the street—suddenly appearing at one of the top events of his sport. A top-flight sandlot baseball pitcher who suddenly found himself on the mound in the World Series could not face any greater trauma than an O'Linger at the U.S. Open. Except that O'Linger can't call for a relief pitcher. And his scores will be in every paper in the country.

That is what the "Open" in U.S. Open means—anybody, theoretically, can do what O'Linger has done: Stop smoking and drinking, get in top shape, hone his game for a solid year, then win an Open spot in a qualifying tourney. "I don't want to play on the pro tour," said O'Linger, whose father, Mus, is head pro at the popular Ocean City club. "I just play in Middle Atlantic sectional events. The U.S. Open was just as much a dream as you'd think it was."

O'Linger began his clean-living kick months ago—his friends now call him "One-Beer O'Linger." "Everything was geared to having the stamina to play thirty-six holes in one day of qualifying," said O'Linger, who had tried to reach the Open and failed in other, more halfhearted, years. "You'd struggle around all day with guys who had no business in the tournament—it looked like the Yellow Cab Open. I saw a guy shoot 99 once . . . with an eagle. You'd spend the whole day searching for these guys' lost balls and come in with cockleburrs all over you."

After his own personal boot camp, O'Linger shot 142 at Manor Country Club in Bethesda, Md., winning one of four Open spots out of a field of thirty pros. "I was whipped by the final nine. But I was awful happy," said O'Linger. "No, I didn't celebrate. I just drove home three hours to Ocean City. My dad was pretty excited—he lit up his pipe for the first time in years."

O'Linger set out on the 600-mile drive to Toledo with his-father-the-pro's words of advice in his ear: "Just make sure you're not standing too close to the ball after you hit it."

"I've never seen a course this great," said O'Linger. "It's not like the Elks Club nine-holer in Salisbury." O'Linger's biggest surprise was the information that he would be the Open's dew-sweeper—the first man off, and the fellow expected to set a fast pace. "They'd like me off the course in two hours, I'm sure," he said. "And I'm hitting laterals and obliques all over the place. I told 'em, 'Give me a spotter and I'll play fast.'

"I wouldn't say I was a contender. Not even to make the cut." But O'Linger sees hope. "Oh, I never give up," he said. "Every time you see me, I have a different swing. I may wake up at five tomorrow morning and be hitting it straight again. It's not going to bother me . . . I got here. I'll just beat at it my own way and have a good time.

"You know, every putt, even the two-footers, has a break," he marveled. "You'd practically have to nip your shots out of the sand to make them bite. I'm not nervy enough to hit that close to the ball in a trap. I'd hit it up in the Kool-Aid stand."

Has O'Linger had nightmares about missing his 7:15 A.M. tee time by oversleeping? "Who's going to sleep?" he said.

WHATAYA GOT, BIG CHIEF?

AUGUSTA, GA., April 16, 1979–Deep in the towering sanctuary of pines at the Amen Corner, the wind whispered in the stark silhouetted treetops at evening. The sun was nearly down, the Georgia air gathering its first nip of night chill. Fuzzy Zoeller ambled down Augusta National's eleventh fairway, sucking on a cigarette, humming to himself as he looked around at the growing sweetness of the Southern evening. "Lord, this is such a pleasure," he thought. "Out here walking in the woods, got my fishing pole in the car . . . so many people would like to be doing what I'm doing right this minute. Why the hell shouldn't I be enjoying myself?" Out ahead of him, precise, picture-perfect Tom Watson and ramrod-straight, analytical Ed Sneed marched purposefully toward their golf balls on this second sudden-death hole of the Masters.

"Let 'em go," thought Zoeller, shambling with the easy swaying grace of a big cat, a natural athlete, a long hitter. "My ball's way past theirs. Why should I hurry up and then wait for them to hit?"

Zoeller bumped shoulders with his young black caddie, Jerry Beard, then gave him a playful grab in the ribs. "I've been like a blind man with a seeing-eye dog all week," Zoeller told the beaming caddie. "You sure enough got me here. Just read me one more putt."

"Geez, man," said Zoeller, suddenly seeing a sea of nearly twenty thousand people waiting for him just around the bend in the dogleg, "how many people they got at this damn golf tournament?"

Into golf's staid and proper Easter Parade today walked Frank Urban Zoeller, Jr.—chain-smoking, longing for a beer, cussing innocently with every fifth word. Sneed's quiet introspection and Watson's workaholic ethic—two of the hallmark temperaments of the PGA world—did battle with Zoeller's flippant joie de vivre in the Amen Corner today.

Frank "Fuzzy" Zoeller

It was a great victory for What-the-Hell.

Zoeller, playing in his first Masters, never dreamed he might find himself in such a supposed caldron of nerves. On the first tee Thursday, "I had trouble breathing, but I was paired with Lee Trevino and he had me laughing all the way around. I've been fine since."

Only once today did Zoeller act like a normal harried man. When Sneed hung his final agonizing six-foot putt on the lip of the seventy-second cup to finish the worst collapse in Masters history, Zoeller could not bear to watch. "They had me a good post position to watch," said Zoeller, who grew up in Indiana, near Louisville, Ky., and horse country. "But I had to move away. . . . I knew Ed had to play an awful bad round today to lose . . . and my caddie had told me, 'He better hit that putt firm or he'll get bit again.' But I just can't stand to watch golf when it gets that tough."

Zoeller only shies away from watching others suffer. As for himself, he loves tight spots. "On the first playoff hole, Watson and Sneed had the pin covered with their second shots. I couldn't see any room for my ball. . . ." So, like a Robin Hood in his own private Sherwood Forest, Zoeller gunned a hooking eight-iron dead on the stick, but fifteen feet short. "I missed mine first, and I thought the party was over," he said. "Didn't think both of 'em could miss it."

Zoeller would never twist his guts over so inscrutable and fickle a thing as a putt. He spent too many bachelor years studying too many interesting women to fry his brain over unanswerable problems. His approach to moments of crisis was perfectly demonstrated on that eleventh fairway, which became the last hole. "Just like always, I wrapped those white knuckles on an eight-iron and said, 'Where the hell's it going this time?' "

Where Watson might have run through a mental index of Byron Nelson's theories on eight-foot putts, where Sneed might have agonized over the memory of other missed shots at the devil's hand, Zoeller just asked Beard what to do. "He read every other putt for me," said Zoeller. "Why not the last one?"

When the last shot of the Masters disappeared, "A million thoughts went through my mind," said Zoeller, "what little mind I have." He fired his putter so high in the air, spinning, twisting, that it caught the last rays of evening light, hanging like a brilliant sword blade forty feet in the sky above the huge scoreboard.

"Hell, that putter might have landed in the pond," said Zoeller, suddenly remembering the trusty tool nearly two hours after it had done its work so well. "I'll fish it out. That'll just teach old Betsy a lesson. You can't let a putter think it's indispensable. I keep another identical one— named Number 2—in the car trunk. I switch at least once a year, just to prove to Betsy that she can be switched." Sounds like a lesson learned in some other endeavor.

No Masters champ ever has enjoyed the first hours of his reign more than Zoeller. His face aglow amid the silver bowls and aristocratic silver hair in front of the Augusta clubhouse, Zoeller found just the right words. Well, by Fuzzy standards. "Jesus, I wish I could tell you what this means to me," he blurted. "I'd like to thank . . . well, I'd like to thank Tom and Ed for missing all those putts. . . ."

Zoeller touches many types. He grew up in New Albany, Ind., next to a fairway at Valley View Country Club, where his father was president. "He owned a veneer company," said Zoeller. "That's veneer, not manure." Zoeller also has married into millions. "I guess maybe our marriage was a little overdone," Zoeller said of a now legendary bash that resembled a convention more than a wedding. "We invited a few people . . . well, 950. My father-in-law, Mr. Thornton, likes to do things right."

"Can he afford to?" Zoeller was asked. "Well," said Zoeller, not one to refuse a straight line, "he owns Thornton Oil."

On the other hand, Zoeller's taste in friends is extremely egalitarian. Mike's Tavern, the Old Pike Inn and Flaherty's in New Albany were happy places on Easter night. "Yes," said Zoeller, "before I got married, I was in all of 'em. In one night."

When Zoeller's unorthodox crouched swing—"Some people say I look like I'm praying"—develops a problem, he does not go to a famous high-priced pro. He goes crosstown to Moe Demling at Shawnee Golf Course—a predominantly black public course. That's where Zoeller, a born hustler and tall-tale teller, feels at home. Zoeller also knows he is accepted down there. At the ritzier clubs, he hears: "When are you going to win a tournament?"

"I'll tell ya, babe, I don't care for that at all," said Zoeller, whose first win came at San Diego earlier this year. "That comes from people who know nothing about the life out here. . . . I wasn't at all tight on the playoff because I know what I believe. That win-win-win stuff doesn't cut it with me. If I finish second, that's a win for me. If I finish third, that's a win, too. And I'd have felt that way today. You don't come out here and blow these guys' doors off. They're too good. And you can't hate yourself for finishing second.

"I play the game the way it gives me pleasure. If I've got a fifty-fifty chance to pull off a shot, I say, 'Hell, let's go for it.' "

MAMARONECK, N.Y., June 17, 1984–No one won the U.S. Open at Winged Foot today and no one will forget it.

Sports had one of its perfect hours. And golf gained a marriage of moment and player worthy of legend. Place Greg Norman's putt at

Winged Foot on the page next to Tom Watson's chip at Pebble Beach in the leather volume of Open events worthy of preservation. Put a photograph of Fuzzy Zoeller there as well, waving a white towel of surrender over his head in an act of cheerful sportsmanship that may, with time, etch him in golf's memory more than any shot he ever hits.

Years hence, the USGA record book will, no doubt, show only one name in boldface type beside the year 1984. That champion will be either the burgeoning Australian star Norman or the vibrantly decent Zoeller, both of whom finished seventy-two holes of Open play in 276 strokes. The issue between these keen and feeling sportsmen will be settled Monday; this fifth day of labor will provide a victor, but it will be almost impossible for it to equal this gray day for substance. Norman's 69 and Zoeller's 70 are just numbers that fail to touch the experience. This time, the golf maxim was wrong; this time it was how, not just how many.

When has there been a better example of the ethic of competition or a finer illustration of the courage required to thrive in the moment of crisis that lies at the center of athletics? For once, every spectator here and millions of television viewers were forced to understand that the core of golf, like the nub of any fine game, is not the crowning of a champion but the capacity to show man when he is most truly and completely alive.

Norman, who sank a forty-foot putt for par on the seventy-second hole to escape defeat; who, in fact, made nearly miraculous saves of par on each of the last three infamous finishing holes, was reduced to a blissful inarticulateness.

"I could not put into words the feeling I had when I made that putt at the last [hole]. One of those greatest feelings in the world," he said, having trailed Zoeller by four shots after six holes, by three shots after twelve and by one with just two to play. "Golf is very hard to explain. I could feel it in my hands. I knew I was going to make it. . . . I just knew."

His putt to save par broke five feet from left to right, but "From the time it went over a bare spot twelve feet in front of me, I knew it was in the hole." When Arnold Palmer and Jack Nicklaus were twenty-nine, they knew such things, too. When that dying putt dropped in the heart of the hole for par, Zoeller stood stunned in the fairway as Norman took a kingly parade route around the green, arms over head, face aglow.

Zoeller, immersed in his own problems, had lost track of Norman's miseries. "I turned to my caddie," he recalled, "and said, 'My God, he's made birdie out of this mess.' "

That's when Zoeller surpassed himself. Perhaps a few other golfers, realizing that Norman had probably forced a tie and a playoff, would have made some gracious gesture of approval. Perhaps there is even one somewhere who would, like Zoeller, have smiled and waved that white flag, prompting Norman to grin and salute back down the fairway. But is there anyone else in golf except the blithe Zoeller who would have waved that towel thinking that he probably had just lost? After all, no one ever has birdied the seventy-second hole to win an Open and, surely, Zoeller must have doubted that he could be the first.

Yet, he waved. And smiled a bit. What the heck, it was just the U.S. Open and the estimated million dollars in fringe money that it brings. If only a nation full of screaming Little League managers and ref-baiting high school coaches and run-'em-till-they-drop big-time football coaches could have watched and understood.

"I know what I felt like today, but I can't put it into words," said Zoeller. "Momentum swirls . . . Golf is not a fair game. It's a rude game. But I know I played my heart out."

MAMARONECK, N.Y., June 18, 1984–When Fuzzy Zoeller and Greg Norman left Winged Foot Sunday night, they were tied on the scoreboard but Zoeller was behind. When you squander a four-shot lead in the final round of the U.S. Open, when you lose a three-shot margin on the last five holes, when the other fellow sinks a forty-foot gasp of a putt on the seventy-second green to snatch the greatest prize in golf from your hand, you're not tied. In your mind, in every mind, you enter the next day's playoffs as an emotionally battered underdog.

If the Smartest Fan here on Sunday had owned a crystal ball, gazed one day into the future and known that he could bet on Zoeller today and give seven shots, he might own the World Trade Center now. If he'd said that Zoeller would win the 84th U.S. Open, which he did today, by the biggest landslide margin of any eighteen-hole playoff in major tournament history, he'd have gotten a Bronx cheer. If he'd said that Zoeller would lead by three shots after sinking a sixty-eight-foot birdie putt at the second hole, by nine shots after sixteen holes, and would finish with an eight-stroke victory, 67–75, he'd have been ruled eligible for relief: brain under repair. After all, in twenty-seven previous Open playoffs, dating back to 1895, no one had ever shot lower than 68. Zoeller, who waved the white flag of gracious surrender on Sunday, set an Open playoff scoring record today.

In fact, counting this round, the thirty-two-year-old Zoeller is the only man ever to break par for any of the four Opens played at Winged Foot. He was seven-under-par for ninety holes, a feat that should grow with the years. "I whipped this great course for five days," said Zoeller. "It got Hale [Irwin] yesterday. . . . It got Greg today and it might have gotten me tomorrow. But I whipped it."

Few final acts in golf have been more improbable than this afternoon, which ended with the quipping, populist Zoeller walking up the eighteenth fairway to chants of "Fuzzy! . . . Fuzzy!" "That walk was the warmest feeling and the coldest streak down my back of my life," said Zoeller.

The odds on everything that happened here, from Zoeller's birdie, birdie start to Norman's double bogey, bogey, bogey collapse at the second, third and fourth holes, would have been longshots, indeed, a day ago. However, strange things happen in the night. The men who leave the course one evening are not necessarily the same men who return the next morning. The mind, given a chance to escape from the flow of events and regain its equilibrium, can restore its own health. Certainly Zoeller's could. "I didn't sleep well at all. I was still awake at 3 A.M., smoking a cigarette, and the fire alarm in my hotel room went off," he said.

Sure, Zoeller had insomnia, but he also had ideas. "I thought about it and I figured that coming back on Monday was a break for me. You never know what twelve to fourteen hours will do for a guy. . . . After the way Norman finished, he had the momentum. When you get the old putter answering, the way it was for him yesterday, you're hard to beat."

Also, Zoeller, who looked hangdog and fatigued during the final fourth-round holes, came to the first playoff tee nervous and determined to atone. "My guts were in a knot, there was a lump in my throat. Don't ask me for a hole-by-hole. I don't remember what I was doing out there . . . I was in a zone of my own."

Norman's night-to-day progression was just the opposite. He rode out the rough-hewn front gates of Winged Foot after the fourth round as a hero and a blossoming star. He returned around noon today as an uninspired mortal. "My adrenaline wasn't pumped up. . . . I felt too relaxed," said the mystified Norman. "I needed something special. It didn't happen."

This is called being "flat" and it happens in many sports many times. "Hey, I thought I got him with that putt at the eighteenth on Sunday," admitted Norman. By the eighteenth on Monday, "I just wanted to get the hell out of there," said Norman, who exited with grace by waving a white towel in surrender as he approached the final green, thus mirroring Zoeller's magnanimous gesture of Sunday.

Actually, at the eighteenth tee, Norman asked Zoeller, "Double or nothing?" Retorted Zoeller, "Okay, if you'll hit your second shot where you hit it yesterday"—i.e., into the bleachers.

"Arnold Palmer always gave the crowd what it wanted," said Zoeller, who gave the press fifteen bottles of champagne at his press conference à la Tony Lema. "I like to think I'm giving some of that back. If it weren't for people like him, I'd be playing in front of trees for $200 a week.

"If what Norman did yesterday under pressure—my hat's off to him —doesn't get your adrenaline flowing when you're sitting in a chair watching TV, I don't know what would."

Once, in college at Houston, Zoeller's coach told him to stop being so cheerful and encouraging to his foes. "You're relaxing the other players; we don't want that," the coach said. Zoeller's reaction was to make a basic life decision. "I decided I was going to play my way," he said. So he left the team and the school. And would wave a towel whenever he wished.

Chalk one up today for a twinkle in the eye and champagne on the lips.

Ponte Vedra, Fla., March 1985–Fuzzy Zoeller spotted a familiar face in the crowd at the Tournament Players Club's remote thirteenth tee and headed that way, completely unconcerned that he couldn't remember the gent's name. "Whataya got, Big Chief?" said the reigning U.S. Open golf champion to the small middle-aged man.

"Oh, just workin' hard," said the delighted, nonplussed man, trying to match banter with one of the more famous quipsters in sports. "How you doin', Fuzzy? Coming to our tournament in Atlanta?"

"Yeah, if I'm still walkin'," said Zoeller, who learned last fall, barely two months after the biggest win of his life, that he'd have to have one disk chiseled out of his chronically bad back and have another repaired. "I'm doin' pretty good. Have my good days and bad days. Today's not so good. I hate this slow play. When I start waiting, my back tightens up and I play like a klutz."

"Getting to bed early?" asked the fan, who had hoped for a nod of the head and was getting a life progress report.

"Got to. No choice," answered Zoeller, smoking and stretching his back as he waited on the backed-up tee. "I tried to stay up until ten o'clock one night at Doral [Country Club] and the next day—oooh, did it hurt.

"Ten to twelve hours in bed and I'm in pretty good shape the next day."

Next to Zoeller, Tom Watson was using the dead time to take about fifty practice swings—some with no club, some with a club turned upside down so he was swinging the handle. He was in his famed "rubber room" of concentration, oblivious to the fans and the course.

Seve Ballesteros was there, too, locked in the characteristic great-man-at-odds-with-the-universe sulk that comes over him when he's seven-over-par and about to miss the cut on another tough, tight course.

Zoeller looked at them, then turned and walked away as though Watson's ambition and Ballesteros's funk were both equally useless to him. Zoeller whistled to himself and gazed straight overhead at the Spanish moss hanging from the gnarled limbs of a live oak tree. Miles above, a skywriter was printing out the word "S-L-I-D-E-R" in a cloudless sky.

While Watson thought about golf and Ballesteros about himself, Zoeller looked at the world around him and decided, again, that it was wonderful.

"Nice place to be," he said, then stepped to the tee and hit his ball in a trap. "Ooops, that wasn't very good." The crowd by the green moaned as though the ball had been hit by Arnold Palmer. Nearly two hours later, Zoeller's ordeal of delays finally ended as he saved par at the eighteenth hole with a great sand shot and made the cut by a stroke. In relief and exasperation, he pulled his tap-in out of the cup and threw the ball into the lake. The crowd laughed because Zoeller was smiling. They hardly guessed that he was aggravated, exhausted and stiff, just as they never knew he played the first ten years of his career in nearly constant pain— wearing a corset, taking twice-daily shock therapy in the lumbar region of his back. Zoeller never said why he let his caddie get the ball out of the cup some days—because he couldn't bend over.

At the scorer's tent, Watson's wife and baby daughter kissed him as a CBS minicam whirred two feet from their faces. Zoeller went out the tent's back door and signed autographs for fifteen minutes after Watson and Ballesteros were gone. Only as Zoeller walked through the crowd, answering every cry of "Hiya, Fuzzball!", did he reach his own wife and two small daughters. Zoeller was interrupted constantly, but the less significant the person, the more attention he got. "What did ya shoot?" asked one man who, when told it was 74, was as silent as if Zoeller had said his dog died.

"Hell, better'n 75. Made the cut. I'll be back tomorrow," said Zoeller, who shook his head after the fellow walked away. "Never been able to understand that attitude. Things can always be better, but they can also be worse. Why not look on the good side?"

As he walks, Zoeller answers questions so graciously and patiently that you could forget that he's been asked the same dull litany for six months. "I didn't know I was makin' a comeback. Everybody makes such a big deal out of me winning at Bay Hill [three weeks ago]. Well, I should have won another one, too.

"The biggest trouble I've had is in my head, not the back. I fall asleep on too many shots. Gotta keep concentrating. The back? It is and it isn't a problem. Sitting is tough, waiting is tough." But Zoeller's back was "tough" for years, so it's all relative. "You won't see me over there much," says Zoeller, pointing to the practice tee. "The doctors tell me it will take two years and two months until I'm completely back to full strength. I'm doing exactly what they tell me, even trying to lose a few pounds. I'm up ten from when I won the Open. This is one time I'm not a free spirit."

The closer Zoeller gets to the clubhouse, the more buzz surrounds him. "Hello, Smiley," says one player.

"Tooth and nail, coming in," moans Zoeller to one person. "Well, thank you," he says, stopping to look someone else in the eye after a compliment. "Head, head," he says, spotting someone about to decapitate himself on a low ledge as he walks and gawks at Zoeller.

"These guys are real glad to see me back," he says as he steps into the locker room. "They just wanted me to come back and talk to 'em. Nobody in there will talk to each other, all so serious. They need to have somebody who will give 'em grief and who will appreciate it when they give it back."

"The Hoosiers gonna win the NIT?" a shoeshine man asks Zoeller, a rabid Indiana fan who watched thirty college basketball games a week during his first bedridden month after surgery ("That's what kept me sane").

"Those cockroaches better win," says Zoeller, then brightens as he spots Ben Crenshaw. "Are you buyin' my dinner at the Masters this year or not?" says 1979 champ Zoeller to the man who had finally won his green coat. "New man has to buy for everybody, but I haven't seen any 'Ben Crenshaw Dinner' invitation in my mail."

"That went out three weeks ago," protests Crenshaw.

"Doesn't matter," says Zoeller. "We're all sendin' you the bill, anyway."

Another reporter gets Zoeller in his sights, asks how he feels.

"Wore out. Goin' home," he says.

"One question."

"You get uglier every year."

"What's the one shot in your career you wish you had back?"

"You asked me that yesterday. I said I couldn't think of one."

"Figured overnight it might have come to you. Now, don't strain, Fuzz. We don't want you to have to have brain surgery, too," says the reporter, who would hardly feel comfortable saying such a thing to any other top star.

"Every shot I ever hit has been perfect," says Zoeller.

Crenshaw, overhearing this, says, "You should ask me that. I got plenty I want to take over. Every time Fuzzy gets in contention, he wins."

Zoeller winks devilishly. "Well . . . if it ain't just the truth," he murmurs.

Former Open champion Larry Nelson is nearby and says, "When Fuzzy first became known, after he won that Masters, I thought he was funny from trying to be funny. But now I'm convinced it's just natural. He's like Lee Trevino, but Lee's humor is more cutting. Fuzzy is softer. There's a truth in humor and Fuzzy will take it right to the edge of being questionable. Lee sometimes goes over."

"I think it's tremendous that he could come back," says John Mahaffey, the former PGA champion who has had his own will-I-ever-play-again moments. "Maybe it's lucky that he came back on tour so fast. What ever that special thing is that you have when you're winning—I don't know if it really has a name—he still had it. That magic, I guess. What's so special about Fuzzy is he's just genuine. Can't teach that."

Zoeller is walking out the clubhouse door when six-foot-four, 210-pound Andy Bean grabs him in a hammerlock from behind and starts bending him backward playfully. Bean used to wrestle alligators and is renowned for not knowing his own strength and not always using good judgment. That's not quite correct. Actually, Bean is known for having less common sense than God gave a box of rocks.

Zoeller goes along with the joke, but his eyes get big. If he had a white towel to wave in surrender, he'd use it now.

"Let him loose, Andy," snaps a veteran player.

"We need him."

THE
CARDIAC CLIFFS

Ask every professional on tour what his five favorite golf courses are in the world, and the one name that will be on everybody's list is Pebble Beach.

Tom Watson, practicing for the U.S. Open

PEBBLE BEACH, CAL., June 16, 1982–As he walked to the tee of the tiny, precipitous, sand-locked, surf-rocked, wind-wracked 110-yard seventh at the Pebble Beach Golf Links, Jack Nicklaus paused to look at the vista before him. Standing at the top of the tip of this peninsula, Nicklaus, playing a practice round before the U.S. Open, had the full panoramic sweep of Pebble Beach around him.

To his right was a sheer cliff drop down to Stillwater Cove, and, in the distance, the cypress-wooded promontory of Pescadero Point. To his left was blue-black, kelp-clogged Carmel Bay lapping on a mile of white Monastery Beach and, beyond that, the long rocky reach of Point Lobos. Around the tee was impenetrable barranca, full of wildflowers, Scotch broom and sea grasses. On those huge ocean rocks not washed with waves were perched hundreds of sea birds. Behind Nicklaus, the foothills of the Gabilan Range began their climb, their heights covered with fog. Straight ahead lay the Pacific.

"This sure is beautiful," was all he said.

Like many who come here, Nicklaus has learned the foolishness of trying to hem in Pebble Beach with words. Robert Louis Stevenson called this Monterey Peninsula "the greatest meeting of land and water" anywhere on earth—and Stevenson got around some.

Even photographs are inadequate to the sight. They catch only a narrow arc of the place's 360-degree impact. And, inevitably, they tend to

Pebble Beach is the constant haunt of the famous and powerful. Here Speaker of the House Thomas P. "Tip" O'Neill and former President Gerald R. Ford share a golf cart in bipartisan amicability.

flatten what is, in reality, a wild and craggy place. Take two steps off the right side of the eighth fairway and it's 200 feet straight down to the rocks and driftwood.

Occasionally, something in the world of sport actually surpasses expectation. Once in a while, Peggy Lee's wrong; that isn't all there is. Pebble Beach is natural, wild, stark and capricious. That's why it is, perhaps, the ideal U.S. Open venue. In February, at the annual Bing Crosby Pro-Am, Pebble Beach is wet, green, close-cropped and pretty, even if the weather is raw. But, in summer, with high rough and the general brownish tinge of longer grasses, Pebble Beach has the mean look it deserves. "It reminds you of a lot of British Open and Scottish courses. Yup, lotta Scottish golf in this course," said Watson. "From the seventeenth tee, for example, all you see is sky and ocean and flat grasses. It's a beautiful blue-gray setting."

"This is, basically, an unscorable golf course," says Craig Stadler. "It doesn't need to be tricked up or protected. If you can keep it in the fairway, you've got a shot at a real good round. If you don't, you're in a lot of trouble."

Rounds here have a compelling internal chemistry because Pebble Beach has such a well-defined personality. As Watson says, "There are a lot of birdies early on the first seven holes, and a lot of bad scores late."

The first five holes are completely inland and, by contrast with what follows, bland. The first, third and fourth are all short par-fours of less than 400 yards, the snug fourth being only 325 yards—just a one-iron and a flip wedge; but all punish a shoddy drive severely. The 506-yard par-five second hole is, for top pros, a gimme birdie hole. "This course has no weak holes, except number two," says Watson. Even the notorious 170-yard fifth hole, sarcastically called "the only dogleg par-three in the world" because the tee shot had to be hooked to avoid trees, has a new tee and now provides a fair shot.

The truth of Pebble Beach begins with the majestic, uphill 515-yard sixth hole that begins in dense inland woods and culminates in a headlands heaven. In minutes, you've gone from the calm and familiar to a stretch of breathtaking holes that are the heart of this links. If Augusta has its Amen Corner, then Pebble Beach has its Cardiac Cliffs. From the seventh through tenth holes, tournaments here are almost always decided.

The treacherous, wind-beaten 110-yard seventh sets the tone. Here, the balls start bouncing off rocks into the Pacific. Here, Sam Snead took a putter and deliberately bounced his ball down the hill into the front bunker to avoid an honest shot.

The eighth, ninth and tenth may be the best stretch of hard par-fours on earth. He who comes to the eighth tee without a cushion of previous birdies may well end up wrecked; "Homero Blancos played the first seven holes six-under-par in 1972," recalls Watson, "but he finished the round even-par."

The 433-yard eighth is the most visually intimidating hole in America. The uphill tee shot is blind. The second shot must clear a 160-yard gorge that is so deep and beautiful that the only defense is not to look at it. From the green, approaching players look like specks as they swing atop a bluff.

The 467-yard ninth and 424-yard tenth—with their fairways tilting ridiculously toward the cliffs and ocean on the right—are actually tougher holes. They are impossible; the eighth just looks that way.

From the eleventh through the sixteenth, Pebble Beach regains its sanity once more, weaving inland again, but this time offering stern pars, not birdies. Even the 565-yard par-five fourteenth hole is an honest par.

Finally, comes the signature finish. The 209-yard seventeenth, into prevailing winds, looks bleak, barren and intractable. Every other hole is aesthetically pleasing; the nasty, charmless seventeenth is, in the best British sense, hideously ugly. "Take your bogey—if you're lucky—and shut up," it says.

The eighteenth is better. Better than what? Better than you think it is. Better than its photographs or its reputation. And its reputation is that it's the best finishing hole on earth. What TV doesn't show is the complete sense of desolation and vulnerability on the exposed tee. All around you is crashing surf. Between there and home is 548 yards of prehistoric sandstone and tumbled rock. You know the fairway is way over there on the right, but every misguiding instinct in the subconscious is going to pull you left to oblivion. Pros say this might be the most difficult shot to align properly in all of golf.

The man who comes to this seventy-second hole on Sunday of a U.S. Open and survives it for victory, is, in the truest sense, the American champion, because he has won the title on the course that may be this country's most beautiful—and thorough—test.

AFTER
THE GRAIL

A smart fella once told me that a fine golfer only has one fine thing, and that's his fine golf—and that if he forgets it, he's a fool. Tom Watson never forgets.

Byron Nelson, Golf Hall of Fame

TOLEDO, OHIO, June 12, 1979–Ascension is in the air. This is the hour when the outwardly freckled but inwardly fierce Watson, with his deep voice and deeper drive, should move from his plateau of wealthy excellence to his game's mountaintop. Certainly, the time is ripe. "Tom's the top star of this sport . . . period," says Nelson, expressing the golf consensus. "And he has been since he beat Nicklaus head-to-head in the 1977 Masters and British Open."

Nevertheless, Watson seems reluctant to take the last step forward. He had better hurry. "I must win the U.S. Open to be considered one of the great players. . . . Right now, I certainly don't have the career of the names like Nicklaus, Hogan, Jones," Watson acknowledges. "Just winning money is not enough. In this game, you are measured by your major titles. And that's fair . . . I'm no different than anyone else. I want to be recognized as the best player in the world."

But with the next breath, Watson is determined to avoid the issue, the pressure, of the majors—perhaps even in his own mind. "My only goal is to improve my golf swing. I have a lot to work on. Then everything else will take care of itself," said one of the most fanatic workaholics in a sport of drudges. "I'm trying to limit my distractions and save some private time for myself and my family. Sometimes it's impossible. Look where I am right now," said Watson, signing autographs, smile fixed on his face, as he tried to nudge through a crowd before TV crews could cut him off at the

Tom Watson

locker room door. "One thing is of primary importance to me—my swing, my improvement as a golfer, my consistency," said the Stanford graduate in psychology. "I want to make this game easy. That one idea—improving my swing—is a simplifying principle. It eliminates a lot of clutter, a lot of false issues."

If golf, that sport of theorists, has one old priest who talks with more influence than any other, it is Nelson—often called the father of the modern swing. And if the humbling game, the sport of flagellates, has one young monk who follows his ablutions and devotions with more diligence and intelligence than any other, it is Watson. The two make a perfect athletic marriage—a pair of purists.

"Lots of people will pay attention to you, but they don't really listen," said Nelson, whose swing was so ideal that when a machine was built to hit golf balls for research, it was designed on his swing mechanics—the Iron Byron. "Tom listens better than anyone I ever saw. He'll look right at me, like this," said Nelson, doing a touching imitation of Watson's devoted, almost beaglelike stare. "Now, my swing was shorter, firmer, slower and with more loose leg action than Tom's. Mechanically, they're not that similar. But underneath, we're searching for the same thing—a consistent, repeating swing with a personal rhythm that doesn't change from takeaway to impact."

Ah, golf's Holy Grail—the perfect repeating, always dependable swing. Old heads nod—even Nelson's—when a young buck sets off after that chimera of golf which has destroyed more players than whiskey and the yips combined. "I used to worry about Tom," said Nelson. "I thought he was more critical of himself than anyone should be. You can't always hit it just the way you want. I was afraid he was too much of a perfectionist." Could Watson derail his career by trying to acquire by labor what Nelson had been granted by nature?

"Tom's got such a brilliant mind that his intelligence always saves him," said Nelson. "He's able to keep some balance and not get down on himself when his swing deserts him a little. He always finds the flaw, because he's the most observant young man I know. He was over to my house for dinner after not being there for a while. We have some ancestral bone china that my wife loves, and since the last time Tom was there, I'd found a lady in Belgium who could make these dainty little place mats to match the pattern in the china. Tom walks right straight through the house to the kitchen, and as he passes the table he says, 'Hmmm, place mats to match the china,' and goes right on. I never saw my wife Louisa so impressed."

From week to week, Watson's meticulous method, his gift for catching his own creeping terrors, serves him well. "If I continue to play well," he said, "it's just a matter of time until I win. It takes care of itself." Like

Nicklaus, Watson wants to be so persistently at the top, that winning is not a feat, but an inevitability. Also like Nicklaus, few players are so utterly undisturbed by an anonymous second-place finish. At the Tournament Players Championship, where he was runner-up, Watson simply said, "I'm making progress. Perhaps I'm sometimes a little distracted by the aesthetics of trying to hit a beautiful shot, rather than a functional one."

But the U.S. Open, the Masters and the PGA will not take care of themselves. They dictate. They give the orders. And Watson deeply resents it.

The notion that one tournament, one week, can have a special importance in a whole career is anathema to Watson's system of subduing the game by laborious, never-relenting practice. "Of all the top players, Tom Watson is probably the most bothered by all the commotion that surrounds a major event," said pro Dave Stockton. "It's to his credit that he has learned to overcome it."

That is the generous point of view. "There is no question that Tom is playing far better golf than anyone in the game," Nicklaus said, "but . . ." That eloquent "but" simply means Watson has not proved that he has the champion's knack of playing his best when the stakes are arbitrarily the highest. Watson, however, cannot change his method and never would consider it. His whole career has been a slow upward battle, not a gift of talent.

"By and large your golf game mirrors your personality," said Lanny Wadkins. "Tom's certainly does. We all approach things differently. Tom's methodical, organized, mechanical. What makes Tom different from the other great players is that he has no weaknesses. Even players like Nicklaus and [Arnold] Palmer were never more than adequate wedge and bunker players. They never had to be. Tom would never tolerate a weakness. He'd go to the practice tee and beat at it till the darn thing went away."

Watson and Wadkins are almost perfect golf opposites of the same age. Wadkins is a streaky "rhythm," or "touch," player with an unorthodox swing who trusts no one to give him advice. "When my swing is in trouble," said Wadkins, "I go back and look at old films when I was hot. Tom would probably never do that. He's always pushing forward, trying to reach some new level, make some improvement. The idea of going back to recapture something would make him sick." Wadkins, and his heroes—hot-and-cold touch players with unorthodox swings like Palmer or Lee Trevino—wait for their periods of inspiration when they play in the exalted way that they feel. For them, the golf course is a place for adventure.

"When I'm like that, golf has no strategy," said Wadkins. "I drill every shot at the pin. I wanna hole out from the fairway."

Not surprisingly, those players—suddenly soaring above the mundane, strutting the fairway with a special exhilaration—are called charismatic. They glow. Watson always carries the sweat of the practice range with him. One can almost hear the clicking of the tumblers in his swing that looks like an aggressive ever-repeating metronome. "The range is my place," said Watson. "I practice after every round. Even if I'm leading by five shots."

Perhaps no one can understand Watson, respect him sufficiently or sense his limits until they have stood with the gallery on the practice tee, just arm's reach from his workshop. "Home, home on the range," that's Watson. "I'm not hitting it well at all," Watson grumbles. "I need a lot of work. That's the only way to make things too easy for pressure to bother you. I would like to come to this Open very confident. . . . I took two weeks off just to practice, but my driving just got progressively worse. I'm not pleased. I can't force it to happen. I just have to let it fall in place."

Before each practice shot, Watson's lips purse in a winsome pucker of determination—he might still be fifteen years old, the perfect dutiful schoolboy. Other players practice alone. Watson, never. Someone is always behind him, observing. Whether it is his caddie, just a passing pro, or his lifelong hometown teacher from Kansas City—Stan Thirsk, Watson must have someone to whom he directs a little comment after almost every swing. "Did I lay the club open a little at the top?" he said. "I'm a little ahead of that one, right?"

If the PGA tried to dream up—in a nightmare—the least useful type of player to be its showcase man, it would be the assiduous Watson: short on colorful personality, long on unseen character and adamantly allergic to fame. "I don't like to be on display."

"Tom and I chitter-chatter about a lot of things," said Nelson. "The thing that concerns him most is probably all the outside disturbances that come with being a celebrity—press, commercials, fans. He knows he needs to pay full attention to golf. This game is like a horse . . . if you take your eye off it, it'll jump back and kick your shins for you. . . . I think Tom has handled himself well. He smiles big and tips his hat. Who says you have to shout and jump up and down? In fact, to me, he's more exuberant than Jack. Even though he's as intent as [Ben] Hogan, he's a much freer and friendlier-type person.

"But, no doubt, the hubbub affects Tom—maybe doesn't hurt him, but it affects him. I tell him that his focus of attention has to be elsewhere, that he has to do all these little duties of a star in a subconscious way. Nicklaus was the best ever at it." Perhaps Nicklaus's greatest gift—over the long haul—was his ability to be the calm eye at the center of the constant Nicklaus hurricane. Watson must constantly work to create his own precariously maintained golfing calm—he battles for it in the solitude of that practice tee. Hurricanes, like the one this week, crash at the walls of his monkish peace of mind.

For years those storms defeated him. Watson led the 1974 and 1975 Opens in the fourth round, as well as the 1975 Masters. He backed out of the lead all three times, earning a now-discarded reputation as a choker who was too smart for his own good. Watson also has lost in playoffs in his last two major tournaments. At the Masters this April, he had an agonizing half-dozen birdie putts slide past the hole, including three in sudden death, any one of which would have won a green coat. Watson seemed stunned, almost disbelieving, that he could play the game properly, strike the ball better than his competitors, yet be betrayed by the mysteries of those twelve-foot putts that can only be coaxed, never commanded.

As Watson always has insisted, "The biggest person I have to overcome is myself. . . . It's not like the Nicklaus versus Palmer days anymore. There is no rivalry like that now."

Ironically, and perhaps significantly, the only major title that Watson has won in his own country came on the only occasion in which he abandoned his icy, precise style, and admits that he became fighting mad—at Nicklaus. In the 1977 Masters, when Watson's choke reputation was at its peak, he and Nicklaus were in the thick of a final-day battle, with Nicklaus playing in the group ahead of Watson. After Nicklaus birdied the thirteenth hole, he appeared to pull the ball out of the cup and wave it at Watson, as though saying, "Stick that in your ear, kid." Nicklaus insisted he was waving at the crowd. Watson did not think so. "I got very angry with Jack and then later I got hold of myself. I thought he had waved at me. But I was out of line and I apologized." Watson was so angry he went nose-to-nose with Nicklaus in the scorer's tent after the round until Nicklaus's shocked expression showed Watson his mistake.

Does Watson the Purist need a rush of emotion, an infusion of self-forgetfulness, in order to play his instinctive best under the greatest pressure? When he isn't head-to-head with Nicklaus, just head-to-head with himself, can Watson place a crown upon his own brow?

Augusta, Ga., April 12, 1981–As Tom Watson's final five-iron shot floated toward the eighteenth green at Augusta National, checking up safely pin-high to the right, the huge crowd let out a roar. Their gutty golf darling was home free, winner of his second Masters, and a man-to-man victor over Jack Nicklaus, to boot. All Watson needed was a routine two putts for a final 71, a 280 total and a two-stroke triumph over Nicklaus (72) and Johnny Miller (68).

Actually, this is a lie. The bare facts of what Watson called his most "indescribably delicious" victory are true, but the embellishments are false. To be accurate, the crowd was not so terribly huge. When Nicklaus, who managed a tenacious but homely par round, had burned the lip at the last hole with a thirty-foot birdie attempt, most of the mob of 58,458 began to go. If Nicklaus's last far-flung chance for a twentieth major championship was gone, they, taken as a group, weren't much interested in watching the last formalities of a Watson win, even a brilliantly courageous one.

In the further interests of sporting fact, it should be noted that when Watson's iron shot landed at the eighteenth, the roar was not very loud. In fact, there was no roar. In fact, there wasn't even a cheer. A yawn would have sounded ear-splitting. When Watson himself arrived, he received the perfunctory applause due a man who had just corralled his fifth major championship; it was a proper champion's welcome, perhaps, but hardly a hero's greeting.

Twenty years ago, when Nicklaus was in the process of displacing Arnold Palmer, the "sophisticated" golf folk here resisted the notion, seeing in Nicklaus a fat and talented man of few personal charms. Now the process is being repeated. Again, a great player is asserting himself with an entirely personal signature. And, again, he is being largely misunderstood and underappreciated. The misconception about Watson is that he is merely a dogged technician who, throughout his career, has been unable to face up to competitive tasks in the premier events of his sport. He arrived here this week at age thirty-one with a record of one-for-twenty-three in major American golf championships. When Watson's game was perfectly honed, he won; when he had to show some guts, he choked. That was the label. And, sadly, it still may be.

Watson showed again today that he has gradually become the reverse of his public image: his lingering, ineradicable weaknesses are technical as he wages a perpetual battle with a swing that is too fast and too unpredictable, while his strengths are those of a profoundly determined competitor. Time and again today, Watson's golf swing—despite the thousands of hours he has invested in it—got him in Dutch and only his fierce will could save him. Watson, who started the day one shot ahead of Nicklaus, may have led this final round wire-to-wire. But it wasn't that easy.

On the PGA Tour, there is an expression: "a Watson par." It means that you have visited sand, trees, water and briar patches, yet somehow you salvage your score, even if you have to knock the ball in the hole from the fairway. On the final ten holes this day, Watson epitomized that inexplicable gift. At the ninth, Watson faced the most vicious downhill putt on

A typical Watson par.

the course. "As soon as I tapped the ball, I reached in my back pocket and started putting on my glove again." The ball rolled 100 feet past the pin, off the green and back to the fairway. Just minutes before, that same fate unhinged Lon Hinkle, who was so humiliated that he took triple bogey. Watson chipped to eight feet, then rammed the bogey putt into the heart.

The back nine was to be one long succession of "Watson pars." At the twelfth hole, he walked round and round a ten-foot putt for par, then sank the slick little devil ("A helluva putt—if I do say so"). At the thirteenth, leading by just one shot over Miller, Watson sliced a four-iron shot into Rae's Creek—an abysmal shot. Watson took his drop like a little man, wedged over the creek to six feet and made another of his six heart-stopping one-putts for the day.

The final test of Watson's combativeness came at the seventeenth— his nemesis hole—on which he scored bogey and double bogey on Friday and Saturday. Once again, he misclubbed himself and knocked the ball in the front bunker. "I could have played it like a dog . . . blasted to fifteen feet short," he said, "but I hit an aggressive [potentially dangerous] blast to five feet." And what did he do with that evil, hard-to-read, bastard-length villain that had tormented players here all week? "Well, I never considered the possibility that I wouldn't make it."

From where do such certainties come? "Inside," said Watson.

"The best part of Tom Watson's game is his mental toughness," said Nicklaus. "Above all, he doesn't like to lose. And the place that that's reflected is in putts between four and twelve feet. He makes putts when he has to make them, and that's the mark of a competitor. Today Tom was there when he had to be there."

"It's sweeter the second time," said Watson, who won here in 1977 and finished second in 1978 and 1979. "It was more of a fight this time . . . a fight against myself . . . and I did it. I felt so nervous all day that I thought I would jump out of my skin, but I was determined not to hit two bad shots in a row, and I didn't. . . . I'd be lying if I didn't admit that it was special to beat Jack today. It means more to go head-to-head with him and win."

For a moment, Watson's mask was down. He wasn't talking about his pursuit of the perfect, repeating swing. He was talking about himself. Was it possible, it was asked, that the real Watson was not a stylist intent on "swing arc" and "late release" and similar quasi-scientific foolishness, but a raw battler who loved nothing more than to attack a Bear and chew its leg off? Watson grew quiet, thinking. He has never asked for praise, never milked a crowd. He plays the game for its own sake.

"Well," he said, "I might chew off a toe or two."

PEBBLE BEACH, CAL., June 20, 1982–Fifteen years ago, when he was just a teenager and Jack Nicklaus was already established as the king of golf, Tom Watson would find a way, on Sunday mornings, to be the first player on the Pebble Beach Golf Links. "I'd drive down here from Stanford University and tee it up at 7 A.M., when I'd have the whole course to myself," said Watson this evening. "Honestly, I did fantasize about coming down the stretch head-to-head with Jack Nicklaus in the U.S. Open. Then I'd get to the last couple of holes and say, 'You gotta play these one-under-par to win the Open.' Of course, I'd always play 'em two-over. And I'd say, 'You have a long way to go, kid.' "

Tom Watson has had to come a long, slow, arduous way. But today all his fantasies, plus one piece of magic so outlandish that even a boy playing at sunrise would never dream it, became reality. And history. With one shot that will live in the retelling as long as golf is played, Watson wiped away—like a Pacific fog along the cliffs evaporating with the morning sun—the last blemish on his great and growing record.

Years from now, it will probably be forgotten that Watson won this 82nd U.S. Open by two shots over Nicklaus in a vibrant back nine duel. In time, the details of this misty, Monterey evening may fade—even the trenchant fact that, with Nicklaus and his 69—284 total already in the clubhouse, Watson finished birdie, birdie on the seventy-first and seventy-second holes to slash his way out of a tie with the fabled Bear. In nineteenth-hole lore, only a few will recall that Watson's pilgrimage to his first Open title was carved out with a week of creditable work (72-72-68-70) for a six-under-par total of 282. In the end, only one moment—one shot that epitomizes both Watson and his game—will last. Already, Watson calls it, "The Shot . . . the greatest shot of my life, the most meaningful."

It's that one swing, and no other, that prompted Nicklaus to grab Watson in a fraternal bear hug as he stepped off the final green and tell him, "You son of a bitch. You're something else. I'm really proud of you." Naturally, Watson remembers the embrace a little bit differently: "Jack said, 'I'm gonna beat you, you little S.O.B., if it takes me the rest of my life.' "

So, for the moment, we will forget how Watson began the day tied for the lead with Bill Rogers. We will pass over the jubilation that swept this seaside links as the dormant Nicklaus birdied five straight holes on the front nine—the third through seventh—to forge, momentarily, into a one-shot lead. We will negligently dash past the details of how two bogeys by Nicklaus—one perhaps abetted by a former U.S. President—plus a cross-country birdie by Watson pushed the thirty-two-year-old redhead back into the lead by two shots. And, finally, we will gloss over Nicklaus's classy birdie at the fifteenth and Watson's wild drive and bogey at the sixteenth that deadlocked the pair for the lead one final time.

The scene thus set, we must return to the one moment from this Open that will outlast and, unfortunately, diminish all others. Outlined against the blue-gray sky of Carmel Bay, Watson stands locked in ankle-deep rough beside the seventeenth green. In trying for a daring birdie—hitting a two-iron into the breeze at the 209-yard par-three, Watson has, instead, put himself in just the predicament for which Jack Neville built this course in 1919. No shot in golf is a better test of nerves, experience and touch than the "grass explosion" from high, unforgiving U.S. Open rough to a pin on a glass-slick green that is only eighteen feet away.

Watching on TV, Nicklaus, who was going for a record fifth Open title and twentieth major, says he thought, "There's no way in the world he can get up and down from there [for par]. Even if you had a good lie, you couldn't drop the ball straight down out of your hand on that green and keep it from going less than ten feet past the pin. I figured, 'Now he's going to have to birdie the last hole just to tie me and get into a playoff [on Monday].' "

Watson's opinion was different. "I'm not trying to get this close," he told his caddie. "I'm going to make it."

Why shouldn't he have thought so? Perhaps no man since Arnold Palmer in his prime has so consistently willed the ball into the hole from ludicrously improper places. On the tenth, Watson was on a cliffside amid wildflowers; he hacked to the fringe twenty-four feet away and sank his Texas-wedge shot to save par. On the eleventh, he sank a twenty-two-footer from the fringe for a birdie. And at the fourteenth, he was in the frog hair again, and holed out from thirty-five feet. As Nicklaus put it, "Yes, yes, I heard about all those shots. Just another tap-in for Tom."

With this preternatural confidence, Watson stepped into the weeds by the seventeenth quickly and, opening the face of his sand wedge, "sliced across the ball and slid the edge of the club under it. It was a good lie, with the ball hanging in the middle of the grass. If it had been down, I'd have had no shot. . . .

"As soon as it landed on the green, I knew it was in," said Watson, whose whole face was alive with hunger as the ball trickled and broke—a full foot and a half from left to right. "When it went in the hole, I about jumped in the Pacific Ocean," said Watson with a laugh. He ran at least twenty yards around the edge of the green, his putter over his head in victory and his feet carrying him he knew not where. Then, commanding himself, Watson spun and pointed at his caddie and yelled, "Told ya!"

"He was chokin', chokin' bad," Watson said with a grin. "He couldn't utter anything."

Neither could Nicklaus. "When he makes that, the golf tournament's history. . . . I've had it happen before, but I didn't think it was going to happen again. But it did. . . . How would I evaluate that shot? One of the worst that ever happened to me. Right up there with [Lee] Trevino's [chip-in] at Muirfield [on the seventy-first hole of the 1972 British Open]."

An almost certain bogey that probably would have lost his Open and branded Watson a gagger had been turned, in a twinkling, into one of the most gloriously improbable Open-winning birdies in history. Had Watson merely parred the seventeenth, he would have had to birdie the eighteenth to win. And nobody has ever birdied the seventy-second hole of the Open to win. As it was, Watson's downhill eighteen-foot birdie on the last hole was a wonderful crescendo for a day full of tremulously rolling drums. But, had Watson needed to make it to win, it might have been a tougher proposition.

Watson's playing partner, Rogers, said of that soft shot into history, "He couldn't have hit a better shot if he'd dropped down a hundred balls." "Try about a thousand," said Nicklaus drolly. Told of Nicklaus's odds-making, Watson—as superb a greenside magician as Nicklaus has always been bear-pawed—said, "Let's go out and do it. I might make some money."

Watson faced up to every sort of Open pressure today. "I was on pins and needles all day." He woke up nervous, then calmed himself by reading two newspapers "front to back. Ask me anything about the earthquake in El Salvador or the budget problems." His swing was loosey-goosey all day —he missed only one fairway, but his putting was nervous and cold on the front nine, especially when he missed a two-foot birdie putt at the seventh. Perhaps Watson was unhinged by all those Bear tracks he had to walk through. As he trudged through the third through seventh, all he heard was buzzing talk about how Nicklaus, after a shoddy bogey, par start, had been knocking down flags for five consecutive holes. By the time Nicklaus had made two-foot tap-ins for birdie at the fifth and sixth, he was tied for the lead. And when he sank a twelve-foot curler at the gorgeous seventh to take the lead, his caddie—son Jack Jr.—jumped nearly two feet in the air and began applauding.

Nicklaus misclubbed himself at the over-a-gorge eighth and was lucky to make bogey from a hanging lie on the edge of a precipice. That, however, won't be the bogey that haunts him. At the eleventh, tied for the lead, he had a flat, slightly downhill eighteen-foot birdie putt that he slid four feet past and missed coming back. What could have accounted for his only mental lapse of the day? No one will ever know for sure, but lovers of anecdote might enjoy the fact that former President Gerald Ford, a notorious three-putter, walked down from a course-side house and stood conspicuously by the eleventh green as Nicklaus three-putted. Ford then came forward to shake Nicklaus's hand and exchange pleasantries at the twelfth tee—an intrusion into serious work that no normal citizen would, presumably, have dared to attempt. Call it the Presidential Bogey or Jerry's Whammy.

In the gathering dusk around America's most lustrously atmospheric links, Watson was aglow with pride and vindication. Asked, teasingly, "Why can't you win the PGA?", he said, "Up till now, it's been: 'Why couldn't Sam Snead and I win the Open.' Now it'll be: 'Why can't Arnold Palmer and I win the PGA?' Well, I'll stay here all night and talk about it."

Time and again, Watson had to return, as he will have the pleasure of returning for the rest of his life, to the Impossible Shot. "I had no alternative," Watson said, finally, with his best freckled, gap-toothed smile. "For *you*, it's impossible."

From time to time, it is necessary for a sport to rise up and show itself at its absolute best—otherwise, we begin to forget what attracted us to it in the first place. That's what Watson and Nicklaus accomplished at Pebble Beach.

More than virtuosity, more than clutch performance, more than inherent drama, more than the splendor of Pebble Beach in a full foggy funk, this Open isolated the quality that separates, and perhaps distinguishes, golf from all other sports. Golf allows its champions to develop a genuine dignity. They play completely alone, more free of owners, managers and teammates than even professional boxers. They are individuals who must face a three-part task: Their game is man against nature, man against man and, finally, man against himself. Because of their solitude—each reaches moments like Watson's at the seventeenth when he is framed by nothing but sky and history—great golfers seldom find it possible to hide their bedrock character, even if they would prefer it.

The U.S. Open cannot offer the sight of a man being beaten senseless, as a heavyweight fight in Las Vegas may. Nor can it claim the spectacle of a human body being fragmented and incinerated at 200 miles per hour, as Indianapolis provides periodically. What golf offers is the sight of Watson, in his hour of vindication, showing no rancor toward anyone, no envy for Nicklaus. "This makes me feel that my career is one plateau higher. . . . I don't think you could have a better scenario than Pebble Beach and Jack Nicklaus, the greatest golfer of all time," said Watson with the good grace typical of his game.

Finally, golf, at its best, gives us a subdued and beaten, but thoroughly proud Nicklaus saying, "When you get this close to winning, when you think you really have probably won, it's pretty disappointing when it's over and you've lost. I played about as well as I could have. I played a good championship, one that was certainly good enough to win, except for one fellow." Was there any one shot that he wished he could have played differently? Nicklaus was asked.

"Watson's at the seventeenth," he said.

AUGUSTA, GA., April 10, 1984–When Tom Watson chipped in on the seventy-first hole of the 1982 U.S. Open at Pebble Beach, it seemed that golf's heir apparent was ready to become his sport's true king. After a dozen years as a pro, Watson had finally overcome his Open hex and won the game's premier event. "Nothing will stop Watson now," said the sages who study the game. "He'll dominate the sport for years." Watson had already been the PGA Tour's leading money winner four years in a row. What wouldn't he accomplish with the Open monkey off his back?

How little even the greatest golfers grasp how tenuously they control their game and themselves. Since that instant-legend chip shot, Watson has not won a medal-play golf tournament in the United States. Okay, so Watson won the Seiko Match Play tournament; he probably found some way to spend the $100,000 prize. But that's a gimmick event. Also, Watson has continued his private plundering of the British Open, winning that arty but competitively weak event for the fourth and fifth times in 1982 and 1983. However, in medal-play PGA events, which is where golf muscle is most fairly measured on this planet, Watson hasn't made a mark since The Chip. His drought in his own country has now reached twenty-two months and counting.

"I got very discouraged. . . . Wouldn't you get discouraged? Sometimes I wish I could cut this right arm off," said Watson of the misbehaving limb that has caused him to spray his long shots, especially his drives, into uncharted acreage. "I grip it too tight."

What flaws does that activate? "Everything," said Watson.

Watson's misery became so well-known among the golf cognoscenti that the nature of the great man's mail began to change. One fan sent a book with the title *Don't Choke.* "Another guy sent me a book with theories on everything, including how to put the tee in the ground," said Watson. "He said if you tilted the tee forward there would be less friction on the ball at impact and it would go farther. . . . I even received a set of forward-leaning tees that had the target side beveled away."

Once, Watson boasted that he played golf in his own private "rubber room": a state of concentration and confidence so deep that the perils of the course and his own psyche could not reach him. That rubber room disintegrated. "Lately I've been thinking, 'When am I going to hit a good shot again?' " says Watson now. "I haven't been so cocksure. . . . I knew [during the slump that] I probably wasn't going to win. . . . But I never let on to anybody, not even my wife. I don't let that out to anybody."

Once, Watson seemed so secure and even brash that fellow players on the tour, perhaps jealous, nicknamed him "Karnac." As Howard Twitty once said, "We called him that because he always knew the answer before he even heard the question." They don't call golf "The Humbling Game" for nothing. Watson has been reintroduced to doubt. He thought he'd left that behind years ago when, as a youngster on the Tour, "I choked. . . . There were a lot of times when I could have won but didn't. But I persevered and eventually I learned that you don't have to hit the ball perfectly to win; you have to manage yourself better. . . ."

These days, realistic, but extremely uncharacteristic phrases of self-doubt punctuate the thirty-four-year-old Watson's conversation. "I haven't played as well as I did in the late seventies. . . . Maybe that's old age," he says, adding later, "When I'm in a slump, I think so much about my long game that I don't think enough about getting the ball in the hole. . . . I don't practice as much as I used to. . . . Sometimes I'll still practice eight hours in a day, but not as often. . . . I have other responsibilities besides golf. . . ."

"I watch Tom," says Seve Ballesteros. "I don't see many bad things in his swing. But he has lost maybe the confidence a little bit and he loses his temper a little more. . . . This game is all in the mind."

In some ways, Watson seems to have fallen prey to the athlete's most inescapable enemy: not age, but maturity. Greatness at games is, to some extent, kid's stuff. Once, Watson had about him an abstracted and icy bearing. At times, he seemed to remain in that rubber room even after he left the course. Now, with eight major championships on his mantel and more millions in his pocket than he will ever spend, Watson's mind runs to his wife and their two young children, to his many business ventures and to the failing health of Byron Nelson's wife.

"I saw Byron the Monday after the TPC," said Watson, speaking almost to himself. Nelson's health is fragile, yet better than his wife's. "She's about the same," said Watson bleakly. "He's devoting his whole life to her."

Tom Watson's golf game has seen better days. And may see them again. Yet, through his struggles, this less-cocky Watson may have acquired some qualities—who would bother to pin down their names?—that he never had time to develop when he was boring his way to greatness.

SHOOTING
AT CLOUDS

Sandwich, England, June 1981–In 1885 Laidlaw Purves climbed to the top of St. Clements Church, one of the quaint historic sites in the oft-invaded English Channel port of Sandwich, a town that knew its greatest glory in Chaucerian times and has been on the slide ever since. Purves was not a historian, an architect or an archaeologist—all the sort of folk who come here to peruse a medieval Peter's pence box or savor the seventh-century rubble of St. Mary's Church. Instead, Purves gazed out toward Pegwell Bay, the bluffs of Ramsgate and the broad straits of Dover. There, stretched before him, were vast natural sand dunes, covered with a thin layer of loose soil two inches deep. "Behold," said Purves, "the ideal site for a links."

Two years later, Royal St. George's Golf Club had been built in Sandwich. So great and instant was its fame that by 1894 it was chosen as the site for the first British Open championship ever held outside of Scotland. For the next fifty-five years, the only lore created in Sandwich was golf lore.

For more than a millennium, this southeastern tip of England had been a region of far greater events. St. Augustine landed here in 597. King Arthur and Robin Hood each had their adventurous flings in Kent. And everybody, from the Saxons to the Normans to the Romans to the Spanish and French, always landed here when they wanted to start the pillaging of Britain.

However, by the twentieth century, Sandwich was synonymous with two things. It was the home of the Earl of Sandwich, who invented the sandwich, and it was home of glorious Royal St. George's, the heavenly links brought to earth. From 1894 to 1949, the British Open was played here nine times, usually with vivid incident. Harry Vardon and Walter

Hagen each won twice, Hagen celebrating in 1922 by giving the whole of the paltry prize money to his caddie as a tip. In 1938, the year of the gale, every tournament tent was flattened by winds that, history claims, neared 100 m.p.h. And in 1949, the runner-up, Harry Bradshaw of Kilcroney, Ireland, lost in a playoff to Bobby Locke, although, were it not for a bottle of beer, he would have won in the regulation seventy-two holes. Bradshaw's tee shot on the fifth hole, you see, rolled into the midst of what had been an alfresco lunch in the rough; his ball lodged in the broken neck of a bottle. Not knowing that he was allowed free relief, Bradshaw smashed ball and bottle with his niblick, advancing the ball only twenty yards, and took a double bogey.

Typical of Royal St. George's deliberate unfairness—which the British believe to be the most lifelike quality of golf—is the towering white-faced bunker on the fourth hole that looks like one of the white cliffs of Dover. This thirty-foot sheer wall trap faces the driver on the tee like an open maw that could swallow any number of elephants.

In the English Championships of 1979, fifty-four-year-old amateur Reg Gladding was on the twenty-second hole of a match play semifinal when he imbedded his tee shot near the crest of the monstrous trap. To enter the desert from the top would have caused a sand slide and moved the ball (a penalty). So Gladding, with neither ropes nor pitons, began inching his way up from the bottom as though through a deep snowdrift. Once at the top, and at the end of his strength, Gladding swung, lost his balance and tumbled to the bottom in a tangle of ball, club and limbs. "I forfeit the hole and the match," declared Gladding. "I have no idea how many times I grounded my club or collided with the ball while I was falling."

What we see here is the epitome of one of Britain's most basic institutions—the Open. Royal St. George's *is* links golf. And links golf is as central to Britain's notion of its own character as . . . hmmm . . . well, as it is foreign to an American's sense of both golf and character.

Royal St. George's is a world of grass and sky. To compare it to any American golf course is pointless. It is a creation, and an experience, entirely unto itself. The first impression that a great British links makes upon an American golfer is that the place is unspeakably ugly and fit neither for the eye nor the game of golf. An American judges a golf hole by its beauty and by its definition. That is, it should be a specific place, self-contained. A British golfer judges a seaside links hole by its barren, forbidding severity and its lack of definition. If you can tell where you are going, or what you are aiming at, then it's not an outstanding hole.

American golf courses are neat, well trimmed, like the Versailles gardens. Even the rough is regulation. British links are utterly wild. The notion, dating to the earliest nineteenth-century links, is that you take a marvelously unkempt stretch of dunes land, hitch up the team and drag the smallest conceivable landing area for the drive, then clear the smallest possible landing area for the green. The idea is to guide the golf ball through the wilderness, flying it from one safe landing area to another. That those clear areas are grotesquely bumpy and hard—meaning that a perfect shot can carom freakishly into the undergrowth—is, to British minds, the essence of sport. American golfers, Hale Irwin being a contemporary example, are so outraged and fundamentally upset by this British affection for the arbitrary and unfair that they often loathe coming here.

The American notion of golf—one that has produced great uninhibited talents, daring play and unbeatable scores—is: "Let 'er rip. Tear the guts out of the course. Tee it high and let it fly." It is a distinctly New World perspective that is optimistic about the notion of progress and trusts nature, if not as a friend, then at least as a benevolently indifferent companion.

The British concept of golf is defensive. Keep it in play, survive disaster, recover from adversity. It is a weary, philosophical Old World approach that is long on wisdom, short on results. Nature is seen as an implacable and unbeatable enemy that can be endured and kept temporarily at bay. American pros play in short sleeves and associate their game with warmth and heroic derring-do. The British play in sweaters, caps and long underwear and think of their game the way monks supposedly revere their hair shirts.

The charm of Royal St. George's is the charm of minimal art. The dogwood and azaleas, all tended to the limit, try to attack you at the Masters. Here, as you trudge through the dunes, trying to figure out where you are, why you're here and where you're going, you must acquire a taste for the beauties of life among the long grasses. The smell here is not of the salt sea, although odd signs on the course say "To the Sea" lest one become totally disoriented. The nose knows nothing but the rich scent of grasses and wild flowers. Instead of towering trees or lakes or steep precipices, the essence of pleasure at Royal St. George's is an acquired taste for bees and butterflies dancing in a stand of wild lavender clover.

In American golf, the horizon and, consequently, the sky play little or no part. The unit of measurement is one golf hole, surrounded by trees, hills or whatever. The horizon would interfere or distract. At Royal St. George's, the sea, the cliffs of Ramsgate and even the distant, tempting hint of the coast of France are always as close as the next rising dune.

The golf course—the greens, tees and traps—is a minor part of a larger mural. In America, the land exists to emphasize the golf holes that are crafted into its heart. In Britain, the golf holes are an almost ephemeral part of a lasting landscape. Let Royal St. George's lie fallow for one year, you sense, and no one would know it had ever existed.

"Our courses are built without one puff of smoke," say the British proudly, meaning that they have used no bulldozers, no buzz saws, no earth-scorching. Where Americans attack the land, turn it to their hand and their purposes, the Britisher, with almost Zenlike stoicism, resigns himself to what exists and, by an act of mind, turns it into a pleasure.

To an American pro, the greatest contempt he can show for these odd, ugly-duckling British shrines of golf is to say, "Go to the British Open and shoot at clouds." That means that, on a links, there are no targets, or very few. So seldom can you see the flags that, on more shots than not, the target is the third knob from the left or, literally, a drifting cloud. That, to Americans, is unsettling, like built-in bad hops. Or wind.

Yes, wind. It is central to British golf that the golf ball, and, therefore, the golfer, are defenseless against the elements. The wind rules; the player merely uses the wind as best he can, like a tacking sailor.

While American golf soars, emphasizing the long, majestic shot, the ICBM approach, the golf on this island emphasizes the modesty of a bouncing ball. "The freshest element here," says Tom Watson, who loves links golf, "is studying a bouncing ball. In America, we'll do anything to build a shot to avoid a bounce because a bounce is inherently unpredictable. Here, a rolling ball is more dependable than one up in that wind."

"We live with bad conditions," said West German Bernhard Langer. "We should be able to cope with them better than Americans." Therein is contained a world view, and, perhaps, a kernel of contempt. It insults Europeans that a dozen times between 1970 and 1985 a few American pros, hardly half the full U.S. contingent, have taken a week from their Palm Springs-to-Miami life-style to win the British Open. Although they'll never say it, the golfers of Europe don't know how the Americans do it. The fact, perhaps, is that, as a brisk change, golf on these chilly, invigorating dunes is a stirring challenge and an enticement. However, an American player, or even spectator, who labored on these links long enough would soon adopt an Old World droop of the shoulders. These links, perhaps like their troubled island, are a place to visit and appreciate. And then leave.

The British players who labor here for a lifetime bear the marks of their links heritage to the very soul. Tune in on the second round of the 1981 Open here, for instance, and the script might have been written by P. G. Wodehouse. Nick Job, a character worthy of the man who wrote "The Clicking of Cuthbert," led the field and turned Royal St. George's into a sort of musical comedy.

"It's all a total shock to me. The pressure's getting to be hell," deadpanned the strapping thirty-two-year-old redhead with a Byronic profile and quiet, wry voice. "It's embarrassing to come to every green and have to say, 'Thank you, thank you,' and give that jaunty salute to the crowd. I just can't master it . . . and Nicklaus does it so well. . . ."

Job, the son of a Kent golf pro, seemed to epitomize a sort of British character that is compulsively self-deprecating, always anticipating disaster, but in a charmingly amusing way. During this time of economic woes, some folk on this island term that cast of mind "the British disease."

"The English are not the most positive people. Say 'Have a nice day' to us and we'll look at you like you're balmy," said Job.

"The odds on you were three hundred to one before the tournament. What should they be now?" he was asked.

"Four hundred to one."

"Why did you bogey three of the last five holes when you might easily have been leading the entire tournament?"

"The swing was getting a bit hunched, a bit jerky, a bit nervy . . ."

"Why the sudden improvement in your game?"

"I found out recently that for the last fifteen years I've had a bad swing. It was quite a shock to my system. I've changed everything. . . . New swing entirely."

All these things seemingly are said not as wisecracks, but as the labored utterances of a patient and long-suffering Job. Imagine a handsome, fey, exhausted, elegant Peter O'Toole who happens to be near the top of the British Open leader board and doesn't know quite what to make of it.

"What would it mean for an Englishman to win the Open?"

"Be bigger than the royal wedding," said Job. "It won't change me if I win. I'll still be the same nice person."

What does he think of playing in one of the last prestigious twosomes on Saturday?

Job paused, pursed his mouth and said, "I can't see how I'm going to get out of it."

On a more serious note (and at times Job's face was so serious that it seemed washed out from emotion), he said, "People don't know what a normal man goes through in a situation like this. It's fun and it's hell at the same time because you know it's the chance of a lifetime. I have no idea if I can cope with this kind of worry because I've never been through anything like it. The stress comes because I know that if I can somehow pull myself together and play my best golf for two more days, I could win.

"Still," he said, changing mood, "it might be easier if I were American. I say, how do you do it? You seem to eat positive for breakfast and we [English] eat negative. How do you stand on the first tee like this?" he said, doing an imitation of Nicklaus swelling his shoulders, adjusting his glove and giving a flex of wrist to the club that speaks as elegantly as a king's gesture with a scepter.

"It's that old American thing from the Ryder Cup matches. The

This magnolia-lined roadway typifies the traditional splendor of Augusta National.

(Leonard Kamsler/*Golf Magazine*)

The charms and frustrations of St. Andrews can be seen side by side.

(Leonard Kamsler/*Golf Magazine*)

The notorious Road Hole at St. Andrews.

(Photograph by Ruffin Beckwith)

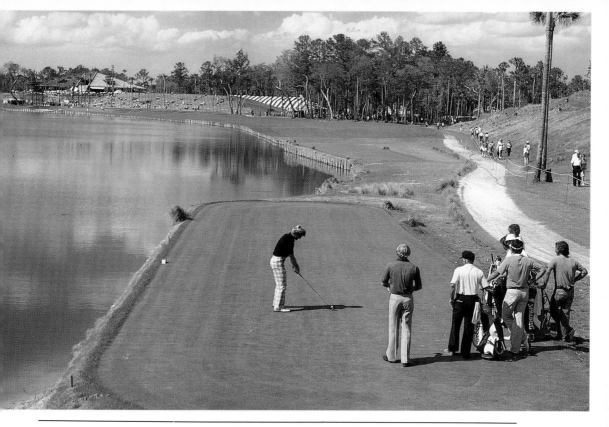

The TPC's designers created a classic test of accuracy under pressure.

Perhaps the greatest hole at one of the world's greatest courses—the eighteenth at Pebble Beach.

Americans wear Foot-Joys and all the English players stand together admiring their shoes, and their slacks and their clubs. How can you beat a man if you can't even afford his shoes?"

Just as many Americans don't know that St. Andrew is as far north as Labrador, so many U.S. golf fans have no glimmering of the international prestige of the British Open. Or the entirely justifiable reasons for that status.

Among the four "major" golf tournaments, only the U.S. Open still stands clearly above the British Open. The PGA can't compare to this extravaganza by the sea, either as entertainment or as a test of golf. And it's moot whether the Masters stands higher than this Open in the golf pecking order.

In 1960, when Arnold Palmer led a legion of U.S. players here—out of respect for tradition far more than hope of prize money—the British Open was a dying institution. Palmer saved it. Now the U.S. Open better watch its step if it wants to remain number one. "This is the real World Series of Golf," says Tom Watson.

This field has much of the best of the U.S. Tour as well as the best players from Europe, Australia and Japan. The day is gone when the hundredth-best player on the U.S. Tour is automatically superior to the best players from the "lesser" Tours. Golf has become truly international, led by players like Greg Norman, Seve Ballesteros, Bernhard Langer, Sandy Lyle and Nick Faldo.

Although the U.S. circuit is the big league of golf, the sport needs a great tournament that's played on what amounts to a neutral site—a place where Americans don't have home cooking, home crowds and home conditions. That's what the British Open is. Just as the game needs a venue where tweed and sandstone replace polyester and chrome, so the sport also needs an alternative to the monotony of the kind of target golf played in the United States. On the U.S. Tour, conditions are so lush that shots into both fairways and greens rarely bounce more than a few yards. You pick a target and land the ball on it. The game is played entirely through the air. The emphasis is on power and accuracy; ultimately, that is the best and most athletic way to design the game. That's why the United States still produces most of the best golfers. But it's not the only way to play.

On the U.S. Tour, your caddie tells you, "One hundred seventy yards, wind left to right, pin's thirty feet behind the front trap." So you pull out your seven-iron, take your standard full swing, draw the shot a little against the wind and land it as close to the stick as you can. For the experienced pro, almost no thought is involved, no basic decision. Golf becomes a game of execution.

In Britain, brainpower and emotional resiliency and creative shot-making and intuitive touch are essential. Power, and even accuracy, are much less vital. "Those little shots aren't all that easy," said Watson. "Downwind, you can bounce through the green and make bogey even though your drive is only seventy yards from the hole. Into the wind, you can check up on the wrong side of a swail and three-putt. This is the way golf was meant to be played."

Well, let's not get carried away. It's one way to play. Especially on an island where the weather is cold and windy and the ground is stony.

The fact that the best players from the U.S. Tour owned the British Open trophy almost exclusively from 1961 to 1983 is proof that the version of the game here is compatible with the abilities of players like Jack Nicklaus, Watson, Lee Trevino, Tom Weiskopf, Johnny Miller, Bill Rogers, Tony Lema and Palmer.

One final charm of the British Open is that it is both the best-organized and the most physically impressive of all the major events. The Royal and Ancient puts the U.S. Golf Association to shame with its competence at detail, its ability to manage traffic and crowds, its speed and accuracy with scoreboards. The USGA should send a committee here and copy, copy, copy. When major tournaments and major titles are discussed these days, the two Opens—U.S., then British— stand securely at the top.

BUCKING
THE SYSTEM

June 1981–Ten years ago this month when he threw a rubber snake at Jack Nicklaus on the practice tee, then beat him in a playoff at Merion to win his second U.S. Open, Lee Trevino became famous.

Famous, yes; known, no.

Many in golf, including Trevino himself, say that he barely became known at all. In June 1971, there on the Main Line, Trevino became bona fide—two Opens are considered proof of golf bloodlines. That thunderclap of success brought Trevino into the glare of publicity. Every corner of his Dickensian life was lit. His early sufferings were considered uplifting, amusing, heroic. Quickly, the myth of the funny man was profitably put in place. Once Trevino was a public personality, anything at odds with that role was left in shadow. Only with the years have the other parts of Trevino slowly come to light, giving balance and humanity to what we knew and appreciated all along.

Still, Trevino may be the least-fathomed superstar in golf. As a melodramatic example, it's been a Tour whisper for years that when Trevino began his comeback in 1978 after being struck by lightning and undergoing major back surgery for a ruptured disk, the second-leading money winner in golf history was almost broke. "I didn't want to make a comeback; I had to make one," says Trevino now. "It got to a point where I was scared that everything I'd worked for would be gone. I'd invested badly. . . . I had almost everything tied up in one [failed] project and, until I got out of it, it was draining everything. I still had our $300,000 home, but it had a $140,000 mortgage. I had eight antique cars, but that doesn't amount to too much. And I had one piece of commercial property all paid for that was worth maybe $25,000. Other than that, all I had was the rainbow."

The rainbow?

Lee Trevino, a very private person, caught between moods.

"Sure, you know, the pot of gold that's buried under the end of the rainbow. I've always believed in that. But I had to get my old tools out and dig for it again."

It's hard to find any aspect of Trevino that is not either completely misunderstood, or, at best, half-understood. Trevino needs to be read like some of the late works of Mark Twain—with trepidation, lest we find that the joke is on ourselves. "People think Trevino's loosey goosey," says Dale Antrum, a veteran PGA Tour official. "In fact, he's tight as a drum. They think he's relaxed. Really, he's so intense he has to talk and joke constantly to relieve the tension. The reason he plays so fast is because he has to. Trevino goes absolutely nuts if play is slow. It can destroy his game and other players know it."

Says Trevino, "There ain't nothin' relaxed about me on a golf course. I'm very tightly wound. All that jabbering is a pressure valve. I couldn't do without it. The competitor inside you knows what has to be done. If the game doesn't eat you up inside, you can't possibly be a great player. I still get mad, but not nearly like I once did. In the last ten years, that's probably the biggest improvement in my game."

Fans think Trevino is naturally gregarious. "Once he steps off the course, he's one of the least-sociable, least-outgoing guys on the Tour," says Antrum. "He never—and I mean never—eats outside his room. He's the all-time loner when it comes to fraternizing with other players off the golf course." Trevino, taking pleasure in being found out, says, "I can count on one finger the guys out here that I've had dinner with in thirteen years. I never spend any time with golfers away from the course. I don't want to hear, 'At seven, I hit it over the green. . . . ' After 6 P.M., I charge caddie fees to listen. . . .

"In a way, my personality is like Muhammad Ali's. In front of a camera or a group, he's loud. But if you catch him alone in a room, it's very difficult to hear a word he says. That's me . . . a completely different person off the course. Neither's an act. They're both real. . . . People think I talk in my sleep. I get 'em to think that. I like to give people what they want."

"The public has idolized and loved two players in recent times—Palmer and Trevino," says Antrum. "While Palmer really needs the galleries and appreciates their affection, I've often wondered just how high an opinion Lee has of the public."

Even in the arcane technical debates of golf theory, Trevino is mysterious. "People think Lee's got a bad swing," says Antrum. "The truth is he might have the best swing. Some players call him the best shotmaker since Hogan. He is the only guy out here who has every shot and will play 'em under pressure."

"Yes, I think I have the best swing on the Tour," Trevino says. "Why

Look at that follow-through. Is this unorthodox swing perhaps the best since Hogan's?

have scores come down in the last ten years? Partly because they're imitating me . . . open position, fade, lots of power and control from the right side. In the evolution of the game, who says they invented the swing right back then? Maybe it's supposed to be flat like mine. The best swing is the one that repeats. And that's what I have. . . . Years ago, I had a one-iron that I could hit 260 yards through a doorway. Now I can hit it through the keyhole."

Perhaps it is time, ten years after the fact, to take a brief synoptic look at Trevino as though we'd never met him before, never taken him at quip value. The bare bones of his life have a chilling quality; like a magic lantern, they throw fascinating, sometimes frightening skeletal shadows. That Trevino is as biting as he is facile, as philosophical as he is funny, should be no surprise. This is a man, totally a creature of his past, who has forgotten nothing, forgiven little, learned from everything and always looked for a way to reconcile a good heart with a smart percentage play.

Trevino never has known his father nor wanted to. His mother was a maid and his maternal grandfather, who was all the father he had, was a hard-drinking, itinerant gravedigger. Trevino grew up in a rural maintenance shack near Dallas with no electricity or plumbing. It wasn't degradation, but it was poverty. He dropped out of school in the eighth grade to earn money for the family. He took the closest laboring job at hand— doing maintenance at the golf course a few yards from home. That is, when he wasn't a shoeshine boy. A solitary child, giving to hunting rabbits or fishing alone, he joined the Marines as soon as he was old enough.

"I was a messed-up kid. I'd fall in love with a fence post. . . . I had the feeling Dallas was the whole damn world and I was going to die without ever seeing anything else except another fairway to cut. So I went."

The Corps taught him responsibility, pride, hard drinking and carousing. In his first tour of duty, he mastered the machine gun, setting a speed and accuracy record that still stands. In his re-up tour, he mastered golf, turning a childhood hobby (he was a caddie) into a vocation. He left the Marines in 1960 with one fixed idea: to become a pro golfer. For years, Trevino denied this seriousness of purpose, telling tales about simply being a public course hustler who played all comers with a twenty-five-ounce Dr. Pepper bottle. Now he admits, "From 1960 to 1967, I did nothing but play golf fifteen hours a day. You don't start playing at 5 A.M. every morning and hit a thousand practice balls a day for seven years just to win some $2 bet."

However, while he found order on the course, Trevino found chaos off it. His first marriage ended, he says, because of his immaturity and drinking. His wife and son moved to Ohio. Within months, he had married a seventeen-year-old girl who was a ticket taker at the local movie house. At every turn, his golf dreams were stymied. For four years, he worked at a rinky-dink par-three course on the theory that it was a back door to getting a PGA Tour card. Then, after those four years, the range owner—the man Trevino considered a surrogate father—refused to sign papers validating his term of indentured servitude.

It took three more years, until he was twenty-seven, for Trevino to make the Tour. Then he played the rube, making fun of his unorthodox swing, claiming it was all luck. Even after he won the 1968 Open at Oak Hill, veteran Bob Goalby said, not critically, just analytically, "In ten years, we'll be playing benefits for that guy." Now, Trevino says, "When I came out here, my game was ready. From the first year, I did nothing but win tournaments and money."

And, from that first year, Trevino kept close tabs on the past and present, keeping the two separate in his mind, not letting one change his memory of the other. "When you're successful, everybody wants a piece of you," said Trevino after that first Open. "I hadn't seen my sister in several years. Now I'm the sweetest guy she's ever seen."

Trevino has never forgotten several personal slights at his first Masters; he has never set foot inside the Augusta National Clubhouse, although he says, "Oh, I think I might've been in there once," and, for a decade, he changed his spikes in the parking lot like a public course hacker to avoid entering the locker room. Now he changes shoes at home. "They say we've already played one major tournament this year," said Trevino after this year's Masters, "but for me, the first major tournament will be the Open at Merion. I don't count the Masters."

His refusal to pity himself may be the hole card that Trevino has been forced to play more than any other. His ill fortune everywhere but on a golf course has never changed and remains brutal to this day. His luck with a buck is so rotten that he's now working on his third fortune; he's lost two. "Everything's okay now," says Trevino, who is in the midst of a large golf course-and-condominium deal in Titusville, Fla.

Nonetheless, Trevino and business seem to be a tragic mix. Three days before this year's Masters, the largest investor in their Titusville project died of a heart attack. A few days later, so did the project's general manager. Let it be noted that Titusville is, nonetheless, working out well, according to Trevino. "I've learned what to do and what not to do in business. The hard way."

In a lifetime of hardships, Trevino has always maintained that one precept—hard work—would see him through, and the loss of that one insight would undo him. Trevino's grandfather, Joe, the gravedigger who could drink "from nine in the morning until dark and still drive away," and who lived just long enough to see him win the Open, was a man of one maxim: "You want a life, you work for it."

"A few years ago, I got to the point where I forgot that," says Trevino. "I got it all too fast. Stardom, recognition, whatever. It went to my head. I was neglecting practice, making excuses, turning into a give-up artist. When I got hit by lightning in 1975 and then had the back surgery in 1976, it gave me almost a whole year to take a good look at myself. I realized that for years I'd felt myself floating away from hard work. I was getting away from the one thing I believed in. Pride in what you do well is what makes a man."

This, of course, is self-hypnosis—a man talking himself into the test of a lifetime. At the age of thirty-eight, after falling to thirty-third place on the money list, with a back so precarious that he says, "If somebody don't lift the bag out of the car for me, I don't play," Trevino started to climb back to the summit. In the morning, he hung upside down on a trapeze apparatus, then exercised for an hour to limber his back. More of the same at night. Between dawn and dusk, he followed the law he had laid down to young pros for years: "If the sun is up, why aren't you playing golf?"

Last season, at forty, Trevino won three tournaments and $385,814—more than $150,000 more than ever before. Just as important, he won the Vardon Trophy for lowest stroke average on tour, his fifth Vardon but his first since his salad days (1970, 1971, 1972, 1974). Trevino's feat lacked only one thing—a centerpiece, a major championship victory, to call attention to all that happened to him since his last major, the 1974 PGA. "I know what you're talking about," says Trevino, when asked about this. "I could still do it.

"I can't honestly say that I have the same goals now that I did ten or twelve years ago," says Trevino. "But the number one goal is still the same —to win the big one . . . I may have spent a lot of time trying to find my game, but I haven't had to try to find myself. I've known who I was all along. If I forget, I look at my driver's license. I'm not one of those freaky cats sayin', 'Hey, man, where you coming from?' and 'Where's it at?'

"I've always been at the same place."

"And where is that?"

"Right here," said Lee Buck Trevino, stomping his proud foot on the firm earth.

NO
HUMAN HAND

ST. ANDREWS, SCOTLAND, July 1984–Not long ago, I came here to make my pilgrimage to the Old Course—the home of golf, the most famous links in the world and the site of twenty-three British Opens. Like Bobby Jones, Sam Snead, Tom Watson and thousands before me, I stood beside the eighteenth green, looked across the bleak peninsula jutting between the Firth of Forth and the Firth of Tay and felt both shock and disappointment. Every American golfer comes here forewarned that St. Andrews will be a colossal letdown. Yet, no matter how low your expectations, St. Andrews (on first impression) is duller, drabber, flatter, windier, scruffier and homelier than you could believe.

"This is the ugliest golf course I've ever seen in my life," I said to my wife. "I wouldn't bother to play it if you put it in the backyard. Somebody's pulling somebody's leg."

When Snead first saw this layout, he wanted to go back home and withdraw without playing. Jones was at first "puzzled and bewildered" and wrote, "I could not play the course, and I did not think anyone else could." One U.S. Walker Cup captain thought, on first introduction, that the Old Course was "the worst." Everybody hates the Old Course. Until he's played it or walked it or studied it. Then it gets 'em. From Granny Clark's Wynd to Ginger Beer and around the Loop, from the Swilcon Burn to the Valley of Sin, over the Elysian Fields and through Hell Bunker, past the Principal's Nose and along the Road Hole to home, you feel like you've been out for a stroll with history.

U.S. Open champion Fuzzy Zoeller, fresh from winning the 1984 U.S. Open, hopped off the Concorde and hit the links early the next morning to see the Old Lady, which has ruled and defined this town since the twelfth century. "It's different," said Zoeller. "Holes, mounds, pot bunkers. . . .

You can't see all that on TV. . . . Think a guy could get lost out there if he didn't know where he was going. . . . You're aiming at a lot of church spires. . . . There sure are a lot of little holes out there that they forgot to put sand in. . . . Some of those things [pot bunkers], there isn't even room to sit down." Such bemused consternation is the required first reaction to St. Andrews.

"Anyone's first impression is puzzlement. It has to be," Ben Crenshaw says. "It is odd. But I've never seen a course that grows on you so much. . . . It puts more emphasis on strategy than any course. There's an A, B and C way to play every shot, depending on your ability or how the wind is blowing or if you want to gamble. . . . Its flexibility . . . its ability to accommodate every class of golfer, from the champion on down, and to present him with every choice and challenge is unique." Then Crenshaw pauses for the sort of smile that many give when they talk about St. Andrews. "And no man ever had a hand in building the course."

This tract, which was centuries old when it was protected by law in the city charter of 1552, has never been touched. Shaped like a huge shepherd's crook, the Old Course hasn't been altered since Mary, Queen of Scots, drew criticism by playing here too soon after the death of her husband, who'd been locked in nearby Loch Leven Castle. Nature made the Old Course and man hardly seems fit to criticize it.

"St. Andrews is the most fascinating golf course I have ever played," wrote Jones, changing his early opinion. "There is always a way at St. Andrews, although it is not always the obvious way, and in trying to find it, there is more to be learned on this British course than in playing a hundred ordinary American golf courses."

To most current pros (except Jack Nicklaus, who's finished second, first and first in three Opens here), this immemorial ground is still mostly a mystery. As for his romance with the Old Course, Nicklaus says, "Yeah, I understand it. I understand that you don't have a clue and it's going to keep you that way. . . . There are going to be situations where you don't know what to do. . . . The phrase 'Golf wasn't meant to be fair' was born here. . . . I don't know why, but I've loved this course since the first time I saw it. . . . It's the number one course in the world for difficulty in understanding [its subtleties]. I don't know which course would be second. There'd be miles between them.

"There's more to be learned here about course design than anywhere. Collection bunkers, false fronts, bump shots. The fundamentals of design became fundamentals because of what's here. And it all happened accidentally. Or maybe accidentally on purpose. . . ."

"The Old Course is a puzzle . . . and no one's ever going to completely figure it out," Watson said. "The more I play it, the more I remember it. . . . It's the most difficult of all courses to figure out where to hit the ball." You can only understand that statement after you've seen the Old Course. No photo, with its foreshortening effect, can begin to give a sense of the amazing lunar quality of the land here. It's said that old Tom Morris, the first pro, looked through a nineteenth-century telescope at the moon and said, "Faith, sir, she looks like the Old Course."

Aside from its strategic appeal and difficulty—only three players have broken 280 in twenty-two Opens here—St. Andrews has two other enormous charms: its beauty once you're actually out on the course, and its capacious lore. Looking out, St. Andrews is ugly. Looking back, it's magnificent. Once you're lost out on the links, the play of light on the burns (streams) and the sight and smell of the heather, broom, gorse and whins (green shrubs with thorns) is fine stuff. The Old Town and the University of St. Andrews, with its Greek, medieval, Georgian and Gothic architecture, make a skyline backdrop so stirring that Crenshaw said, "I have to compose myself and not look at it too much when I'm playing."

This little gray town in the Kingdom of Fife, sitting on its rocky promontory overlooking the North Sea, is so addicted to golf that its cheerful obsession has almost become a parody. Back in 1885, an American student-poet (R. F. Murray) visiting here wrote: "Would you like to see a city given over soul and body to a tyrannising game? If you would, there's little need to be a rover, for St. Andrews is the abject city's name." That state of affairs hasn't changed since the Middle Ages. Old town records are full of stories of bridegrooms teeing off at dawn on the morning after their wedding nights and clergymen giving up the ministry because it conflicted with their golfing vows.

In a place where the feather ball was discovered in 1618 and the Royal and Ancient was founded in 1754, it's easy to fall into a sense of timelessness. Here, modern and ancient anecdotes blur into one. Was it 105 years ago that Maitland Dougall stood on the first tee, waiting for the starter to say, "Play away, please," in the club championship when a storm sprang up in the bay and a ship began to founder? "I'll take the stroke oar," Dougall said as he took to a lifeboat for five hours until the crew was rescued. Of course, Dougall returned to the tee and won the title.

It seems less likely that another quintessential St. Andrews yarn is completely true. It's said that, long ago, two Scots were having a match on the Old Course when, far out on the Loop, one had a heart attack and died. The other golfer then carried his friend all the way back to the clubhouse. Asked if that were not a tiring job, he said, "Aye, it was. But the worst bit was laying him down and picking him up between shots."

If we searched for one symbol of St. Andrews, one slice of the whole which could give us a taste of the place's rich composite of golf lore, strategy and obdurate eccentricity, it would be the Road Hole. The legend of the infamous number seventeen began more than a century ago.

Back in 1885, a chap named David Ayton came to the next-to-last hole of the British Open with a five-shot lead. At the 461-yard, par-four, Ayton hit a good drive and a spanking brassie shot to excellent chip-and-run position in front of the green. Victory seemed a formality. Even when Ayton's first putt failed to stay on line on the green's cross-slope and rolled back in front of the bunker, his problems seemed minimal. Then the realities of what may be the hardest hole on earth began to take hold. Pitching over the Road Hole bunker is an advanced form of golf torture. Dump it in the trap and you may have to play out sideways. Go a few feet past the pin and you slip down a sharp hill and onto the stony road itself.

Ayton, fearing the bunker, went over the green and onto the road. Then he scraped the ball up the bank and had it roll back to his feet. Next, he pitched across the green into the bunker. Too weak, too strong, too weak, too strong. Twice Ayton tried to blast from the bunker and twice he failed. Finally, he exploded onto the green and two-putted. For an eleven. Nine strokes from 100 feet without a penalty. He lost the Open by two shots.

Such terrors have not abated over the years. In fact, the best golfers in the world still call the Road Hole the hardest on earth. The generally understated Open program calls the seventeenth "probably the most famous single hole in the world."

"I got no pride on that hole," says Lee Trevino. "It's a par-five and I play it that way. A four is a birdie." "Into the wind, the hole is almost unplayable," said Seve Ballesteros. "I just try not to pull a Tommy Nakajima," said Greg Norman.

Ah, yes, Nakajima.

In 1978 Nakajima, well up among the contenders, reached the seventeenth green in two shots. And ended up with a nine. Oh, so you'd like to hear about that, would you? Who says that golf isn't the game played by masochists and watched by sadists?

Nakajima's first putt took a left-hand turn and trickled into the Road Bunker. Fearing that he might blast over the green, over the road and over a low stone wall out of bounds (a realistic possibility), Nakajima swung too tenderly. And left the ball in the bunker. Twice. His third blast escaped the sand. His chip reached the green. Two little putts and a quintuple bogey. Easy.

(Nakajima, it should be noted, had prepped for his seven-shot performance on that green by taking thirteen on the par-five thirteenth hole at Augusta National three months before. In that horror, Nakajima had one of his recovery shots ricochet back and hit him in the foot [two-shot penalty]. Then, as he handed his club to his caddie, the caddie dropped the club into the hazard for another two-shot penalty. Nakajima, asked if he lost his concentration, "No, I lost count.")

Let's take a tour of our nightmare. The tee shot may be the most bizarre in golf. For a century, railroad coal sheds extended across the fairway perhaps seventy-five yards in front of the tee. Twenty years ago, the "drying sheds" were torn down, but purists clamored for their return and now they're back. A stupid-looking half-modern, half-antique duplicate of a green shed makes the Road Hole tee shot entirely blind again. Printed across the shed, like a crass advertisement, are the words: "Old Course Golf & Country Club." The trick here has been to figure out which letter in those words you should try to drive the ball over. Fuzzy Zoeller says it's the ampersand. Tom Watson insists that, for him, it's the *C* in Club. Picking a letter can be a test of character more than a test of spelling. If you opt for the safe left side ("Old Course"), then you'll probably bounce into rough or Cheape's Bunker and make five. If, like Watson, you aim for the tight right side, where an out-of-bounds stone wall cuts in, your nerves will be sorely tested. Too much fade and you're in "the wicked whins," rocks that are usually unplayable. A bad slice ends up in somebody's hotel patio.

The Road Hole's second shot is even more difficult. If you're coming out of rough and into a breeze, you may end up well short of the green in the Scholar's Bunker or the sarcastic Progressing Bunker.

If you go at the pin (and it's a fool's play), the deep Road Bunker awaits. For years, players laid up short of this angled green situated on a plateau. However, if you get a bad lie on the left, you would easily wedge through the slender green onto the road. That way, double or triple bogey lies.

In 1984 the field stroke average was 4.84—high for a par-five. Only 10 birdies compared to 219 bogeys and 52 scores of double bogey or worse.

Perhaps only Arnold Palmer really "learned" how to play the Road Hole. In 1960, at the height of his powers, Palmer used a six-iron to reach the green in regulation three straight days. He three-putted all three times. Finally, on Sunday, Palmer knew the truth. He was going to lose the Open (by one shot), largely because he had played the Road Hole in five more strokes than eventual winner Kel Nagle. Faced with an identical approach shot, Palmer refused caddie Tip Anderson's proffered six-iron and insisted on what both knew was an incorrect five-iron. Palmer's shot went over the green, bounced back off the stone wall behind and back toward the pin. And Palmer finally made par.

Every time the British Open is at stake here, many a player steps to the seventeenth tee, gazes out at the sheds and whins, the bunkers and road, the tough and encroaching stone walls and prays for just such expertise as Palmer's.

The entire 1984 Open came down, essentially, to this one hole—as usual. What will be remembered, and told a thousand times from Edin-

burgh to Santander to Kansas City will be the way Seve Ballesteros and
Tom Watson came to the notorious Road Hole—tied at eleven-under-par,
and how their fates diverged there. Ballesteros made par from the rough
on the wrong side of the fairway while Watson made bogey from perfect
fairway position. That's St. Andrews.

All week Ballesteros laughed and promised, "Tomorrow I will par the
Road Hole." On Saturday, after his third straight bogey, Ballesteros
amended his vow, saying, "If I don't par it Sunday, I will come back and
play it Monday until I par it." In victory, his first thought was: "I keep my
promise. I won't have to come back tomorrow."

But it was a near thing. Ballesteros hooked his drive and faced a 200-
yard shot to the pin. "I told my caddie, 'This is the most important shot,'"
said Ballesteros. His six-iron shot landed short of the green and bounced
safely onto the right side, thirty-five feet from the pin and far from the
cavernous Road Bunker. "We got this hole this time," Ballesteros said
before barely missing his birdie attempt by two inches.

Where Ballesteros, with a flier lie in the rough, could negotiate his 200
yards with a six-iron, Watson needed to nail a two-iron to fly his 200-yard
shot to the green. Power is nice. "I pushed it right," said Watson of his
second shot on the into-the-breeze beast. The ball bounced over the road
and off the low stone out-of-bounds wall, leaving Watson with a severely
restricted backswing. An awkward chip thirty feet past the pin was the
best he could do. Two putts later, Watson's chances for victories at all five
Open courses in Scotland—the Scottish Slam—and his hopes for a sixth
Open title to tie Harry Vardon's record were dead.

The Road Hole, like St. Andrews itself, is unendingly confounding
because its intentions—if it has any—are so deeply concealed. Augusta
National, earth's only comparably famous course, is laden with Bobby
Jones's philosophies and schemes; human intelligence created it and can
defeat it. Such cannot be said for ancient, ugly, forbiddingly beautiful St.
Andrews—a place as ambiguous and mysterious as the hand that made it.

COSTLY
CRUSADE

Sometimes chronology can feel like a roadmap to psychology. Know the order of events in a life and, circumscribed as those isolated facts may be, we begin to understand a man's mysteries better.

Severiano Ballesteros was born in the poor little Spanish town of Pedrena in the northern Basque country in 1957. The land was lush, beautiful, like Georgia in the spring; life was hard and pride was the staple of the family diet.

His father was a champion rower, then a small farmer on land adjoining the Real Pedrena golf course. His uncle Ramon Sota was Spain's best golfer, a laudable but not terribly lucrative distinction. One of five brothers who loved sports, Ballesteros fell in love with the game next door.

As a child, Ballesteros's first taste of work, of responsibility, of talent, came as a caddie. Seve, who lived in a small room with no window, got up at 5 A.M. to play the course in secret. With only one club, a three-iron, he hit every shot. To this day, he hits bunker shots with a long iron better than most pros with a sand wedge; pay to learn.

Seve loved the rains in Spain. To the empty course on which he was allowed only once a year, he'd dash and play alone—one club, one ball, the world to himself. "I still practice every day when it rains in Spain. That is when I am most comfortable. Everything is empty." When torrents soaked the 1980 Masters, Ballesteros became the youngest champion ever. What others saw as hardship reminded him of happy hours as a shy child fond of solitary practice.

Smitten with golf by the age of nine, he shot 79 when he was twelve. "I tried soccer, but truly I can only do golf." Not interested in school and

Seve Ballesteros, early in his career, young and full of promise.

aided in technique by his uncle, Seve knew he'd make his name as a golfer by the time he was in his teens. That wild-child youth created a virtuoso with a bold lust for the limits of his game. How far can a ball be hit? What magical tricks of twist and torque are possible? Few players have craved distance more hungrily and gambled so audaciously. Which of his peers doubts that Ballesteros can escape from more dungeons than any living golfer? He loves the challenge of peril. "Fairway, fairway, fairway . . . boring, boring, boring. I am great fun for the gallery. I mix with them and let them tell me what to do."

For him, every shot is adventure. Try the ultimate; adapt to reality. When it works—magic, joy. When it doesn't—catastrophe, depression.

At nineteen, still a socially immature teen, Ballesteros entered the last day of the British Open (Europe's crown jewel) with a two-shot lead. He ended second, his mark made. Handsome as a movie star, exciting as a young Arnold Palmer, he was met by instant adulation. Even the exotic name sounded like a bullfighter or artist.

He had the temperament of both. Poor but proud, he had a social chip on his shoulder from the first; the peasant in him was determined not to be humiliated in high society. He noted slights, remembered snubs. His retaliation was to use his talent to demand privilege, like guaranteed prize money to play. Soon he was paid more just to appear than the event's eventual winner was for low score. Unless, of course, Ballesteros got both. By twenty-one, he'd won titles on four continents.

Seve also wore his nationality on his sleeve. Spain versus Europe. Or Europe versus the United States, whichever the occasion demanded. The view was provincial, a by-product of a rudimentary education, but heartfelt. Seve picked up the fallen banner of European golf and held it high. He'd show that rich Americans weren't the only great players. He would symbolize the entire Third World of golf—Europe, Japan and Australia. He'd go Palmer and Nicklaus one better and be to the world what they were to America.

Why shouldn't he aim so high? At twenty-two, in 1979, he became the youngest British Open winner since 1868 and the first winner ever from the Continent. The next spring—youngest Masters champ. With nine holes left, he had a ten-shot lead. Talk about announcing your arrival. It was predicted, almost *assumed*, that Seve would rule the eighties as Arnie had the late fifties to early sixties and Nicklaus the next fifteen years.

A crowd-pleaser, Ballesteros mastered a military gait and a habit of jumping over small objects which made for nice, bold photos. In each huge mitt he could hold eleven golf balls. "Greatest pair of hands in golf," gushed Greg Norman. "The action he gets on his chip shots is almost freakish."

Everything fed his growing myth. Asked about women, he'd grin and say casually, "Many, many, many girlfriends," although those close to him swore he was more a homebody, often the first in bed. His clinics were charming, funny and almost irresistibly magical; no foe should ever watch one. His public speaking was wry, understated, regal. His vibes proclaimed him the best player on earth *by far,* no matter what some particular scoreboard might say. For Seve, style mattered—designer shots nobody could match. Sign it: "Miracle by Seve." Ballesteros judged himself —and expected to be judged—by standards that were not altogether tangible.

For Ballesteros, golf was not just "how many," it was also "how."

An extra weight in a hard game.

Seve carried two more burdens—a bad back and homesickness. All those years of classic reverse-C swings with his spine severely swayed gave him the miseries endemic to his sport. He just got 'em young because he'd played more. Once he confided to David Graham, "Only I will ever know how bad my back has really been." By twenty-five, Ballesteros refused ever again to mention his back, feeling it gave others a psychological crutch or made him seem an alibier. "My back is fine. No problem." Next subject.

What Ballesteros would admit was that he missed his home, his people. He measured the world in airplane time, saying, "I am fifteen hours from my father." Long after he was rich, his only home was that single windowless room in his family's house. Good enough then. Good enough now. Blue-collar pride.

Asked why he didn't play the U.S. Tour more, since that was the only place he could stake his full claim to greatness, he said, "Ask the American players how many weeks in a row they can play in Japan." To important events like the Masters, he would bring whole Spanish-speaking entourages, including a brother to caddie and a chef to make him his special secret omelettes.

As the eighties began, few would have believed that, well into his thirtieth year, Ballesteros would have won only one more Masters, one more British Open and not a single U.S. Open, PGA, World Series of Golf or TPC. At a comparable age, Tom Watson had only three major titles and Nicklaus just seven of his twenty. The thirties are often a player's best decade. Still, after such a start, Seve was flirting with a reputation as a disappointment.

Legends, of course, bear only a shadowy relationship to reality. Sport feeds on the pleasure of exaggeration. Get on the right side of the myth-making machinery and it fuels your own self-esteem while granting a protective aura that daunts foes. But get on the wrong side for too long and woe be unto you. Even if you don't come to believe in your own invisible flaws, others may. When did Sam Snead start wondering if he would ever win the U.S. Open? When did Tom Weiskopf start to believe that every Nicklaus triumph was somehow taken from his personal column—until, one day, there were none left for him?

If few foresaw Ballesteros's limits as a player, can anybody say that he anticipated Seve's self-destructive feud with the PGA Tour and its commissioner, Deane Beman? In 1986 Ballesteros was actually barred from the U.S. Tour for a season after years of nit-picking and haggling over how much the PGA could dictate Ballesteros's schedule. Try to imagine a man less willing to be told where and when to play. Ah, they want to crush my pride, rein me in, wear me out, hurt my back, deny my stature in the game. *Insult ME, will you?*

For his part, the pugnacious, educated, angle-playing Beman was comfortable in a public stance that amounted to a Bronx cheer: We can do without you, Seve. You're not that hot. Come back when you have the clout to make your own rules.

How Seve's career turned from sweet to bittersweet will probably be seen, someday, as part and parcel of his American Problem. More than any trait in his nature, Ballesteros demanded that his deeds be properly appreciated. Slight his golf and you have wounded him almost beyond forgiveness. And, make no mistake, America slighted his golf.

Just as the American public and press were slow to warm to Nicklaus when Palmer was still on the throne, so they were hesitant to crown Ballesteros. He was arriving just as Nicklaus was canonizing himself by winning the U.S. Open and PGA at age forty. A tendency grew to denigrate Ballesteros's wins by a sort of deliberate misunderstanding. Seve did not win the right way, you see. That's to say, he did not win the way Nicklaus won—with self-control, conservative strategy, methodical Germanic doggedness and endless patience. The virtues of the king can, unconsciously, become the only acceptable virtues.

In 1978 Ballesteros beat Nicklaus in the British Open despite some wild drives. His winning birdie, in fact, came after he got a free drop from an Austin-Healey in a parking lot. That started the jokes about Seve's luck. Want to make a man like Ballesteros so mad he can't see straight? Call him "lucky." For years that's all he heard.

At first, he was a good sport. At the 1980 Masters, for instance, one of his tee shots at the seventeenth came to rest on the heart of the seventh green.

"Where'd the third ball come from?" asked David Graham as he reached the seventh green—his hole. "No one's playing mulligans, I trust. Oh, it's Seve's ball, is it?! Well, good enough, that explains it."

"I am a fine driver, yes?" said Ballesteros to Graham. "This is the first time I hit the seventh green today. I missed it the other time."

"I'd trade balls," said Graham. "Yours is closer to the hole."

Ballesteros then took his drop, hit a seven-iron over the wall of pines —and made birdie. Three times he drove into woods that day and three times made birdie to take the lead for keeps. The idea of luck was locked in place. The notion that power, plus the grit and imagination, might be a legitimate form of greatness was out of vogue. The Bear didn't approve.

So America angered Seve good and proper. Three years later, he was saying, "People here want to see my bad shots. They do not want to see my good shots. I believe that." Of the Masters, he'd say sarcastically, "Oh, you know I am a very wild driver. This is the only course in the world that is wide enough for me. Every fairway is 200 yards wide, so I can use my driver."

Meanwhile, to make matters worse, Ballesteros was amassing a mediocre record in the U.S. Open, the event U.S. pros proclaim the most important, just as European pros say the British Open is tops. One year, Ballesteros came all the way to America for the Open, then missed his tee time —by about fifteen seconds—and was disqualified.

"It's a shame to think he came all the way from Europe just to get disqualified by a few seconds," said Lon Hinkle, who was in Ballesteros's group. "He's not accustomed to our American ways, I guess. But, you know, a rule is a rule and everybody waited as long as they could."

In Europe, Ballesteros might've gotten $50,000 up-front money to show his face in the place, plus a limo driver to pick him up from his free villa and deposit him at the course. In America, he paid his way, got caught in Newark traffic and was booted out like some assistant schmo from Pensacola.

Seve doesn't love America. Bet on it.

Gradually, Ballesteros's triumphs gave him leverage. His 1983 Masters win, plus his worldwide rep, put him in a position to ask the PGA for a special rule change before the 1984 season so he could be a PGA member. "Basically, Seve helped write the new rule," says Watson. It said any foreign player would have to appear in fifteen U.S. events to keep his card. Not something that homebody Ballesteros would love. But he agreed.

Then he won the 1984 British Open—beating Watson in a last-round duel to prevent the American from completing his "Scottish Slam." Ballesteros's place in the game seemed fairly assured; he was moving Watson out of the top spot.

So, in 1985, Ballesteros decided to ignore his fifteen-tournament commitment to the PGA. He played in eight events. Some thought it the kind of a blatant show of strength Ballesteros used to get his way on the European circuit. Beman called Nicklaus. "Deane said, 'How many rules have you asked to have changed in twenty-five years?' " recalled Nicklaus. " 'How many did Palmer or Watson have changed? Zero. That was good for the game. Now it's Seve's turn to live by the rules—in this case one that he made himself.' "

So Ballesteros was banned in Boston. And every other PGA Tour stop. In a sense, it was no big deal to Seve. He could still play the majors; none of them is a bourgeois Tour event. He just couldn't prep properly for the U.S. biggies.

At Augusta in 1986, Ballesteros was on a crusade. First, to embarrass Beman. Who tells Pavarotti where to sing? Next, to glorify the memory of his father, who had just died. And, finally, to stake fresh claim to top-dog rank in his game.

For the first time Ballesteros pulled out a gimmick he'd mastered in Europe. Verbal intimidation. Woofing. "The eighteenth hole won't matter on Sunday. By then the tournament will be over. I win. . . . This tournament is mine. . . . I know this course as good as my house." Even Nick Price, after shooting a Masters record 63, said, "I don't think any course in the world suits one player as well as this one suits Seve. It should have his name written on it. He hits it so long, so high and draws it. He has the touch on the greens and the imagination around the greens. He should never be out of the top five here the rest of his life."

With four holes to play, Seve had yet another green coat in hand. Eagles at the eighth and thirteenth holes put him in front by two shots. Then something happened which may, in the long run of his career, make or break Ballesteros.

It's a secret of the game that golf is a sport with knockout punches, too. Nobody can prove it, or will even discuss it on the record, but around the nineteenth hole after a couple of beers, players will say that Arnie was never the same after he blew that seven-shot lead to Casper on the final nine holes at the 1966 Open. They say that Watson knocked out Nicklaus, head-to-head, twice and put him in long deep slumps both times—at the 1977 British Open at Turnberry and the 1982 U.S. Open at Pebble Beach; the first time the Bear needed three years to recover and win another major, the next time four years.

And they'll say that they are still waiting to see if Watson will get back up off the canvas after the prize that Ballesteros snatched from him the last day at St. Andrews 1984; what looked like The Day of Watson's career—that Scottish Slam plus a sixth Open to tie Harry Vardon—turned to dust as Watson's putter failed him a dozen times in one round. He ain't holed squat, nor been seen since, folks.

As for Ballesteros, his psyche was basically unscarred until that unlucky April the thirteenth in 1986 when Nicklaus, old and all but forgotten at forty-six, ran him down from behind with the most famous back nine 30 in the history of golf. One moment will live with Ballesteros forever. He stood in the fifteenth fairway, 200 yards from the par-five green with a five-iron—golf's most basic club—in his hand. Nicklaus had just gone eagle, birdie to move within one shot of Ballesteros. Still and all, Seve was looking at a fairly easy shot to set up a two-putt birdie; that would keep his lead at two shots with three holes to play. Really, what's the sweat? Hey, why not stick this baby close, make a *third* eagle of the day, take a *three*-shot lead and *then* what can the Americans say?

What Ballesteros did he couldn't have imagined. No more than Palmer could imagine blowing seven shots or Nicklaus imagine Watson chipping in on the seventy-first hole. Or Watson imagine missing ten birdie putts on a bluebird day.

Splash.

Those bubbles were Seve's breath.

With an awful, quick and short swing that never even reached a full follow-through, Ballesteros snap-hooked into the creek. He wasn't within ten yards of land. In pro talk, he missed the world. And made a bogey. Ballesteros finished an almost forgotten fourth. He dashed off the course but, the next day, summed up his feelings.

"They do not appreciate me."

No sport offers careers as long, arduous and twisting as golf. Nicklaus won Masters twenty-seven years apart. No other game lets us watch the maturation or degeneration of competitive personality in such endless detail. With golf, we must remember that, in the picture of a whole career, it's not always how *or* how many. Sometimes it's how you got where you are.

In the traditional novel, it's said that "character is fate." A just world, literature. In golf reality, something as mundane as chronology can be destiny. For Ballesteros that hardly seems fair. Doesn't a hero, who could've walked straight out of a romance, deserve a final chapter worthy of fiction?

DYE,
YOU DEVIL, DYE

PONTE VEDRA, FLA., When Pete Dye first gazed on this swamp, the only eyes that looked back at him were those of deer, wild boar, alligators and "every damn type of snake in the world." So impenetrable was this hideous Florida jungle that Dye, machete in hand, followed deer and small animal trails to find the lowest land in the swamps. Once, while whacking a rattlesnake as it dived into its hole, Dye forgot that "Those things always run in pairs," and the "Momma" rattler nearly got him when he was bending down to finish off "Poppa." "Musta killed fifty or sixty of those rattlers, all of 'em four-to-five inches in diameter," said Dye, who, hopefully, meant to say circumference.

As far as many a pro golfer is concerned, they wish the rattlers had won the day. Instead, Dye lived to build the most wonderfully ugly golf course on earth. His surrealistic Tournament Players Club here is a perverse paean to life's vengeful, capricious dark side. The Players program ought to have a Durer print for a cover—a demented, emaciated knight on a starving horse followed by a carcass-gnawing mongrel.

"Welcome to Pete Dye's Paradise," says fiendish Deane Beman, the PGA Tour commissioner, brimming with pride at what was his genuinely radical brainchild. Perhaps no golf course has ever been surrounded by such controversy in its first five years. That's because no joint ever wanted to be so dang mean. As soon as it opened, veteran Miller Barber cursed the joint: "It's not ready to play on. They'll need to completely tear up and rebuild about eleven greens, because they're too severely contoured to play."

"Too much luck out there," lamented Craig Stadler. "Hit it one spot and it's a foot from the hole. Hit the same shot two feet away, and you roll off the green."

At first, Jack Nicklaus relished the diabolical intent—what he called "the Scottish concept" of the built-in bad bounce and the impossible lie. "Golf is not a fair game and was never meant to be," he said. "A British weekend player would enjoy it, because he's used to hitting shots standing on his head."

Making the pro golf world stand on its head is just what Dye had in mind. "Everything here," says Dye, "is the dead opposite of Augusta. On purpose. . . . Augusta is pretty pretty. This is 'mean pretty.' "

Dye's course, cut out of 415 acres of hell, is designed to intimidate the eye, tighten the guts and defeat the will before the first shot is even struck. Other courses have eighty acres of cleared ground; this has forty. It's called "target golf." Which means, you either hit it exactly where Dye says or you go commune with the flora and fauna. Dye calls these awful regions "waste bunkers. . . . You can find your ball, and you may be able to hit it. But you can't hit it right." Waste bunkers are just part of Dye's signature, along with railroad ties, greenside pot bunkers in the British style and wildly undulating greens. Add to this the vast spectator mounds that look like prehistoric burial pyres and you know why this spa is called the Dyeing Ground.

"This is the hardest-looking easy course around," protests Dye as players demur. "Everything looks more severe than it is. . . . The key is, you must be aggressive. Cautious play is punished worst."

From its first year, the Players Club created silliness and lore, debate and drama. The final "award ceremony" scene at Players I in 1982 was, to say the least, unique in golf history. The photos even made the cover of national magazines. Beman, in his best blazer and tasseled loafers, wallet still in his hip pocket, chose the backstroke. Beman could enjoy this moment of aquatic glory, because, an hour before, he had assigned two guards to keep an eye on the alligators in the lake. Pete Dye, his mouth full of swamp water, opted for a dead man's float, then, while on his back, spouted like a small whale. Finally, his brogans full of wet sand, he did the Australian crawl to the nearest sand trap, where he climbed ashore.

As for Jerry Pate, the hero and culprit of that sundown hour just wallowed like a happy turtle in a favorite bog. With only his wet pate above water, he looked like an old rock with eyes. His smile was even brighter than the orange golf ball that he had struck within half a pace of the eighteenth hole flag to clinch his triumph.

No, golf never had a scene quite like that one as the victorious Pate, fresh from the thrill of spectacular birdies on the seventy-first and seventy-second holes, wrestled the commissioner of golf and the game's most famous architect into the lake by the last hole. Pate had the right. With his brilliant closing 67 for an eight-under-par total of 280 and a two-shot victory, Pate fulfilled all Beman and Dye's hopes for this event, while simultaneously allaying their worst fears. Beman and Dye desperately hoped for last-minute excitement, memorable winning shots and a well-known name atop the leader board. Pate, a past U.S. Open winner, gave them that and more.

No amount of cash could have bought the crowning shot that iced the win. At the eighteenth tee, Pate led by one shot. He had just sunk a fifteen-foot birdie putt at the instantly legendary 132-yard seventeenth hole. "I won the tournament there this week," said Pate, who played that water-locked conversation piece in 2–2–3–2.

Instead of playing cautiously on the seventy-second hole, Pate scorched a draw down the preferred, but more dangerous, left side next to the lake. With 174 yards to the flag, Pate chose a five-iron, the stick he used to hit his famous Open-winning shot from the rough at Atlanta Athletic Club in 1976. At Atlanta, Pate had left the ball a yard from the hole. This time, he did better—twenty inches.

When he walked the final yards at the Open, Pate "felt like cryin'." At Players I, he felt "like I'd conquered the world. You'll never know just how great this stadium golf is unless you're the guy walking up the last fairway with thirty thousand people cheering."

By the Players II, however, the tone of voice around Ponte Vedra had changed radically. "You want controversy, okay, let's have controversy. . . . A lot of guys would like to put a bomb under that thing," said Nicklaus. "These greens are like used car lots. . . . It's a chore to play here," added Tom Watson. As far as Jack and Tom were concerned, there was nothing wrong with the Players Club that eighteen tons of dynamite and a bulldozer couldn't cure in a hurry. Just blow those miserable greens back into the swamps with the alligators and water moccasins, then start running that 'dozer back and forth from tee to green. Have a heckuva golf course.

If most Tour pros had had their wish, a "No Trespassing" sign would've been hung at the entrance and the whole experiment in survivalist golf canceled on account of it was impossible. Nicklaus rooted for torrential rain. "Thunderstorms. That's what we need. About eight days of it. Though I doubt if much of the rain could stick on these greens. . . . I have no idea how I'm playing. I thought my game was in good shape until I got here. Now I don't know. You can't tell out there. . . . You need some room to play golf and there isn't any here."

Even granting that complaints are a constant of the pro golf tour, the TPC suddenly qualified as a special sort of Hades. With raw March weather on the way, the new TPC threatened to make the old horror stories about Sawgrass obsolete.

Sawgrass? Ah yes, the witch of Sawgrass.

In its five years at Sawgrass, the TPC endured every sort of inclement inconvenience. Just a mile east of the Players Club, Sawgrass was the epitome of blustery links golf, not jungle target shooting. No two courses so close to each other were ever so different. Yet equally and wonderfully horrid.

Out-of-control brush fires, caused by arson, which destroyed millions of dollars of timber, burned on the horizon throughout the tournament one year. Each morning, the sooty smoke was so heavy that eyes watered and Sawgrass smelled like a barbecue pit. Two Tour officials had to hie to the roofs of their homes with hoses to douse the buildings with water in case winds should waft sparks onto their property. As a special added attraction, a mass case of food poisoning ran through half the field. Some say it happened when most of the better-known players on the Tour had a seafood dinner on the eve of the tournament. Special of the day: poison.

Sawgrass or the new Players Club? Firing squad or the gallows? Of Sawgrass, David Graham said, "The day we leave, they ought to bulldoze this golf course into the Atlantic Ocean and build some nice houses here."

Why would anybody say something so impassioned about an innocent golf course? Hey, this is Sawgrass—guilty until proven otherwise. "If Sawgrass is a major test of golf, I'm the Pope," Joe Inman once said— moments before a forty-mile-an-hour gust of wind blew over a scoreboard that knocked him cold. "When I grow up, I want to be like this Sawgrass golf course," said Leonard Thompson, after shooting 302. "Long and mean." Tom Watson said you would have to go to Australia to find a course on which the wind blew harder on a regular basis. "You can't stand by the traps or the blowing sand will burn you."

On one infamous day, nobody knew how hard the wind blew. An anemometer was put up to measure the velocity. The anemometer blew over. That afternoon, Ben Crenshaw announced to a locker room full of fellow sufferers, "Your attention, please. We have Jim Colbert in the interview area. Jim, tell us about your 88."

All this began to pale in memory; Dye's course was more fearsome than nature's. "Some players," said John Mahaffey on the eve of Players II, "may jump into the lake this year, too. To get warm."

How tough had the Players become? So tough that defending champion Pate showed up Tuesday, shot 81 in the Pro-Am, then withdrew, saying he had a severe pain in the neck. So tough that Ray Floyd left in such a hurry he neglected to show up at a ceremony where he was to receive a check for $150,000. The only happy ones were the ones who didn't come—medical excuse. Everybody else was in danger of leaving Jacksonville with a compound fracture of the backswing.

Many suspected that all this hullabaloo was exactly what Beman wanted. Build the meanest golf course in creation, make the pros suffer in public for a few years, accumulate some lore, then, on the QT, subtly redesign the joint so that it would be built for golf, not headlines.

"Last year, they said they'd send out questionnaires to the players for suggestions to improve the course, but they never did," said Watson. "I guess they forgot."

"I never was much good at playing four-iron shots to the hoods of cars. That's about the size of the targets you're aiming at on these greens," Nicklaus said. "I like to play intelligently, figure out the smart place to miss. Here, there's no place to miss. You just aim it at the flag, then chase it and hit it again.

"Either they've greatly overestimated the talents of pro golfers, or I'm getting a whole lot worse. . . . I can't, on a consistent basis, play the shots that are required on this course. You try to do so many things that you never repeat a swing. . . . It was twenty holes until I made a birdie. I didn't know there were any out there. . . . An awful lot of guys are going to wonder how they shot what they shot—both the good and the bad.

"I love the basic concept of this course," added Nicklaus. "Shell-wise, it's one heck of a good golf course." In other words, it looks great to Jack from his airplane. If only he could play it from up there.

As the eighties progressed, the central issue of the Players came into focus. Eventually, the TPC would almost certainly take its place as one of the preeminent events in golf. That is, if the players didn't get their hands on the Players and change it.

From its first day, no American tournament could approach the Players for offering the paying customer a dugout view of the action. Beman's concept of "stadium golf" was a stunning success. Before the Players Club was built, golf was the worst of all sports to watch in person. Standing on tiptoe in the sixth row of a gallery, then jumping ahead two holes to stake out a decent seat is not entertainment. But, at the Players Club, any fan, with a bit of effort, could have a dream seat for any shot.

When Hal Sutton punched his eight-iron shot to within inches of the flagstick at the island seventeenth for the final birdie of his 1983 victory, thousands of fans had an ideal view, while thousands more perches went begging. When John Cook, tied for the lead that day, hooked his drive into the lake beside the eighteenth hole, a mountain of people were looking over his shoulder.

Beman asked Dye for a golf course that would do for golf what the 200-m.p.h. crash did for auto racing. They wanted every stroke to demand a shot that only a professional, at his best, could be expected to make. All margin for amateurish error was eliminated. That way the average sports fan, seeing the Players Club, would finally realize what all the fuss over Jack Nicklaus and Tom Watson was about.

"Oh, that's what these guys can do."

The vast majority of the pros are insulted by this opportunity. The mental strain, don't you know. They'd rather play the Hartford Open and spend four days making fifteen-foot straight-in birdie putts. The pros' first act after Players II was to start a petition imploring Beman and Dye to consult them on changes they'd like to make. Quoth Nicklaus: "A hundred pros can't be wrong."

Of course they could be.

The idea at the Players Club was to showcase golf at its most creative and crowd-pleasing, not its fairest. Make the Players Club a model of fairness, like the PGA, and it will never again have the shimmering aspect of danger that made it special in its early years.

"The pros don't like to fight and struggle," Dye said. "But that's what people love to watch. . . . And the players win. My only fear was that I'd built a course that nobody could play. It's been a pleasure to find out they can."

Once it was snakes that Dye had to fear. Now, as the TPC tries to find its lasting place in the golf world, it's a few dozen timid blond golfers who are dangerous. If the Tour can keep the Players unique, then it can transcend golf and attract the interest of the general fan, as the Masters and Open do. However, if the players get a stranglehold on the Players and make it suit their own ease of mind and vanity, golf will lose a great event: its perfect Anti-Masters.

REACH
AND GRASP

FORT PIERCE, FLA., March 13, 1983–This week, Calvin Peete apologized. The straightest man in golf said it was unprofessional of him to quit after nine holes at the Inverrary Classic because he had been baited during his round.

Many on the PGA Tour think Peete has little for which to apologize; in fact, some think it might be the world that owes him a lifetime supply of sorries. The notion that he'd act unprofessionally is beyond the ken of Peete's fellow pros, many of whom consider him their model of decorum and restraint. "Cal Peete is a gentleman," says Jack Nicklaus, who would know.

Perhaps only a person as rigorous in his private standards of conduct as Peete would feel bad for others, rather than himself, in such a situation. For forty years, Peete has gotten the bad rub-of-the-green breaks, yet has always reacted by saying, "You're responsible for your life. I can overcome that."

"I panicked," Peete says, still shaken by the incident. Peete explains that the man who followed him was "not a complete stranger" but someone he had known "years ago . . . like from a previous life." In a statement released by his attorney, Peete said the man was a process server. Something about a visitor falling, ten years ago, on the porch of a property Peete had just bought.

Peete was particularly upset because, although he was not playing well, one of his partners—Payne Stewart—was tied for the tournament lead. According to one of Peete's closest friends, the golfer was worried that either he or his caddie might get in a fight with the person—a scene so far below Peete's rigid code of ramrod dignity that he would rather quit than risk the possibility. The process server's motive was "personal, not racial," according to Peete. In fact, Peete and his wife Christine say that

Calvin Peete

the incident was merely a symptom of a much larger problem that has attacked Peete this season and deeply disturbed him: the approach of full-scale fame.

For six years, Peete was just another middle-of-the-pack pro, one of the Tour's purest swingers and worst putters. Then, late last season, as 1982 wound to a close, Peete suddenly turned one of those mystical corners in sport; he won four tournaments in four months and jumped to the top in every category: money ($318,470—fourth), victories (tied for first) and stroke average (70.33—second). Suddenly, Peete went from a heart-warming human-interest story to one of the half-dozen best golfers in the world.

"The guy who hassled Calvin was just the last straw. That incident came on top of a lot of little things building up and Calvin just bolted," says Peete's agent, Steve Frank. "It took a long time, a couple of days, to get Cal calmed down. He's been living in a different kind of world recently and it's a tough adjustment."

"Calvin's a very, very private person," says his wife Christine. "He needs time to himself, time to practice. He can't stand schedules and appointments. When you make plans for Cal, he looks at you like you're trying to steal his life from him. . . . But now it seems like everything is appointments and schedules and interviews. Everybody wants something from him. Don't our lives still belong to us?" asks Christine Peete, who has quit her job as a high school English and drama teacher in bucolic Belle Glade, Fla., to be her husband's secretary, manager and bodyguard of the soul. "I never knew what 'invasion of privacy' meant until the last few months. . . .

"Calvin had to explain to me the other day, 'Honey, every time I get blue, that doesn't mean it has anything to do with you. It's just all this pressure, all this stuff.' Calvin didn't get into golf to be a celebrity. He wanted to be good at something and be proud of himself. For seven years [on the PGA Tour], I don't think Calvin ever said no to anybody, because he really believes that, when you take something out of a sport, you have to put something back. . . . But we didn't ask for all this. Do we have to take it?"

In the long run, that Inverrary heckler is probably the least of Peete's difficulties. Peete knows that, just when he thought his life had finally reached the plateau he's always sought, he's going to have to surmount a whole new set of obstacles. And, Lord knows, Calvin Peete's already climbed a lot of hills that were steep, even for a stepper.

Born one of nineteen children in the tiny Florida hamlet of Pahokee, Peete fell out of a tree when he was twelve and crippled his left elbow; that permanently crooked, locked-in-place joint ended any future in games—he thought. Peete quit school in the eighth grade to help his family by becoming a field hand, a vegetable picker.

While still in his teens, he financed an old station wagon and became the smallest of businessmen, traveling the dirt roads in territory from south Florida to Rochester, N.Y., to sell clothes, watches and jewelry to itinerant farm workers. Because salesmanship was so alien to his quiet temperament, Peete came up with a gimmick to make himself memorable; he had his top-of-the-line product—a diamond chip—put in each of his front teeth. For a decade, Peete was the Diamond Man, a migrant selling to migrants. He was proud to be "making it," clearing $250 in a good week. Peete even invested in an apartment house, though as landlord he also ended up as handyman, fixing toilets. He was improving his lot, but he was still searching for his fate.

Peete never hit a golf ball until he was twenty-three, when buddies conned him into a game. He was hooked on "straight and long" from the first day; even when he couldn't break 100, his goal was "pro." For the next five years, Peete hit golf balls until his hands bled, staying out until the last recreation park lights in his town were turned off.

Despite being average size (five-foot-ten, 165 pounds), with skinny legs and that deformed elbow, Peete reached scratch in eighteen months and became a pro at age twenty-eight. So much for Golf's Lesson Number 1: Keep your left elbow straight. At thirty-two, Peete got past the PGA qualifying school (on his third try) and onto the Tour. For three rabbit seasons, Peete's average annual winnings of $20,000 weren't even enough to cover Tour expenses. Christine supported their family of four children with her teaching.

With his short, syrupy, unorthodox swing, Peete always had to go to the same teacher: "I go to Calvin Peete." His conclusions took years to reach. "Hit against a firm left side, but hit with the right side. That's the source of power. . . . Mental discipline, muscle memory. Practice until you don't have to think. . . . Simplicity is the answer. I only check three things—my timing, my balance and my [square] hand position at address," says Peete, who in 1981 and 1982 led the Tour's stats in hitting fairways and greens in regulation.

After a victory at the Milwaukee Open in 1979, Peete reached a new plateau; for three years, he averaged $100,000 a season. Then, last summer, when it got hot enough for this man who says, "I love to sweat. I feel like I'm doing some honest work," Peete skyrocketed.

"I've never been one to get ahead of myself. I do everything in stages. When I start forgetting that, my father [a shop steward in a sugar mill] reminds me," he says. "Your reach and your grasp should be the same. That's the way to be happy. Reach for the furthest thing you think you can get. Then reach again. . . . Sooner or later, the things that looked way beyond you are the next natural goal to reach. . . . Sometimes you can't believe how much you have to go through to get to the end thing, but one day it's there."

Like winning a million dollars on tour, which Peete should do by early 1984. Or taking tutoring from his wife so that, last winter, he could pass the high school equivalency test and get his diploma.

"First, I learned to hit a golf ball, then I learned to control it. . . . That took me fifteen years. I've just gotten to the point where I'm comfortable. Until two years ago, I was still working on different swings," says Peete, who'll be forty in July. "Now I've started to learn how to score.

"I should have a long future 'cause I still have so much to learn. I never worked much on my putting or short game. I used to joke I was the worst putter on tour. But I think I just never had time to work on it enough till last year. . . . I can't wait to play the Seniors Tour," he chuckles. Peete, golf's master of deferred gratification, won't be eligible for the Seniors Tour until 1994.

Hand over hand, Peete has climbed to an ambiguous place—one which is both pinnacle and precipice. This mountaintop, which he only half-imagined during the trek, is both familiar and alien.

Peete insists that he always visualized his accomplishments in advance. "You have to train the mind for success. When I first joined the Tour, I didn't think I was as good as I was. Now my mental has caught up with my physical," says Peete. "I'm as good a player as I think I am. . . . If you can't win in your own dreams, forget it."

Off the course, Peete's difficulties are more precarious. Until a few months ago, he lived the simplest and most Spartan of lives. "I'm a very low-key, conservative person," says Peete, who masks his feelings behind a Fu Manchu mustache, long sideburns and sunglasses that he often wears indoors. "I don't really bother to try to fit in anywhere. . . . I'm a loner."

Peete is not antisocial, just unsocial. His family and friends mean everything to him; the rest of the world's opinion counts for little. Sometimes, when he comes home from the road and takes his family out to dinner, "He'll sit in the car outside until we're done," says his wife.

Peete's modus operandi is to offend no one and avoid controversy. This is not his way of pleasing the world, but of placating it, and thus keeping it at the greatest possible distance from his essential life.

Peete's value system is almost entirely personal rather than social. He's attracted to individual good deeds, not collective good causes; for instance, two years ago Christine Peete had a talented but troubled girl in one of her classes. "Her parents didn't want her and Chris thought she could be an outstanding student if she had the right people to encourage her," says Peete, who thought the problem had a simple, direct solution.

The Peetes adopted the girl as their foster child. "She's been living with us for about a year.

"A wise man doesn't concern himself with things he can't control," says Peete, who can sum up his entire theory of race relations in thirteen words: "There are good people and bad people. Just try to determine the difference."

"Calvin's not experimental—he's a meat-and-potatoes man," his wife says. "I'm the opposite—outgoing, talk to anybody. . . . Cal always tells me I overdress. I say, 'Calvin, this is the style.' He says, 'Why do you want to do what everybody else does? Be your own person.' So I just go around thinking, 'What am I going to do with this dress? Calvin doesn't like it, so why would I want to wear it?' "

Peete preaches to his teenage children that "Education is everything." Nonetheless, when fed a perfect straight line about his "other interests," he says simply and with no embarrassment, "I still think about nothing but golf."

"If people could peep through a hole and see us in private," says Christine Peete, "they'd say, 'No, that guy can't be Calvin Peete. He's having too much fun. Calvin Peete is dull.'

"That kind of thing makes me so mad," she says. "Now, all of a sudden, people want to get him a speech coach. Calvin may not be as refined as he could be, but he's himself. I have a degree in speech and drama [at Florida A&M] and I don't think he should change. He's not being difficult; he's being real. You have to remember who you are, and we all have to remind each other."

Being himself has become a war for Peete since he became a star. He's not encountering anything different than any other suddenly prominent athlete: a jillion interview requests, cameras and microphones in his face, fans wanting an autograph or a conversation, can't-resist chances for business deals, old friends calling in chits for appearances or favors.

"It's so easy to forget that the one important thing is his golf," says Christine.

Now Peete is meeting parts of American success that he never foresaw in his dreams. For the moment, these unexpected and ungraspable phantoms—all the various kinds of heckling and hasslings that superstars endure—seem like a nightmare to him. Ten days ago, they combined to make him dash off a golf course and drive across Florida to the sanctuary of his home here.

Once more, Calvin Peete must reach and grasp.

SCHOOL
OF HARD KNOCKS

PINEHURST, N.C., June 5, 1977–Perhaps there has never been a more unlikely site for a torture chamber than this cloistered little town. For generations, golfers have sought this sanctuary. The loudest sound in the twisting streets is the jay bird and the only bright night-light is the moon.

But for the last week Pinehurst has lost its resemblance to a golfer's abbey where monkish hackers wander through the Pinewoods tending to the health of their souls. The 414 novitiates, here at the PGA qualifying school, have taken no vow of silence. Their howl began Tuesday with the first bogey and it will not cease after Sunday's sixth round.

The kids, given golf clubs fifteen years ago by fathers who idolized Arnold Palmer, have grown up. They are all here. For these children of the golf boom, now in their twenties, the PGA's twice-yearly qualifying school is a winnowing final exam to determine the twenty-five who will receive their Tour cards and a chance to play the multimillion-dollar pro circuit. For many, this qualifying school is a first awakening to the enormous odds against them in the profession they have chosen. For others, it is a final, failing grade.

The golf mythology that flourished in Palmer's wake was seductive and the players here admit it. Golf promised a long career, potential riches, no exhaustion, no injuries, no boos. Simply hit that little white ball around in the sunshine. It was seldom mentioned that golf offered little room at the top other than an elite 100.

So this week they gathered—the best golfers in the world outside the pro tour. Their patience was slain, their self-esteem put to the rack and their confidence tattered. Some deserted the tournament before the first

What fun it is to be a golfer!

hole, fleeing at the sight of the rockets launched by their competition on the practice tee. Others threw away their clubs and their hopes in the middle of the first round and stalked, head down, to the parking lot and drove off. Forgotten in a blur of fury was their $300 entrance fee and the letters of recommendation from three pros back home.

One perhaps apocryphal story, told around Pinehurst's grill, The 91st Hole, captured the tournament's blend of unremitting pressure and bleak humor. One player, call him the Unknown Qualifier, went berserk on the pride of Pinehurst, the sacred No. 2 course. Faced with elimination when the field was cut to 120 on Thursday, he suddenly lost control as his drive disappeared into deep pines. The tormented young man dropped his pants and began screaming madly at the course, the qualifying school and the game of golf. He was escorted from the grounds in a police car.

For every player here who has up and called it quits, a dozen have begged to stay. Everywhere tournament director Labron Harris went on Thursday, young hands plucked at his sleeve. "It's not fair," they pleaded. "I've worked for this for a year, for a lifetime really. I'm just getting rolling. You can't cut me now." Harris had a soft word for each. "Take two weeks off and think," he would say, an elder monk imposing a penance.

But thinking is harder than dreaming. "It's sad to see so many fine young men fail," said Harris, his face drained by the week of good-byes and admonitions. "You'd like to see them all get their cards."

However, the professional golf world is small. Baseball and football each provide a living wage for perhaps 1,000 athletes; golf finds a comfortable place for little more than 100. "We tell no one that they are not good enough," said Harris, himself a U.S. Amateur champion and a twelve-year Tour veteran. "The course tells them that. . . .

"The pro tour is as open as possible to every capable player. No one can look at the Tour and say, 'That's not right.' We are probably the most accessible of all major sports. You are not judged on background, race, technique. It's strictly that number you shoot and no one can question how you got it."

If golf fosters the illusion that every man can become a Lee Trevino, hitting thousands of balls until the mysteries of the game become clear, it also makes inflexible demands. The qualifying school is that brutal rite of passage. "This is where you judge whether your dream is realistic," said Harris.

It was raining on the famous No. 2 course. David Brownlee was watching. Late-afternoon mist rose from the fairways. Lightning cracked in the distance.

Brownlee's thin legs and feet were propped up on the Pinehurst Country Club veranda. A white golf visor, a little worn, trapped his disheveled blond hair, cut low over his washed-out blue eyes. "I've wanted to be on the pro tour as long as I can remember," he said, calmly. "I don't have a name. I don't have any amateur experience. I don't have anything going for me. But I'm gonna get there somehow."

It is of Brownlee, dressed in corduroy pants carrying an old canvas golf bag, and others, that Pinehurst club pro Jay Overton is speaking: "Some of these guys don't have anywhere to go when they leave here."

Precious few of those here have any chance of ever making a living on the PGA Tour. Most know it. As Brownlee says, almost proudly, "The odds are awful." For every one a Tour card is a potential passport to heaven. At the same time, it means absolutely nothing. A card, plus a dime, will buy a few tees. The card simply allows a player to enter the Monday qualifying for any Tour event that is not an invitational. It allows him to be what the golf world calls a "rabbit," a golfer who hops from tournament to tournament, hoping to make ends meet.

The hundreds here who are in Brownlee's netherworld category know that even if they obtain their cards, the probability is that they will lose them again after their first season because they cannot win the $5,000-a-year necessary to meet the PGA's performance standard for rookies. This qualifying field is littered with players who previously received their cards and lost them. Others, as did Brownlee, bombed out of the qualifying school more than once. "This'll probably be my last try," said Brownlee, twenty-seven. "I'm gettin' the hint. This is it, or find a job. . . . I do okay in the mini-tours. But when it comes to the qualifying school, my game leaves me. My brain stops functioning after a few days. As the pressure mounts, you don't really know what's wrong. You just don't make the shots any longer."

If Brownlee stops making shots, it is not for lack of trying. One year he spent eight months practicing twelve hours every day to prepare for the qualifying school, which was in Brownsville, Texas, that year. "I'd putt from 7 A.M. to about 11:30," says the five-foot-eight, 150-pound native of LaVerne, Cal., who points out that he is the same size as Ben Hogan. "After lunch, from 1 to 5 P.M., I'd hit range balls . . . 400 to 600 shots . . . all with my irons. No drives. I don't practice my driver. Then, from 6 P.M. to 9, I'd run and weight-lift. That was a typical day. I never went on a golf course for almost a year. Just practiced."

The results? Disaster. "I was awful at Brownsville. I had overworked myself."

In January, Brownlee borrowed $300 from his father and set out for eleven weeks chasing the California mini-tour. "I won $466 the first week and paid my dad back." After that Brownlee stayed one jump ahead of the McDonald's cashier. When it came time to head for Pinehurst, Brownlee drove cross-country in his old Dodge. Against all common sense,

Brownlee is now playing the best golf of his life. After a career round of 65 on Thursday, only four players stood ahead of him on the huge scoreboard.

A touch of success only made him more reflective, more skeptical about his obsession. "It's so tough out here. I'm realizing it. There are forty or fifty Tour-quality players here who won't get cards. It's just whoever gets hot. I guess if I blow up in the last round like I have before, I'll sell my car, get a good meal, head for the mountains and never return," he laughed, not joking.

"I can't see myself doing a normal job. I tried stuff like that—loading sacks in a candy store, golf course maintenance—and I couldn't do it. Golf is what I do best. What do I do next best? Sit, I guess, or backpack in the mountains. . . . After I retire from the Tour"—he laughs, self-effacingly —"I'd like to live in the mountains, sit back and relax."

Will this be his last qualifying school—one way or the other, his last grand assault on his dream? "Absolutely," he said. "But then, that's what we all say."

Curtis Strange sits in The 91st Hole; beside him is his young wife Sarah in a T-shirt emblazoned "One Putt."

"Missing my card last year by one stroke was probably the worst thing that will ever happen to me in golf," said Strange. "It cost me a year out of my career. I finished the tournament bogey, bogey, bogey. Figure out how that feels," he said, running his hand through the gray hairs in his twenty-two-year-old head. "It can make you old in a hurry. . . . If I lost the U.S. Open someday by one shot, I suppose it would be more important, but, personally, on the inside you treat yourself just as bad either way."

A year ago Strange, an all-American at Palmer's alma mater, Wake Forest, was ready to roar on to the Tour. He had sponsor exemptions and invitations lined up all over the circuit. A bad rookie season seemed almost impossible. Then he hit Brownsville. The resort site of the tournament had declared bankruptcy two days before the PGA school started. The greens were abysmal. Bad weather made the course a house of horrors. Strange collapsed after being in serious contention. "I have to face it," says Strange bitterly. "I can't play on the Tour unless I get through this damn school. I have to play well this one week or . . . well, I refuse to talk about the alternative."

Many here this week have cloaked their ambitions, hoping that by keeping their backs turned on their goal, they might advance by rowing backward. But Strange's plan is direct. "I'm going to win this whole tournament. I know I'm not going to let what happened last year happen again."

Friends of Jimmie Ellis's watch him with trepidation. "If he doesn't get his card this time, they'll have to take him out of here in a strait-jacket," his buddy Marty Joyce said. Ellis is king of the Florida space coast mini-tour circuit. He won $42,000 in the golf bush leagues in the last two years. He hates it.

"I'll never rest easy till I get out there with the big boys," says Ellis, twenty-five, who has botched four previous qualifying schools. "Money isn't enough. It's getting so people ask me, 'What happened this time?' " Again, Ellis has seen bad signs. "My game is a week-to-week deal. Either I drain every putt [knock it down the drain] or I don't. This week I'm missin' five-footers. Every year at this school it's new faces, new names, but they can all play. I can't spot these guys a dozen five-foot putts."

Those afflicted by what is called "the School Jinx" seek each other out. Strange became best friends with Phil Hancock, another player who also missed his card by a single stroke last year. Ellis is a close buddy of Beau Baugh, also trying his fifth qualifying school. "Golf's format is fair, but the odds are terrible," said Baugh, older brother of LPGA star Laura. "Five times. . . . Yeah, you gotta start wondering." After three days here, Ellis and Baugh were both a dozen shots off the lead, desperate. "I feel like I'm at the back of a bar with 100 guys ahead of me and I've got to fight my way past all of them to get a beer," said Ellis.

No one wants to fight Jim Thorpe. Fortunately, no one has to. The other 413 players here nod appreciatively when the Falls Church, Va., slugger blasts another 300-yard drive. They simply wait for Thorpe's first mistake. The clouds of frustration roll across the brow of the George Fore-man look-alike and soon the sound of golf balls hitting trees resounds over the course. "Being a big hitter isn't that important," says Thorpe, a man who has learned the hard way. "The woods are full of them," he grins sheepishly at his pun.

Nearly 400 years ago, Montaigne wrote: "To be disciplined from within, where all is permissible, where all is concealed—that is the point." Thorpe, who earned his card once and lost it, knows that such inner disci-pline is the key to "this exasperating pressure game where the most im-portant thing is to relax." Although he knows it, it is the hardest rule to follow. "I cut the heart of thirteen fairways today," said Thorpe on Wednesday, trudging off, dragging a 75 behind him. "Every one 300, maybe 320 yards."

But one drive found the pines. "I had a little opening, so I went for it," said Thorpe. The pines won. Thorpe took a double bogey. "If I could only learn to react differently between the green and the next tee box after I have a bad hole," he laments. "But I just want to bust the ball." The result: another double bogey on the next hole. The rest of the day was spent in repentance.

Thorpe chose golf, in part, because it suited his need for an environment where "nobody gives you anything, but nobody takes anything away from you." Despite golf's long history of racial prejudice, Thorpe finds the Tour close to an equal opportunity. "I know that in golf I'm a black face walking through a white man's world. It can make you jittery. But I've reached the point I don't feel like an outsider. I know half the people I meet. When your back is turned and the other players still speak to you . . . or when they're fifty yards away and yell, 'Hey, Zorro, that's not a sword! Slow that swing down!' . . . you know you are accepted.

"It may be harder for a black to raise the $25,000 a year it costs to travel the Tour while you're learning how to win some money. But on the whole, out here, you're your own boss. I'm twenty-seven now and I'm not about to quit. You just gotta keep beating the ball, grit your teeth and make birdies."

Because so few of these 400 seekers will ever be heard from as professional golfers, it is probably most valid to look at this week as a qualifying school for maturity. Most passed with high marks.

Marty Joyce, who (thanks in part to a golf cart that would only run backward) may not have survived the first cut. But on the last hole before his elimination, he scored an ace of sorts. His playing partner, Chris Haines, whose score was right at the cutoff mark coming to the fifty-fourth hole, drove out of bounds left, then out of bounds right. "Let's go," said Haines to his caddie, starting to walk off the course. "That's all."

Joyce stopped him. "What will Bob Toski [one of golf's famous teachers] say when you go back for your next lesson? He'll ask what you shot and you'll say, 'I quit.'" Young Haines finished the hole, although he waited to stop crying before he went to the scorer's tent to sign his card.

"This week is so sad," said Mary Harris, wife of tournament director Harris. "Every day you see them fighting back the tears. You want to comfort them, tell them life goes on, even though right now they don't think it does. Maybe it's good that golf sets up such clear-cut standards. It tells them the truth.

"I don't believe this is a sport that ruins lives. It just ruins dreams."

THE
CUT

PONTE VEDRA, FLA., March 22, 1981–Professional golfers make money the old-fashioned way.

They earn it.

In most other American money games, an athlete can live off his past like a camel living off his hump. In baseball, a player who has one decent year can—with luck, a shrewd agent and a pliant owner—parlay a smidgen of competency into a multiyear, million-dollar contract. Any NBA player who isn't rich and secure far beyond his desserts is the exception. Even the NFL, that bastion of unblushing owner monopoly, has its fat long-term contracts. On the PGA Tour, you cash a check as long as, and not one day longer than, you retain the ability to sweat blood over a six-foot putt and drain that rascal down the hole's unfeeling heart.

There's no scene in pro sports like the cut. A golf locker room at sundown on Friday is a bleak place as half the players in a tournament await word that their pay for the week will be $0. To them, the cut is the essence of their game; it epitomizes the sharp edge of true competiveness that gives their sport distinction and themselves a special dignity. For the vast majority of pro golfers, the cut is what the game is all about.

"Because we dress well on the course, people think we're all millionaires," said Ed Sneed, who in a dozen PGA seasons has won an average of $50,000 a year. "The truth is that there is less money in pro golf than in any well-known sport. Out of the 144 guys here, at least 100 are extremely concerned about their next check."

As Sneed says this, his face is drawn from tension and annoyance. Currently, he is where he has spent most of his pro life—fiftieth on the

Tom Kite holds the record for making the most consecutive tournament cuts.

year's cash list and perpetually concerned about the state of his game and
the vicissitudes of the leader board.

At this particular moment, his two-day total in the Tournament Players Championship is 77–76—153. Half the field is still on the course. "I
think I'll miss the cut by a stroke, but if the wind whips up, I could get
lucky. Anybody who thinks I'm indifferent to this is crazy. I came here to
play. Hell, good rounds on Saturday and Sunday and I could go from last
place to the top ten." At evening, the wind dies. The cut demarcation dips
to 151. Sneed's gone. His expenses for the week are nearly $1,000. A week
of his life has been a waste. He'd have saved money if he'd stayed home
and fished.

"In golf," Sneed says, "there is no team bus, no team meal, no team
hotel. When I see a player in another sport who's making $800,000 a year
guaranteed, and you know that he's not really giving 100 percent, it galls
me."

Players are magnetically drawn to the scoreboard on Fridays, trying to
walk past it nonchalantly as they count the players with better scores than
theirs. The cut is always "top 70 and ties." Sometimes, however, a pro will
simply sit and stare for an hour at those numbers as they grind him down
and then boot him out of the tournament.

"Last year, Tommy Aaron [1973 Masters champ] came into the press
tent at Westchester and sat down next to me," recalls Tour official Steve
Rankin. "I barely knew him, but he started talking . . . had to have
somebody to spill his guts to. 'I just can't get over the hump,' he said.
'Whatever it takes to miss the cut, that's what I shoot. If my putter would
just start coming around. . . .'

"I kept thinking," said Rankin, "that for every Watson and Trevino,
there are dozens of guys out here who have to battle their brains out every
week."

"It costs me $50,000 to $60,000 a year just to live on the Tour," says
Jim Simons, who had a typical $85,527 season in 1980 (forty-eighth place).
"I suppose I could live a little cheaper if we cut to the bone, but this is my
family's life. We're on tour a lot more than we're home. How can I ask my
wife and two children to live in motel rooms most of the year? I don't live
fancy or eat fancy, but if I have to pay $800 a week for a condo where
we're playing, I'll do it. If it's a choice between flying or driving 500 miles,
we'll fly. I'm not going to make us all unhappy and mad at each other just
so I feel a little more secure. After all, if the babies are crying and Daddy
can't sleep, then Daddy's not going to make any money that week."

Perhaps the oddest aspect of Tour life is the way it fosters indepen-
dence and dependence simultaneously. "Because you have to dig every
dollar out of the ground yourself, you don't feel beholden to anybody,"
says John Mahaffey. "Because you're a one-man corporation; you're very

independent. But it can make you feel very alone. In 1977 I fell to $9,000. I had house payments and wife payments. You know, an ex-wife doesn't want to hear that you've developed a slice. She wants to see that check in the mail. I'd won over $100,000 in three different seasons, but I had reached the point where I could see the bottom of the bank account. Another bad year and I was broke. . . . It's strictly merit out here, but there's also something very, very tough about this life."

In no other sport are standards more sternly fair. Golf has no quibbling about statistics or intangible values. Your score is an absolute. Your style, your strategy is your business.

For instance, on Thursday, Johnny Miller was in seventh place in the TPC. However, he also wanted to see his college, Brigham Young, play in the NCAA tournament that night. So he flew to Atlanta, watched his team win, then flew back to Sawgrass at 3 A.M. That morning, his tee time was before 8 A.M.; Miller started with three bogeys and shot 74. Maybe his decision was dumb. Maybe it will even cost him a championship. But nobody could fine him, fire him or even criticize him. As always in golf, it was his affair.

Oddly, such complete self-reliance doesn't always carry over into other facets of life. "Players tend to become too dependent on golf," says Labron Harris, former player and PGA official. "Too many are reluctant to branch out and discover their other skills." One who has recognized that pitfall is Simons. "I get very tired of playing competitive golf. Every part of the game is a continual battle," he says. "My wife says, 'The longer you play, the more you work.' I admire the way Nicklaus drives himself, strictly for pride. But I have to do it mostly for money." But not entirely. "I'll miss the adrenaline flow in competition," says Simons. "I've searched for something else that will juice me like that." For him, it proved to be becoming a licensed stockbroker last winter. Yes, he's going to make money the old-fashioned way.

In an era when many—perhaps even most—sports have a problem convincing fans that their athletes are not pampered and complacent, golf retains a sort of cruel purity—a knife edge called the cut.

On Friday evening here, Ray Floyd came into the press tent after dark to stare at the huge scoreboard. Just a week ago at Doral, Floyd won $45,000. He lives in a $2-million home on Biscayne Bay and is one of the few with the wealth and prestige to relax if he wishes. Floyd looked thoughtfully at the board, digesting the numbers and the names that went with them.

"What are you doing, Ray?"

"Just looking for my friends," he said.

SOMEWHERE, U.S.A.

Nothing in American sports is even vaguely like the life on the pro golf tour. To get a sense of the loose-knit gypsy caravan, we must look largely outside athletics for our analogies. The Tour is like a traveling repertory company that puts on the same basic show in forty towns a year, but with a different ending each week. The cast of characters is familiar—the same leading men retaining their luster for many years with predictable foils around them. The best players have the presence and panache of actors. Other athletes sweat or sprawl in the dirt. Golfers never have a hair out of place, seldom crinkle a cardigan. They seem coiffed by PGA central casting.

No other major sport allows its audience to get so close—frequently within arm's reach—during play. The first row behind the gallery ropes has the same footlight excitement as the best seat in the live theater. The Tour, however, does not have, nor want, the solemn dignity of the theater. It also has something of the scatterdash quality of circus.

The striped tents go up, along with the huge scoreboards. A familiar golf course suddenly has something of the splash and festival quality of a medieval joust. We half-expect clowns and jugglers to lead Watson and Player to the ceremonial first-tee introduction, rather than caddies and a half-dozen brightly uniformed scorekeepers and officials. The milling crowds, munching and preening, prosperous and relaxed, seeing and being seen, hiking or lounging like picnickers, also lend a sea-of-humanity aura, as though a carnival fairground with hot dog stands and vendors had suddenly been moved to the middle of a landscaped woodland park. As we wander through this welter, Lee Trevino or Arnold Palmer is apt to appear suddenly, face-to-face, saying, "Excuse me, folks. I have to get to the practice tee."

An itinerant Pro Golfer with the tools of his trade, including a Pepsi, a candy bar and a pack of cigarettes. He's been here a while.

No sport in this country has such a similar look and feel, week to week, as the golf tour. Not only the players, but the supporting troops of officials, directors of this and that, publicists, agronomists, secretaries and even the chap who draws the cute cartoons on the leader boards, travel the circuit and reappear everywhere.

To those who have only seen the Tour on TV, everything seems strange and new. Each week, throngs gather behind the driving range to gasp and nudge each other at these prodigies who make a one-iron disappear at synapse speed. Every player looks vastly different—Andy Bean or Bruce Lietzke far larger than expected, Jack Nicklaus and Tom Watson much smaller. Yet, for those who have watched this week of ritual at a dozen different venues, there is an almost haunting sameness, a disconcerting sense that an entire encapsulated community has transported itself ("Beam us down to the Greater Greensboro, Scotty") to a new location without ever knowing how it got there or what surrounds it outside the social out-of-bounds markers that delimit the country club universe.

Tennis might offer a mild comparison, but there the sites, within a month, might change from Rome to Paris to London, while, in the same month, the PGA Tour might venture from Houston to Dallas to Fort Worth. If, on the international tennis tour, the courts seem the least interesting spot in town to linger after a match, on the American golf tour the nineteenth hole may seem the most glamorous spot in Tallahassee, Tucson, Hartford, Jacksonville or Augusta.

For a typical pro, who spends most of his life (perhaps thirty to thirty-five weeks a year) on tour, the potential for a comfortable insularity is great. The Tour is such a self-contained, first-name world, with its own castes and cliques, manners and mores, that one wire service golf reporter and his wife essentially have no permanent address, but might as well list their residence as The Tour, Somewhere, U.S.A.

The players fly in the same planes, some with their whole families in tow. They stay in the same motels, or in the same sort of rented houses near the golf course. The first order of business in each new town is to get a map that shows the airport, the course, the motel and a good restaurant. There won't be time for much else. For those who don't like maps, courtesy cars link these four vital locations so that a player, hypothetically, never need know where he had been, where he is or where he is going. Every player knows the danger of this possible stultification. The first resolution of most players who reach stardom, from Jack Nicklaus on down, is to spend less time on tour.

When on tour, however, the ritual is similar for almost every player. They practice together, constantly critiquing each other and making side bets. They brunch together on the verandas of dozens of country clubs overlooking dozens of practice putting greens. Sometimes they and their families eat dinner together. They even chitchat together in the same playing groups, making small talk for five hours at a time.

Since golfing careers are so much longer, as a rule, than those in contact sports, the PGA perennials know each other better than the teammates on most pro baseball or football teams ever will. No detail or quirk is beneath observation. Mimicry of gesture, speech or playing pattern is an art.

"Thirty-six," said Dave Stockton to J. C. Snead in the locker room at Augusta National as both changed their spikes, each casually glancing at a TV monitor of the play in progress at that moment.

"Incredible," said Snead. "His record is fifty-nine in a sand trap in Houston."

What are they talking about?

"Oh," said Stockton to a stranger, "Hubert Green just fidgeted thirty-six times, sneaking a peak at the flag, as he addressed a shot. Hubie's the king of the peekers. Someday he's going to be wiggling and waggling, turning his head fifty times as he gets ready to pull the trigger, and he's not going to be able to hit it. He's just going to keep on turning that head until it falls off, or until they send somebody out to bring him in."

"The worst I ever saw . . . must be the all-time record . . . was seventy-one waggles by that guy Gilbert from Richmond," said Snead. "If he'd backed off and started over, I'd have killed him with my wedge."

Baseball players are masters of imitating each other's swings and habits. But they can't touch golfers, whose whole sport is keyed to the ability to analyze and dissect the most minute and nearly invisible component parts of a golf swing. Many a PGA pro can duplicate Arnold Palmer's slashing swing. But Ed Sneed can go one better—he can do it backward, from the finish back to the address, at full speed. He can also duplicate an entire Gary Player press conference, with the wee South African apparently the soul of modesty, yet promoting himself constantly.

This Tour life is a charged and schizophrenic atmosphere—part comradeship and old-fashioned honor, and part gamesmanship and desperately serious competition. Far from being teammates, these men, who know each other better than they know anyone else in the world except their families and a few close friends, are adversaries in what may be the most brutally winnowing of all our games.

Faced with the economic realities of professional golf, one might expect the Tour to be an ugly Darwinian jungle of one-upmanship. In fact, it is the opposite. The golf tour is probably the most sporting, the most honorable, the most open to the sharing of knowledge of all games. Pro golfers have many common enemies: travel, boredom, pressure that frays the nerves and spirit and—above all else—the fickleness of the golf swing itself and the built-in capriciousness of the game. In short, everything that is meant by "the rub of the green"—both in sport and in life—binds those on tour into something of a fraternity. Not a chummy fraternity, perhaps, but one that is more than civil.

If anything, pro golfers comprise such a wide-open laboratory—like dozens of mutually supportive scientists who wouldn't dream of holding back the march of knowledge for mere personal glory—that the game seems a bit shy of tooth-bared competitiveness.

The bestowing of blessed "tips" and the gift of crucial clubs are commonplace between players. Ask Trevino how he won the richest of tournaments, the TPC, and he'll say it was because J. C. Snead walked up behind him on the practice range and straightened out his game with one observation. Players can joke about their gamesmanship because there is so little of it. "I should get some earmuffs so I can't hear these guys jangling change in their pockets while I'm putting, or saying bad things about me while I'm driving," said Snead playfully. In this gentlemanly realm where no one is surprised if a player penalizes or disqualifies himself because of an infraction that no one else has seen, a fellow who jangled change would be ostracized back into line in a hurry.

Without question, the Tour does its best to enforce a cautious, conservative tone in all that it does, as though it were an exclusive prep school or a great corporation. Comical dress and beard regulations exist, as does a system of fines for "comments detrimental to pro golf." So much for free speech.

As might be expected, in an atmosphere where the range of socially acceptable thoughts is limited, the range of expression for those familiar thoughts is extremely inventive. In other words, golfers have mastered the art of saying nothing with wonderful style. A low, screaming shot, for instance, "left paint all the way down the fairway," while a proper high shot which lands near the pin "is turning down the stack."

Out of the mouths of America's most clean-cut group of athletes, except perhaps bowlers, comes a rich vein of slang that makes the hyped-up wild men of the NFL seem bland. This is not a surprise. The Tour has more than its share of paradoxes. From the outside, it seems the most elite and glamorous of all our sports—a leisurely, luxurious path to all the perks for which other athletes break their bones. Few golfers, however, completely come to pleasant final terms with this itinerant life-style. Just as they battle with their swings, they struggle with a rootless life. At a Tour stop not long ago, Tom Watson veered off the course, bending under the gallery ropes and marching into the backyard of a condominium that adjoined the eighth fairway. The condo, you see, belonged to him, at least for the week. It was home, sort of.

In the yard, his wife Linda played with their daughter, their first child. As the spectators gawked, wondering if Watson had suddenly gone haywire between shots, the tiny child threw her arms around her father's neck.

A minute later, Watson had marched back under the ropes onto the course.

"God," said Watson to no one in particular, a smile splitting his face, "is her hair ever going to be red."

CLASS
STRUGGLE

Golf is the gentle killer.

The air here at lush Doral Country Club in Miami is as soft as though the breezes blew Chanel No. 5. A single room can cost nearly $200 a day, and the $30 steaks in the Conquistador Room are two inches thick. The lakes are blue, the sand white, the grass a deep July green in March. An enormous flower bed in red and gold carnations spells out the word "Doral" in letters six feet long. In all of sports the Tour, the PGA Tour, comes closest to looking like the promised land. The hours are short—four hours, four days a week. The pay is huge—$30 million in 1986 purses. The career can last forty years—Sam Snead proved it. More than fifty players earned $150,000 on the Tour in 1985. For them the air is perfume, the steaks thick. For practice balls, they hit new Titleists.

But the tropical elegance of stops like Doral is a mask of the Tour, which is, in fact, pure laissez-faire capitalism and Social Darwinism placed behind a thick glass partition of good manners. The public does not have to listen to the screams. From outside, golf looks like a homogeneous world of prosperous pros living a luxurious life. That's one of the great sport's lies.

Actually, golfers are divided into three castes: the stars, the stalwarts and the starving. Nowhere in American pro sports do people who rub shoulders every day live such utterly different existences. Nowhere are the gaps between classes so great. Nowhere is it tougher to go from one level of the game to another—tough, that is, on the way up. Easy on the way down.

Nobody knows all this better than Jim Thorpe. In the last three years, he has lived all three lives: hobo, hopeful and hero. Let his experience provide a preliminary sketch of the golf tour's three starkly separate

A graphic portrayal of golf's "caste" system—from Nicklaus with his seven birdies to the obscure Rose and Byman, with their names written in crayon.

castes. As recently as the start of the 1983 season, Thorpe still drove to every event, even coast-to-coast—D.C. to L.A. at a gulp—like some migrant following the golf harvest. He'd often call a Pepsi and a pack of crackers a meal. At road's end, he knew which Days Inn charged $11.88 a night, which cost $12.88. That dollar mattered. "I was one-quarter hungry, one-quarter tired from driving, one-quarter lonely from missing my wife and daughter and the rest of me was burned out from the pressure of playing."

His first five years on tour, Thorpe won $200,000. Sounds okay? After expenses and his sponsor's cut, Thorpe's share was zero.

Far from being a rarity, Thorpe was the rule. Most of the 250 or so players on tour, then and now, are in this class. They'd make more money as fry cooks, feel less exhausted jockeying a jackhammer and spend less time away from home if they were in the merchant marine. "Prayers, hard work and believing in yourself" was all that kept Thorpe at it. That and his wife's silence. If she'd ever once said, "Why don't you just get a job?" he probably would've.

Finally, in 1983 and 1984, Thorpe moved into the Pack—that group of perhaps sixty to eighty players who have won a tournament or three in their lives and earn in the respectable neighborhood of $100,000 a year (more than half of which goes straight into Tour expenses).

These gents—with names like Inman and Halldorson, Fregus and Hinkle, which barely tickle the edges of our sports consciousness—aren't much richer than good plumbers or electricians (and they have far less security), but they've got public identities and private hopes. At least they're contenders. "I finally started to see a little gravy," said Thorpe, who won tournaments in Houston and Boston, cashed about $125,000 a year and became his own man. By early 1985, he had a nest egg and the beginnings of some peace of mind.

Most Pack players never leave this netherworld of grinding and striving, worrying and swing-fiddling, hedging against age and injury. By forty, they're history and back to a club pro job. Not Thorpe. At thirty-six, this son of a greens superintendent made the leap to stardom he'd dreamed of since he hit balls by the back porch light as a kid. Now, as Thorpe speaks, recalling this whole odyssey, he sits in a private villa at the Kapalua Bay Resort in Hawaii. He's flown in from New York with his wife and daughter. Tickets: $3,200.

Yes, he's one of the hottest golfers on earth. Over the last half of 1985, after the Fourth of July, in fact, Thorpe won a third of a million dollars in eleven events. He can afford room service now. Thorpe's a star. Or very close to it. He's one of the thirty to forty names who define the sport, draw the crowds and have a chance to become millionaires if they play their clubs and their angles right. Who are these fellows in the brahmin caste? Simple. They're the winners—the guys who average a victory a year in their primes. Check cashing is nice—for the Pack; that's their pecking order. But stars only go by the glory; they ask each other, "What'd ya win, buddy?"

Golf has always sold itself as a strict star system. Come see Snead, Hogan, Palmer, Nicklaus, Watson. First place gets the kiss; even the runner-up gets the kissoff. You want the names of the stars—*exactly?* Believe it or not, it can almost be done. The castes are that precisely drawn: Nicklaus, Watson, Trevino, Palmer (still), Strange, Wadkins, Peete, Thorpe, Floyd, Pavin, Sutton, Mahaffey, O'Meara, Stadler, Ballesteros, Langer, Kite, Zoeller, Green, Norman, Irwin, Bean, Nelson, Morgan, Miller, Graham, Crenshaw, Pate, Player. Throw in a few fogies who still play occasionally and, at the moment, that's the lot. What's shocking is that, in a Tour locker room, this list would barely draw an argument. Everybody knows.

When you finally do start winning on tour, everything changes fast. "Now I get to a tournament, they got a car waitin' for me. An exhibition or clinic is lined up. I'm in the Pro-Am, meeting businessmen with connections," chuckles Thorpe, who was the number four man ($379,091) in golf in 1985. "I remember when nobody noticed me. They could care less. Now somebody's looking for me to give me a courtesy Cadillac. You can hear whispers, 'There's Jim Thorpe. He did this or that.' You go into a good restaurant and somebody walks over and takes your check. When you really need it, you can't get it. But as soon as you get halfway on top, when you're finally gettin' over, it just comes to you. That's the system. I told my wife today, looking out at Hawaii, 'I like this part of it. It's a great life.' "

And Thorpe laughs. Laughs like a black man who's labored his way up from hardscrabble hustlers' games, beating taxi drivers out of nickels and dimes on their lunch break. In three years, Thorpe has gone from the Days Inn to the rainbow's end. Almost before he got used to reservations at the Hyatt and three good meals a day, he suddenly had folks offering to rent him their lovely homes for the week that the Tour's in town.

"People tell me, 'Jim, now you got it made.' I know better. I know where I came from. Now I got to work three times as hard to stay where I am."

More than any other quality, it is this caste system that defines and sets the Tour apart, both for better and for worse. In other sports, one lifestyle fits all. For instance, the poorest major league rookie earns $60,000 a year and everybody travels in the same pampered-to-death style. You could go ten years without ever touching a suitcase, a steering wheel or a check. "Compared to football, basketball and baseball, I think you gotta say that golfers are the ones who play for the love of it," says Thorpe.

"Guys in other sports, everything is taken care of for them. You could play a whole career in the NFL or NBA and still be a baby. To stay out here, you have to be an adult."

The PGA Tour is a Reaganomics meritocracy where performance is quickly rewarded and the rich get richer; but it's also a jock ghetto where economic and psychological pressures on the lower castes amounts to a cumulative edge for the entrenched haves. "The hardest thing is to *believe* that *you* can get to the top," says Thorpe. "Lee Trevino is the one who kept telling me, kept making me believe."

Jack Nicklaus comes to town in his private jet, stays at a mansion on a seaside cliff, practices alone on a deserted course and has a $400 million fortune behind him. How's a guy feasting on Pepsi and crackers gonna beat him? Anybody who thinks that pro golf is fair, that everybody really tees it up equal, has dustbunnies for brains. Yet does this system breed revolt? Hardly.

Ask pros in each caste if they think they get a fair deal, and, basically, they say they do. For instance, John Mahaffey has been from the bottom to the top, back to the bottom, back to the top, back down to the middle and now has returned near the top. "I've seen every side of this coin that they have out here," says Mahaffey, who's had serious injuries and a divorce, lost his confidence, changed his swing and changed his attitude. "I'd say our game is about as close to the American Dream as you can get. The harder you work, the more respect you get. Desire means *everything* out here. Isn't that what our economic and political system is about? Individual initiative?"

Ask players if they feel that snobbery or gamesmanship embitters feelings between the classes and they claim that, within the parameters of human nature, golfers act about as decent as you could expect. "This is going to sound corny," says Thorpe, "but the Tour seems to be pretty much one big happy family. Sure, certain guys are exceptions. But not many players act like they think they're above the rest. More likely, they'll talk about how we've got to look out for each other down the road or how to invest a dollar when you've got it. I've never seen a fistfight out here, never heard of a drug or drinking problem."

If there's one sadness that recurs, it's the way that the caste system separates friends. "You do lose touch with people that you care about," says Mahaffey. "It's not that you, or they, change so much as the way the Tour is structured. . . . I don't have the words for it, but it's just the situations you're put in."

"It just happens," shrugs Lanny Wadkins, who's been in the top ten money winners seven times yet has fallen out of the top fifty six times. "When you move up, you're going to stay at the nicer hotels, eat at the nicer restaurants and those other guys won't be able to." What's more

George Burns felt inspired by playing with a higher caste of golfer.

shocking is the reception a player can get from the Tour world when he's been high and is set low. "You find out who your friends are," says Wadkins. "Some people didn't have much to do with me when I was down. I've got a long memory."

On tour, it can be out of sight, out of mind. Players from different castes seldom ever play together. The strugglers are dewsweepers or sundown beaters, playing very early or very late before the small crowds. The stars—i.e., tournament winners—are paired together in early rounds in an explicit system created to increase fan appeal. "It really is like I had suddenly joined a different caste," George Burns says of the aftermath of winning his first PGA event in 1980. "It rubbed off on me. What you see with Watson or Trevino or Floyd is their hearts. They're fighters."

If anything, golfers have inordinate sympathy for each other, even across caste lines. They know how their sport seems to lie in wait to destroy a man's confidence—not just to humble but to humiliate him. "I remember standing on the practice range next to Hubert Green back when he'd fallen out of the top 125 players," says Thorpe. "Everybody had written him off for good. We were both struggling then. He looked me in the face and, for no reason, said, 'Hubert Green *will* make a comeback.'

"Man, I could see it in his eyes."

You'd think that, if anything would annoy golfers, it would be a player who was "miscaste"—i.e., someone who got more or less of the gravy than their golf game deserves. This does exist and does cause some prickly feelings. But less than might be expected. A few players never seem to travel in the caste appropriate to their accomplishments: Gil Morgan, Bruce Lietzke, Larry Nelson, Miller Barber and Wayne Levi are recent examples. Sometimes it's because they exude what might be called negative charisma. Barber, Morgan and Nelson are among nature's noblemen. But they just don't have that sexy Palmeresque spark. Call them Mr. X, Mr. Y and Mr. Z. Sometimes, as in the case of Levi and Lietzke, the problem is a lack of major attention. When the "majors" roll around, they disappear. You get more name recognition for leading the Masters after two rounds than for winning the Pleasant Valley–Jimmy Fund Classic.

At the other extreme, a few men have stayed in the top echelons of the game without totally legit credentials. Chi Chi Rodriguez has only cracked the top twenty in money twice in twenty-five years on tour, but his humor, his trick-shot knack at clinics and his endless self-promotion have made him a popular Tour fixture. He has his detractors; others say he's just the sort of live wire the Tour lacks. Peter Jacobsen is such a brilliant mimic and such a charming fellow that it's been said that he's "a billionaire waiting to happen." Despite just four modest wins in nine seasons, Jacobsen has a superstar's outside income with more five-figure exhibitions than he can handle. Yet, he's seldom resented. Jerry Pate, haughty

Chi Chi Rodriguez (far right) used his colorful personality to achieve a celebrity his performance did not warrant.

when he was on top, has done nothing for three years, yet he still plays a star role. Most players just shrug. Anybody who jumped in lakes after his victories was obviously never a shrinking violet.

"The gravy may still keep coming for a while after your game's gone bad," says Mahaffey, "but it disappears pretty fast once people catch on."

The most extreme case of total mis-caste-ing is Andy North. It's been axiomatic for generations that a fluke could win one Open, but never two. Another cliché bites the dust. In thirteen seasons, North has three wins; he's deep Pack material. But two of those wins were Opens. For years we'll read: "Other prominent pros who shot 73 yesterday include Andy North. . . ."

Golf's class structure has several wonderful oddities. One is the way an occasional college phenom can join the Tour as a star and have to play himself out of that category. Bobby Clampett has managed to go way back into the Pack, thanks to paralysis from analysis.

By contrast, every couple of years a lifelong journeyman is suddenly touched by a one-season benediction, as though to tease all the other Packers. In 1985 Roger Maltbie won $360,554—about as much as he had the previous seven years. In recent years, Rex Caldwell, Bob Gilder and Mike Reid have also pulled such top ten stunts, then relapsed.

Even more perverse is the way stars—in perfect health and still young —plummet to the poverty line in earnings. Bill Rogers and Ben Crenshaw are there now. Johnny Miller, asked years ago how he could go from number 1 on tour to number 111, said, "I had climbed the mountain I'd always dreamed of climbing—and I wanted to rest and enjoy it." It's taken Miller a decade to clamber back to the level of minor star. In a sense, there's been more dignity in his second climb than his first. "It's a little tougher every time, comeback after comeback," says Mahaffey. "It's so damn hard to get back up there."

Despite the obvious broadbrush structure of the Tour's class system, the stories at the individual level have an infinite level of detail.

Greg Powers, golf journeyman, is forty now. But, thinking back just a few years, he still remembers the most important day of his career—the day he escaped his caste—almost.

He woke before dawn that Sunday. Through the dark glass of receding sleep, his fanciful dream came back to him. Nicklaus and Tom Weiskopf were waiting for him on the first tee to play thirty-six holes on the final day of the Doral Open. The 7,000-yard Blue Monster was waiting. The national TV cameras were waiting. That gorgeous, towering scoreboard, showing Powers just a couple of shots off the lead, in prime striking range, was waiting.

Then, in a flash, Powers remembered it was all true. The chance to win more money, more recognition and more security than he had in his whole struggling twenty years of golf were all waiting for him. Three times he had worked his way up the golf mountain to the pinnacle of the Tour. Twice he had fallen to the bottom, losing his Tour card without ever leaving a ripple on the golf scene. This day, this tournament, would be his break. With two decent rounds, he could win enough cash to secure his card. And what if he *won?* Finally, his luck was turning.

At 8:12 A.M., Powers stepped to the tee. Nicklaus and Weiskopf had long, illustrious introductions. "Next to hit is Greg Powers," the announcer said. After a pause came: "The Tennessee sectional champion." Powers's first drive on the 543-yard left-curving par-five was a sickening hook that careened lakeward until only ripples remained. "I was numb," Powers said.

Powers's mind gradually became a sort of groggy blur. After dropping a new ball into the dewy, tangled rough two club-lengths from the lake, Powers gouged an iron shot out of the grass—and again into the lake. Nicklaus and Weiskopf looked away. Such visions can be contaminating. Powers lashed again. And again hooked into the drink. Three swings, three different clubs, three splashes. As the third ball went under, it might as well have been Powers who was drowning. "I thought, 'Oh God, I'm going to be on this hole all day. They're going to leave me here in this rough.' " When Powers took his third drop, the ball buried itself again in an impossible smothered lie. "Honestly," Powers said, "it passed through my mind that I was going to take a 20 on the hole, walk off the course and go back to bed." When the counting was done, Powers had used up all his fingers. His score for the first hole was 10. That's 10.

Out of pity, the teenager carrying the threesome's scoreboard took down Powers's score, leaving only a blank hole in the sign next to his name. Eventually, Nicklaus explained to Powers that he need not have dropped his first ball in the wet rough, but might legally have dropped it in the fairway. "It helps to know the rules," Powers said. "That one thing would have saved me four shots. . . . It would have saved my whole tournament." His final check: $365.

Though locked in ten hours of combat with Weiskopf, Nicklaus chatted with Powers as though they were old buddies. When Nicklaus eagled one hole, Powers was so comfortable with him that Powers laid out his hand, palm up, for a luxurious, fifties-style "gimme-some-skin" slap. "Jack calmed me down and told me at least I had a cheap greenside seat for his battle with Weiskopf," chuckles Powers. "But the truth is I never recovered any part of my game after that. After that . . ." Powers did not finish the sentence.

Powers has no illusions. A steady country club job awaits him in Nashville. But he keeps giving the Tour one more fling. Only young once.

Bob Eastwood, however, is different. He's still sure he is a great athlete. At age twenty-one he won the medal (first prize) in the qualifying school to get on the Tour in 1969. He was called "Bobby" Eastwood then, and people said, "That boy can ring up some low numbers." Nearly fifteen seasons later, Eastwood still traveled the country in a mobile home, trying to scrimp and make ends meet. Drive from California to Florida? Sure. "Some guys couldn't look at those four walls," he'd say. "They'd go crazy."

But Eastwood's vision of his talent held him together. For years his wife stayed back in Stockton as his two youngsters grew up. He thinks of his little boy playing with a sawed-off three-wood in the backyard. "I miss 'em," he says. "But I belong out here. I can play this game."

Eastwood has almost the same body as Nicklaus—huge legs, Popeye forearms, excellent golf size (five-foot-ten, 175 pounds). He starred in a half-dozen sports. Baseball scouts wanted him ten years ago. "My position? I played 'em all." But if it wasn't for bad luck, Bob Eastwood would have no luck at all. Take the year he made a hole-in-one at Doral. On Wednesday a $15,000 Porsche sat beside that fifteenth green—the prize for any man making an ace there. Did he win a Porsche to keep his mobile home company? Of course not. On Thursday the car dealership discovered it couldn't get proper insurance to cover the car. And withdrew it.

"I'm not surprised," said Eastwood. "I have one other hole-in-one on the Tour. They gave away a Mercedes on that hole the following year. I was a year too soon."

"It's lonely for most of us out here, even when we're on the course," explains Maltbie. "Nobody cares what you're doing. You can be very successful and nobody knows you. People pay to see Nicklaus. Even if you're in his group and have a huge gallery, hundreds of people are scrambling to the next tee after he putts out—even if you still have a three-footer. Face it, you can feel very alone in the middle of a whole lot of people."

Greg Powers never got his break, but, almost as it seemed too late, Eastwood did. In 1983–1984–1985, approaching forty, he put it together—sort of—over $500,000 in prizes and three titles, including the Byron Nelson Classic. "Incredible," he said. "It was just a matter of time for me to get everything together."

Only fifteen years.

Tom Watson was still on the practice tee at sundown. He had just missed the cut by three shots. Cynics in his gallery said he looked disinterested, like a man tired of golf and anxious to bug out. But Watson wasn't on a plane out of Doral. He was drilling two irons.

"Rik, can you come help me?" Watson said to Rik Massengale. "Am I crossing the line?" The two pros stood for twenty minutes, Watson first hitting the ball, then turning to this relative unknown to get critique. "The club face feels like it's shut at the top of my swing. The swing's just not in one piece. The takeaway feels all wrong. See?" Watson said, almost pleading as he showed Massengale the angle of his wrist, the plane of his swing, the pronation of his wrists after impact. Massengale commiserated and then went back to his own bucket of balls.

Watson hit a dozen more balls. Massengale left. Watson spots an unknown tour rookie, Lee Mikles, who hasn't won as much money in his life as Watson has in one week. "Hey, Lee," Watson calls, "can you come watch me?"

No man is at peace with the game of golf. Always there is the nightmare of a tiny injury that will change the magic stroke, or the subtle aging of the body, or the hundred things that can make the mysterious golf swing disintegrate. "All the vital technical parts of the swing take place in back of you, or above your head," Maltbie says. "It's terrifying to think of all the gremlins that can creep into your game. Our margin for error is infinitesimal."

The one inflexible law of the Tour is that the hot player of today is a better than even-money shot to be in eclipse six months later. "It's no illusion that we all seem to be on a roller coaster," says one player. "Dave Hill—a great student of the swing—won $117,000 one year and $17,000 the next. Think that doesn't scare people? It can happen to anybody."

The Tour's hundreds of have-nots are a constant—the rabbits ye shall always have with you. And a handful of Sneads, Hogans and Nicklauses span generations. But the Tour's great middle class, its most fascinating and agonized members, are the players in transit: going down, or fighting their way up.

"You become accustomed to good living," says John Mahaffey. "You scrimp and save on the way up as a kid. You don't mind staying at less-than-the-best motels, and cutting corners, and long drives between tournaments. You expect it. But once you make it, you take the good life for granted. When you crash, like I did, it's a lot harder to go through that scrimping and saving the second time. You are used to living high and spending fast. I didn't know what I had when I had it. I was a fool."

Golf is the gentle killer, teasing its pursuers, giving up its secrets, then taking them back without warning.

"Good times, bad times," says Maltbie, who's won five times in a dozen years. "They're both hard to grasp."

Once, incredibly, Maltbie won two weeks in a row. Could he be changing caste? The thought could unnerve almost any golfer. Maltbie, given a $40,000 first-prize check, had a few drinks and somehow let the prize fall out of his hip pocket at the bar at the Pleasant Valley Country

Club. He was reimbursed, but the check is framed and mounted over that bar in Sutton, Mass.

"When I left the golf course, I had $500 in cash and a $40,000 check," Maltbie says. "When I woke up the next morning in another town, I went through my pockets and didn't have a dime."

MAJOR
MISUNDERSTANDINGS

All right, you've made it through qualifying school and gotten your card. Then you've started earning a living by making the cut. You've also learned that your new gypsy life will be like traveling the Tour. And you've even found your place within the caste system of pro golf.

What's left? Not much. Just trying—for that core ten or fifteen years of your career—to leave your mark. You want to do something that matters within the game, something that'll be remembered.

Win a major.

So you've paid your dues at every level and you think you're ready. You know what it takes to win the Masters or one of the two Opens and you think you're the guy who's got it. Okay, you'd settle for the PGA or even a TPC. But if you could have your dream, you'd wear a green coat for life or see your name forever on one of the sport's two major trophies. What happens when experience and circumstance—work and luck—come together and your hour rolls around?

You're not Jack Nicklaus or Sam Snead. No, not that good. You're not going to get scores of chances to contend and a dozen or two gilt-edged opportunities to win. You're only self-made excellent, not flat-out born-to-be-great. What happens when you finally get to the top? Or miss by an eyelash?

Maybe, like Ben Crenshaw, you fail for a dozen years in the majors. Then, when you finally win the Masters, it's not quite what you thought. At all.

Like Curtis Strange, you grind for twenty years, from childhood, following your father's example and trying to escape your twin brother's shadow. Then, in your hour of an athletic lifetime, your judgment fails you. Into the Rae's Creek you go—twice. And that doesn't turn out to be in the least what you expected either.

Perhaps, like Larry Nelson, you take up the game ridiculously late, as an adult. Then one day you make a miracle putt and, before you know it, you're U.S. Open champ. And that—that's not one tiny bit like what you dreamed.

Perhaps, like Greg Norman, you fantasize that nothing is beyond you. These days on center stage are your natural place. On the tee in the British Open, you think of holes-in-one—on par-fours. But one day you wake up on the far side of thirty and realize that, though you are indeed a Great White Shark, you have not really caught very much worth keeping. You've landed one British Open. But look at all that you've let get away. You thought you'd turn out to be Hogan or Jones, and now you look in the mirror and see—no, that couldn't be Tom Weiskopf, could it?

Finally, perhaps like Ray Floyd, you remain consistently excellent for more than twenty years. Sooner or later, you win just about everything— the Masters, the PGA, the TPC, the Vardon Trophy. Only one thing remains—the greatest prize in golf, the U.S. Open. If you just had that, your career would feel complete. Instead, for twenty-two years, you make a buffoon of yourself at the Open. Never in the top five. And, for fifteen years in a row, never even in the top ten. "The Floyd Jinx," they call it. Now you're too old—older, in fact, than anyone who's *ever* won. You've given up. Well, almost. . . .

Then one day, out of the blue, out of the pack, you reach the eighteenth green, look at the leader board and see that you've won.

No, not what you expected at all.

Never is.

• • •

Time was, Curtis Strange could make the hair on the back of your neck stand up with irritation just watching him. On a golf course, little suited him, not much was fun, noisy gnats got on his nerves. A grumpy grinder, weaned on the game and obsessed by it, Strange was too high-strung, afraid of defeat and leery of others. "People thought I was gruff and a grump," says Strange. "Hey, I've seen pictures of myself. Man, I always looked so serious."

When Arnold Palmer got fed up in 1982 and wrote a protest letter to the Tour about the "discourteous and ungentlemanly behavior and thoughtlessness [of young pros] . . . which is despicable to me," somebody had to take the fall. The "abusive language and displays of temperaments" that made Sir Arnold hot came home to roost on Strange. He was not the only sourpuss with a short fuse who'd mouth off at a woman scorekeeper or a noisy cameraman, but he got busted on the Bay Hill rap. He made the public apology to Palmer and got the bad rep.

So who's this fellow impersonating Curtis Strange these days?

Who's this guy with a ready smile and a nice way with a self-deprecating story? Who's this handsome thirty-year-old at the top of the 1985 money list who's becoming a crowd favorite? Above all, who's this guy who loses a four-shot Masters lead on the back nine and handles the whole miserable deal with such candor, dignity and good humor that he gets sympathy from around the world?

Could it be Curtis's identical twin brother, Alan?

Nope, it's Curtis.

Three years ago, Strange wasn't a bad guy, just a troubled one. He knew he was strung too tight. And he knew why. "All my energy, since I was a boy, has been focused on golf," said Strange, whose father was a pro, owner of a Virginia Beach club and a Virginia state champion. By the age of eight, Strange was playing every day. After his father died when Strange was fourteen, he just redoubled his resolve to be great, becoming two-time NCAA champ on a Palmer scholarship at Wake Forest and hitting the pro tour as Mr. Hot Shot incarnate.

Being good but not the best stuck in Strange's craw. Up the money list he clawed: eighty-eighth, twenty-first, third in 1980. But the price was great. "Starting young, wanting it so much . . . you're hardened by that. I know I was." Near the top, he stalled, semi-burned-out and so nervous that insomnia left him weak on the course. His hair was turning pepper-salt gray and friends worried. "I tried to change. I tried so hard to be laid-back that it probably hurt my game for a couple of years."

In the spring of 1985, with two quick victories, he finally seemed to have hit the happy medium. At Augusta, after an opening 80, he staged what might have been the greatest comeback in the history of the Masters, going fifteen-under-par over forty-five holes to take that big lead. Then he shot 39 coming home and Bernhard Langer won.

"I didn't know what to expect when he came home," said Strange's wife Sarah, who'd just had their second child.

The first hint—to others and to him—was his post-loss interview. "That week was the first time I'd ever had fun with the press. They had finally gotten to know me a little. I've gotten that 'Tour clone' stuff. But you can't complain about being stereotyped if you don't try to correct it. I said, 'Let's don't mess this up.' " To his surprise, talk was therapy.

Jack Nicklaus took him aside and said, "This'll ruin you or make you a better player." Strange got the message: How he reacted to defeat was more important than the fact that he'd lost. On his first day home, he took his family boating, then headed to his Kingsmill club in Williamsburg to show his friends that he wasn't hiding under the bed.

Then the real surprises started. "If you could see the notes and tele-grams I've gotten. People are awfully sensitive, awfully nice. It's nice to see, nice to be a part of. It's been incredible. In six weeks, not one person has been negative and said, 'Ya screwed up.' Actually, they feel like they're bringing up a sore subject, almost like a death in the family. . . . I gave a little speech in Bristol [Va.] and afterward I asked for questions. No hands from 250 people. I said, 'How many of you saw the last round of the Masters?' Every hand goes up. I said, 'And you don't have any questions?'

"If I felt as bad as some people have felt for me, I'd still be in seclu-sion at home. . . . The only reason I'm not is that I don't want to ruin a whole year by getting in a depressive state and losing the money title, too. But I'm not going to say I'm not bothered by it [the Masters]. I still think about it every day. I waited three or four days before I could watch the replay. . . . One night I had one too many beers—that's what it took—and watched it. I came away feeling better than I thought I would. I hit too many good shots, made too many good putts, to feel real bad. Everybody talks about my second shot at the thirteenth. Hell, I never had any doubt about going for the [par-five] green [in two]; still don't. I hadn't missed a shot in two and a half days.

"If I'd laid up and lost, I'd really have killed myself. I had 208 yards with a four-wood. Basic golf shot. I never had a decision to make. I just stepped up and said, 'Where are we gonna aim this gypsy?'

"There was one person standing in those golf shoes. That was me. If I can live with it, everybody else ought to be able to."

Since the Masters, Strange has "read every story that was written about it" and examined the ordeal from every perspective. Yet he keeps coming back to the same paradox. He lost, yet, as a result, his opinion of other people has improved while their opinion of him has gone up, too. "If I'd won, it woulda been some story, wouldn't it," he says with a laugh. "But if I'd won, nobody would have seen the sensitive side [of me]."

Not so long ago, if Curtis Strange had gone into the water at the thirteenth and fifteenth at the Masters, it might have been the ultimate grinder's nightmare. It might indeed have ruined him. Now, although his golf game hasn't yet returned to its Masters level, the trauma actually made him better.

"Where are we gonna aim this gypsy?"

Why not right at the top?

• • •

When Ben Crenshaw got back to his rented house in Augusta, Ga., after the 1984 Masters, he opened the front door and saw his best buddies —the singing group the Gatlin Brothers.

They were standing on their heads.

The whole corny golf world felt like standing on its head when Gentle Ben won his Masters. The most popular, sweet-tempered, friendly, star-crossed, emotional and honest golfer of his generation had erased a dozen years of disappointments in a day. The good guy who couldn't win a big one had won the biggest one.

The trouble with happy endings is that life goes on.

Just when Crenshaw thought he'd gotten the monkey off his back, it was replaced by a gorilla. When you see Crenshaw now, exactly one year later, it's enough to make you wonder whether it is wise to set one tangible goal in life and then reach it.

Since that golden anniversary green coat was draped around his shoulders, he says golf has brought him "embarrassment, hurt, anger and frustration." A month after his 1984 Masters victory, Crenshaw said, "It was like the life was just drawn right out of me."

And the life isn't back yet.

Golfers have slumps, but what Crenshaw has been in for the last eleven months is a black hole. He ranks 160 on tour in scoring, 150 in greens in regulation, 160 in driving distance and 134 in putting. Crenshaw has worried so much that he's lost ten pounds and, no matter how much he eats, can't gain an ounce on what was always a slim frame. Even Crenshaw's legendary putting and boyish looks seem in jeopardy.

"The putts just aren't falling," he said. "When you struggle with the putter, it gets into the rest of your game. It's an extra strain on yourself to try to squeeze that ball in the hole." Crenshaw "doesn't even have an excuse. My health has been perfect." Some would like to point out that, since his Masters victory, Crenshaw has gotten a divorce, but he insists, "It's been a long time since the divorce [in October]. If anything, that was a relief."

Last April 15, Crenshaw shot 68 and wrote his name large in the big leatherbound golf history books he loves to read and collect so much. "This is a sweet, sweet win," he told a gallery that perhaps approved of his victory more than any Masters triumph since Arnold Palmer. "I don't think there'll ever be a sweeter moment."

Just a few weeks later, at Jack Nicklaus's Memorial Tournament, Crenshaw was still floating on his golf high, still seeing his name on the leader board every time out. "I can even remember the shot when it changed," he said today. "I tried to hit a wood out of a trap. Hit it sideways, made eight on a par-four and it was like somebody turned out the lights." Crenshaw shot 79 that day, 79 the next. Golf has been a mystery and a misery ever since. "The thing that kills me is that there's no in-between," he says. "Some days I'd just like to shoot par." But he can't. "I

Ben Crenshaw's victory in the Masters turned his world upside down.

need help sometimes because I can get so negative sometimes it's unbelievable."

Hypnosis? "That could be next. . . . You know, golfers' results are like a mirrored images of themselves. You just feel like it's your whole life out there."

Perhaps Tom Watson put his finger as close to Crenshaw's problem as anyone when he said today, "In all sports, you see athletes who attain a certain goal and it stops them. There's always a goal better than that goal and you have to find it. If you don't think that way, you're in trouble." Watson's goal? "To hit the perfect shot every time I swing at it." So much for attainable goals.

Crenshaw, as sentimental as Watson is sensible, has never been fascinated by process and practice. He's always played by touch, been motivated by emotion and swallowed the whole magnolia-and-dogwood Masters mythology. From the day as a teenager that Crenshaw first set foot on the Augusta National, he wanted to win the Masters more than anything else on earth. "This represents everything that's best in golf," he says. Crenshaw came so close to winning major titles so often, and failed so agonizingly, that the frenzy and futility of this quest fed on itself. Five times he was runner-up in a major—twice in the Masters, including 1983. Then came 1984.

"So many moments told me it was my week. . . . On the last day at the twelfth, the hole could have been that big," said Crenshaw, holding his fingers exactly golf-ball size, "and I would have made it [for birdie]. Sometimes you know you're going to produce a shot. . . . After winning here last year, I asked myself many times, 'Can I go through this again? Do I want to go through this again?' "

Does Crenshaw almost regret his greatest victory? "No no, I won't go that far. . . . You bet I'd do it over," he says with a grin, suddenly dismissing his black cloud and getting matters back in perspective. "I still can't tell people how much the tournament meant to me. Not a day goes by that I don't think about how wonderful it was. Just returning here is a positive for me. . . . You know, all a streak player like me needs is a couple of holes to lose it or a couple of holes to get it back. See a few [putts] drop and a lot changes. I wouldn't trade that [day] for anything. If I suffered a while, that's okay. One day, my game will just come back."

Each year here the new champion holds a dinner for all the past champs. This Tuesday, the Texas motif was yellow roses and hot, hot peppers.

Next year, the Masters dinner won't have Ben Crenshaw's name on it. But he'll still be invited.

Even after he won the U.S. Open, Larry Nelson couldn't get any respect.

• • •

When a man works for fourteen years and reaches the top of his sport, when he wins the most prestigious crown in his game, he expects to pick up the paper or turn on the TV and get a little pleasure. If he is a golfer who just won the U.S. Open, he expects to be graciously received, especially if he's a polite, decent man without a blemish on his record as a citizen: military veteran, responsible husband and father, quietly religious doer of civic good works.

If this man also happens to set an Open record of 132 (65–67) in the final two rounds and if he sinks a sixty-two-foot putt on the seventieth hole to beat Tom Watson by a stroke, then it might be assumed that his portrait would be drawn along flattering lines. You know, stuff about how he never swung a golf club until he came back from Vietnam at age twenty-two; a little human-interest angle about how he hits a ball as purely and consistently as almost anyone since Ben Hogan but couldn't putt a beach ball into the ocean. ("I play along every year, waiting for one week, maybe two, when I can putt.")

Well, that's what Larry Nelson thought when he won the 1983 U.S. Open at Oakmont near Pittsburgh.

This humble fellow—who figured he'd celebrate his victory by eating at McDonald's, then spend the evening alone in his hotel room before flying the next morning to speak to a church group—got a tremendous shock in the days following his greatest moment. A shock it has taken him a year to absorb and digest and forgive.

"I've taken a lot of bad lumps. I couldn't believe the way I was ripped. Just terrible, terrible things . . . you'd have thought I did something wrong. I was called bland and dull and boring." On the evening news, he felt he came across as a fluke instead of an established veteran who had already won a major title (the 1981 PGA). Sports section riffs on "Just How Dull Is Larry Nelson?" came at him from all quarters. The notion that his personality somehow epitomized what was wrong with golf hung in the air for weeks. Nelson even called one Detroit columnist at home and asked, "What did I ever do to you to deserve that?" As Nelson explains, "What's portrayed is what people think you are. But that's not what you are. My 'image' is not anywhere near who I am."

Many athletes might be permanently embittered by this experience. Nelson, however, was lucky. He had the perspective to see himself from the outside, as well as pity himself from the inside. Though that hurt, too. "I've had the same accountant for ten years and he was interviewed a couple of times after the Open," said Nelson. "He was asked, 'What is Larry Nelson really like?' And he said, 'I just don't know who Larry Nelson is.' "

Nelson pauses after telling this, then adds, "I thought that guy was probably about my closest friend. . . .

"That's when I started to realize that I was keeping too much to myself. That's not a healthy way to be. Except for my wife and children and family, I just wasn't letting people know who I was. I'd love to be a glass person. You know, so everybody could see inside. But I'm an introvert. Sometimes I feel more at home in Japan, where 85 percent of the people are like me, than I do here in America, where I've read that 85 percent of the people are extroverts."

Nelson decided he had a choice: "I could withdraw even further or I could go forward and try to reveal more of what my personality is." So, for the past year, he has been a classic example of a man turning the other cheek.

"My wife told me that I couldn't expect more out of anything than what I put into it. And I wasn't putting much into my contact with the press and the public. She told me to stop giving one- and two-word answers and make an effort to explain what I thought. . . . You only make jokes around people you feel comfortable with and I got defensive as soon as I saw a notebook or a microphone. My wife said she could see my back bristle. . . .

"I've learned a lot in the last year. I realize that's the way it should be. . . . I'll stay until the last person has asked the last question he can think of. I may not have anything too great to say, but I'll try. If that results in one person having a better idea of who I am . . ."

This approach doesn't mean that Nelson now thinks he got a square deal a year ago. It just means that he comprehends what happened. He will say he got "as much recognition as I wanted," but he can't bring himself to say he got as much as he deserved.

He has learned how to be feisty without being testy. "I'm exactly the same size as Tom Watson, but everybody talks about my lack of hair and my 'small' stature," he said. "This week, I'd like to read about 'short Tom Watson.' "

Nelson is gradually developing a public face that partially resembles his private demeanor. "My wife thinks I'm the funniest person she knows," he said sheepishly, knowing that his wife will probably get to retain an exclusive on this opinion. Part of Larry Nelson is going to stay in a shell. He's a methodical, analytical, private man with a tart honesty and an aversion to smooth social compromises. Asked why he seldom drinks liquor, he said, in his odd mixture of conciliation and candor, "Oh, it's not a moral issue. I just think it kills brain cells."

Nelson wants desperately to rework the final image he leaves in the collective golf mind. From now on, he's got a new attitude: "Here I am. Let's get it right this time."

• • •

When Greg Norman stepped to the tenth tee of the Old Course in the first round of the 1984 British Open, he had an unusual thought. As he gazed at the green, he claims he said to himself, "Just aim it at the hole and it might go in."

Norman's only other thought was to make sure that he didn't swing too hard because, with the club he had in his hand and the breeze behind him, he figured he could "hit the ball another thirty yards [past the hole]." Norman then drilled his shot at the flag, missed the stick by a yard and left a twelve-foot putt. What makes this unusual is that the tenth hole is a 342-yard par-four.

Just at the moment, Greg Norman is the only man on earth who thinks about making holes-in-one when he's playing par-fours. He's hitting his ball like somebody from Up Above, not Down Under.

"Actually, the wind was from the wrong direction for me," he said. "If it turns around [tomorrow], I've got a good chance of driving four of the par-fours—the ninth, tenth, twelfth and eighteenth." Those holes are 356 yards, 342 yards, 316 yards and 354 yards. When nature laid out this links, it obviously hadn't figured on the evolution of a Norman who's been reaching all these holes in practice rounds, though he says he needs a good bounce "off one mound" to reach that tenth hole with wind in his face.

Norman's first-round-leading 67 included eight birdies and was typical of his June–July rampage in which he has suddenly thrust his name to the forefront of his sport. With each passing week, the question becomes framed more clearly: Is Norman this good or is Norman just this hot? Norman has decided to leave no doubt as to his opinion. With a refreshing Australian audacity, he's letting everybody know that he thinks the Norman Conquest has begun. When someone commented that he "seemed to be in an exceptional groove," Norman quipped crisply, "Seven years," meaning he'd been hot for his whole career.

"Actually, I don't think I'm playing as well as I was at the end of last year, when I won seven of ten tournaments around the world. I'm not doing anything different. You just get a helluva lot more coverage when you win in America," said Norman, who has won the Kemper and Canadian Opens and lost playoffs at the U.S. and Western Opens within seven weeks. "I'm not scared of winning because I've beaten every one of these players on their home turf. It's a confidence factor. I breed on that," said Norman.

This is a fellow who, after winning at Kemper, said, "They can watch out now." This is the guy who sank a forty-foot putt on the seventy-second hole of the U.S. Open to force a playoff. This is the good sport who, after losing that playoff by eight strokes to Fuzzy Zoeller, waved a towel in mock surrender when he approached the last hole. This is the cocksure bloke who wins friends just by being himself.

"It's fun to see Greg winning and enjoying it so much," said Peter Jacobsen. "It's tremendous for golf. . . . You can't help but pat the guy on the back, he's so fresh and honest about it."

When Norman arrived at the tenth green at the Old Course for his eagle putt, he played to the crowd, flexing his muscles, then jousted with every player on the green. Fellow Australian David Graham, who was playing the adjoining eighth hole, said facetiously, "A bump-and-run shot?"

"No, I just pitched it there and backed it up," teased Norman.

Jack Nicklaus also was on that huge double green but, after three-putting four consecutive holes, wasn't in the mood for banter. "Jack just stood there looking at me," said Norman. "I don't know what he was thinking."

Nicklaus may have been pondering how great Norman might have been if he'd tried the American Tour at age twenty-one instead of waiting until now, when he's twenty-nine. "I first played with Norman in Sydney eight years ago and I advised him to play our Tour," said Nicklaus. "I've always thought a lot of his game. But, in his own mind, he didn't think he was good enough or mature enough. Even after he married an American girl, he didn't come over. Greg has to lead his own life. Everybody has to answer to himself first of all. Maybe the way he's playing now means that he did it the right way."

The player Nicklaus believes has really messed up his career progression is Seve Ballesteros. "Greg and Seve are a lot alike. Seve's just a helluva player. They both are, really," said Nicklaus. "They both came to play the [U.S.] Tour [full-time] this year [for the first time]. But Norman had an advantage. America didn't know much about him, even though he's won thirty-some [international] tournaments. He wasn't expected to win. Seve was expected to win, so there was a lot more pressure on him. Now Seve's going back the other way, toward the European Tour. I really didn't envy Seve's position. He should have come over a couple of years sooner."

This business of blooming golfers is the trickiest of subjects.

How many candidates have we seen for Next Great Player? In 1974 Johnny Miller couldn't miss. Ben Crenshaw was close for years. Craig Stadler looked as if he was a Walrus whisker from eminence two seasons ago. Wasn't it just last year that Hal Sutton was called the Bear Apparent? In no other sport are getting to the top and staying at the top such entirely separate issues.

At the moment, Norman looks at par-fours at the Old Course and thinks hole-in-one. "When one thing is working, it helps the next thing," he says. "You just go from strength to strength." Norman should relish these magic days when "every shot went where I wanted it. I never felt uptight at all. Just enjoyed my game."

And we should enjoy such days, too. You never know who will turn out to be the next Jack Nicklaus. Especially since no one has.

• • •

The walls of Raymond Floyd's den in his $2-million Miami home are decked with dozens of magazine covers of him in handsome living color. Behind glass cases stand huge silver trophies for victories in events including the Masters, where he holds the course record; the PGA, which he's won twice; and the Tournament Players Championship, where he picked up a $325,000 check for an afternoon's work.

Old Tempo Raymondo, the loosest and most genial of golfers, is not a vain man—just a proud one. The rest of his showpiece home gives little hint that he ever struck a ball for cash. But Floyd knows that a professional athlete needs at least one room to which he can go for reinforcement. As the birthdays pass, you sometimes want to be reminded how great you are, because it wouldn't help the mortgage payments if you forgot.

Only one thing is missing from Floyd's sanctum: a U.S. Open trophy.

That's the one he wants most, and now he has himself in position to do something about it, with his third-round 70 for a 213 total, three strokes behind leader Greg Norman going into Sunday's final round.

With the exception of Sam Snead, no great player ever has had such an awful record in the world's most prestigious event. It's not just that Floyd hasn't won the Open. He's never finished second, third, fourth or fifth, either. For comparison, Jack Nicklaus has been in the top ten at the Open seventeen times. Floyd: twice. And one of those was a sixth place twenty-one years ago. Since then, Floyd has an eighth in 1971 and nothing over the last fifteen years. In twenty-one Opens, he has won barely $50,000.

When the great mysteries—not only of golf but of all sport—are discussed, Floyd's Open jinx should rank fairly high. And, among his fellow pros in the locker room, it does. But Floyd's secret seldom gets out. He's enormously popular and nobody wants to rip him. Besides, there's a weird flip side to this conundrum that baffles logic. Floyd has finished between twelfth and sixteenth in the Open—which is quite good—nine times. If you play the numbers game that way, he's been in the top sixteen more often than Lee Trevino, who is considered a great Open player.

The final twist? Floyd is one guy who ought to eat up Open stress with a spoon. The book on his whole life says he's Mr. Pressure. Last week, Floyd became only the fourth man ever to win $3 million on the pro tour. "My philosophy," he said, "has always been: 'What difference does it make?' If you play every week, you're going to have bad days, too. I think that's why I have the reputation of playing well under pressure."

Except for Nicklaus, no golfer of the last quarter century has a gaudier reputation for having ice water in the veins. That's because Floyd may be the best high-stakes gambler on earth. He'll clean out your pockets and your backers' pockets, then reach in his wallet to peel off a couple of Grovers so you can get yourself home in style. If you still have a home.

With the years, the Open mystery has deepened. Floyd is long and straight enough off the tee. He's fabulous in sand and always tops in putting stats, which measures the whole short game. If you think others are perplexed, just ask Floyd. "The record speaks for itself. The Open hasn't been my cup of tea," he said this week after a second-round 68. "Even at the British Open, where I haven't won, I've been second twice and also third and fourth. I've contended. I've never even been in the hunt at the Open. It's either slow starts or slow finishes. I just haven't ever really played well. If I get close, I'll shoot 75 or 76 that last day. Honestly, I've tried to figure it out for years. I can't. I ask myself, 'Why don't you perform in the Open?' I wish to God I could figure out the answer because if I could, maybe I'd still have time to do something about it."

There is one possible explanation for his Open problems. First, Floyd is both a precisionist and a bit of a sensualist. He loves golf because it's a gloriously pleasant way to earn a living. The U.S. Open is the one American event that removes both precision and pleasure from the game. Everybody's going to meet disaster and nobody's going to have much fun. If Floyd has one flaw, it's that he has little knack for the miracle recovery shot; it's just not in his bag.

The difference between Thursday and Friday here this week showed a lot about Floyd. "With the wind, rain and cold on Thursday, I had no feel. I was all bundled up, just trying to get back in without hurting myself. Then, on the fifth or sixth hole [Friday], the sun came out and I took my sweater off. Suddenly my mind clicked in. I thought, "It's golf. You better perform. It's here. There's a chance to express what we're trying to do out here.' "

Of all tournaments, the Open does the best job of slashing an artist's painting, of denying the expressionist a chance to create something beautiful. Floyd always has been the quintessential front-runner who never hands back the lead. He just finishes the masterpiece. The Open won't even let him get the first brushstrokes in place.

With the years, the Open has become a sort of fixation for Floyd. This is the one time each year he can't say: "What difference does it make?" And that is a huge burden for a man who always has loved to smell the flowers, taste the best food, kiss the prettiest women, build the most beautiful house on Biscayne Bay and, generally, revel in every minute of life as long as he can take his sweater off.

Last week at the Westchester Classic, the forty-three-year-old Floyd was tied for the lead entering Sunday's round. For one of the few times, he blew up with the cash on the table, shooting 77. "I wanted to win so badly that I wasn't Ray Floyd out there," he said this week. "I don't know when that's ever happened to me before." Except at the Open.

Some athletes almost incorporate a whole view of life in their style of play. Floyd is one. His swing is syrupy and locked to his relaxed molasses temperament. He lets that right elbow fly at the top because he trusts life just like he trusts his swing. "Let her rip. Things always work out for the best," he seems to say.

If it doesn't happen this time, Raymond Floyd probably never will win the U.S. Open. But, when you look at his whole life, his whole career, you tend to agree with the man himself.

What difference does it make?

• • •

Don't say that to Floyd, of course. It matters to him—matters more than anything in his whole career that, the next day, he shot 66 and became the oldest man ever to win the U.S. Open.

AGING
WITH GRACE

Augusta, Ga., April 9, 1983–Gaining even a partial victory over age is harder than defeating other men. That's why this Masters has a resonance beyond golf. These days, in their different ways, Arnold Palmer, Sam Snead, Jack Nicklaus and Raymond Floyd have shown us, through their golf, how gently a man can age, finding a posture and a tone appropriate to each stage of his life.

On Wednesday, in the par-three tournament, Snead—playing in his forty-fourth and final Masters—drew a large gallery. At seventy-one, he is still able to bring delight to others. Not with nostalgic jokes or corny dated clothes, but with his marvelous swing, with his golf. At the next-to-last hole, Snead lofted his ball over the water to a tiny green, then sank his putt for a birdie. The perfect tempo, the lashing hands at the moment of impact, were a legitimate, dignified farewell. He shot 79 in the first round, then gracefully withdrew.

This week, Palmer, fifty-three, Nicklaus, forty-three, and Tom Watson, thirty-three—none knowing what the other had said—all made nearly identical comments. "I play with Sam every chance I can so that I can imitate his tempo. I always play better after I play with him," said all three, their pressroom quotes almost eerie Xerox copies of each other. "Sam Snead still has the best swing in golf."

In golf, unlike any other sport in America, it's possible to stay on top for twenty-five years, then continue as a dignified competitor for another decade and, finally, remain a presentable facsimile of yourself right up to the gates of old age.

Arnold Palmer has not lost his competitive edge with advancing age. Note the dangling shirttail.

Taken over an entire lifetime, golf is, by a clear margin, the most lifelike of our sports. Normally, the kernel of meaning hidden inside our games is somewhat bitter. The achievements of athletes are tinged with a quasi-tragic element. We find our heroes doubly piquant because their time in the spotlight is so short. The average professional life span of an NFL running back is four seasons.

In golf, all the ages of man are given an almost Oriental respect.

Particularly at the Masters.

Here, past champions have a lifetime pass into the small field. If Doug Ford insists on coming out and shooting 85, then it's permitted. No one scoffs at the Bob Goalbys, Art Walls and Billy Caspers who make the cut one year in five. They have their place, and even their followers. Gene Sarazen is eighty-one and still tees it up here every year for a few holes; the young watch with genuine interest, since the lineaments of that double-eagle swing are still faintly discernible in the old man's action.

The Masters, however, is not a testimony to old codgers, but, rather, to the capacity of men to grow in experience and knowledge every year. "This is the most subtle course we play," said Watson. I keep learning about the wind—where it turns corners, how it can double back on itself when it goes down in a hollow and then comes back up. A little breeze is the toughest because you have to learn how it shifts and changes. At the fourth hole [205 yards], you can hit what you think is a perfect shot and be 50 yards short."

This week has been especially good for watching the ways that golf allows its champions to arrive at the pinnacle a bit later than in other sports, then stay on top much longer. When we see Raymond Floyd, forty years old and at the very peak of his career, we sense that life is not such a desperately urgent affair. Tempo Raymondo never got serious about anything until he was past thirty. Now it seems he was cheated of little. He's so content, so responsible, that we almost suspect that a man must grow sated on wild oats before he can be so genially adult.

"I think that, in golf, your physical and mental capabilities aren't really compatible until you're thirty-five to forty-five. Those, to me, are your peak years. You feel so much better-adjusted to everything," said Floyd. "When you're young, you're blessed with strength and raw ability, but, unfortunately, you don't have brain one to go with it. I can't hit it 300 yards in the air anymore, but I've learned a lot of the little things. In the last few years, everything in my game has started complementing everything else.

"Every other player I've talked to has mentioned the same thing. Look at the careers of Ben Hogan and Snead and so many others. Jack Nicklaus is the only one I've ever known who came out at twenty-one and had the maturity to play his best immediately. They say Bobby Jones was like that, too. . . .

"My wife was the one who turned the light on," said Floyd, who was number two on the money list in 1981 and 1982. "When we got married, I was thirty-one. She said, 'If you aren't going to be serious about what you're doing, maybe you should do something else.' You might say she said it a little stronger than that. I never had any realism like that put to me. . . . You have to be honest with yourself. It was kinda frightening."

At thirty-two, Floyd—almost overnight—accepted his role as husband, father and earnest golfer and put his extended childhood behind him. "At some point," he said, "you say to yourself, 'I want to be the best.' But when you honestly make that commitment, you have to realize all the dedication and time that it takes."

Interestingly, Nicklaus also had a sort of Road to Damascus revelation when he was thirty-one. Then he was still fat Jack. His doctor had always told him that "There'll be some day in your life when you know it's time to lose weight and you will." That day came for Nicklaus when he'd played thirty-six holes of golf for three days in a row. "I was tired from golf for the first time in my life," he recalled. That night, Nicklaus told his wife that day had come. He called his tailor the next morning and told him, "I'll need a new wardrobe in three weeks." In that time, he lost twenty to twenty-five pounds and has never put it back on. Now Nicklaus takes long brisk walks (jogging kills his back), plays tennis and even skis. "Someday Craig Stadler will go through what I went through," said Nicklaus, "and he'll lose that weight. He'll know when the time is right."

Worse than stiff muscles and excess midriff and yippy nerves is a gradual loss of desire—even in the greatest competitors. "I got tired," says Palmer bluntly. "After fifteen, seventeen years of pushing, day after day, year after year, I really didn't care. . . . The whole thing just deteriorates. I needed to stop, just walk away. . . . Jack [Nicklaus] is in that period now. . . . Sooner or later, you hope you can relight the candle. . . . Two, three, four years ago that desire—that fire—came back. More than ever."

In golf, little of significance is won on the PGA Tour after a man's forty-fifth birthday. Despite this, there's a wonderfully dignified middle ground that a few fortunate players can reach.

The great player, far past his prime, can still have his day—or week— on a major stage. At fifty-one, Snead finished third in the Masters; at sixty, he shot an opening round 69. Hogan, at fifty-four, brought Augusta National to its feet with a splendid 66 that, for many, is one of the finest moments in the history of the game. The legends of those days when time freezes are rich. In fact, old hands here remember that when Hogan shot his 66 he held court for reporters in the clubhouse. Near Hogan, tying his shoes ever so slowly so he could hear the Wee Ice Man's ruminations, was a young chap who was then the number two money winner in golf. That fellow, filing away memories, was—according to the tale—Arnold Palmer.

This Thursday, the fifty-three-year-old Palmer began the Masters with a 68. It was his best round here in nine years, his second-best score in eighteen years and his best opening round in twenty-two years. Some are now dreaming about a Palmer victory. Those with a feeling for this paradoxical game—this sport which both humbles the young and yet leaves the old their pride—know differently. They realize that Palmer has already won his Masters.

WASHINGTON, D.C., September 4, 1986–On Tuesday, Arnold Palmer made a hole-in-one. Yesterday, he returned and made a hole-in-a-million.

Same golf course: the Tournament Players Club at Avenel in Potomac in preliminaries to the Chrysler Cup. Same hole: the 187-yard number three. Same club: five-iron. And, amazingly, same score: 1.

An instant after he hit his ball yesterday, Palmer knew the game was afoot. "Don't go in the hole again!" he called out. "Don't do that."

That's how golfers, even the best, do their rooting. Backward.

The ball smacked the base of the flagstick on the fly with a hollow, distant clank, dove down into the cup and took old Arnie, a week shy of his fifty-seventh birthday, into the record book one more delicious time in his athletic dotage.

Everybody, including Palmer, asked the same question. Had it ever happened before? And the answer was the one everybody wanted to hear.

Palmer, probably the most popular golfer who ever lived, had become the first pro in the history of his sport to make a hole-in-one on the same tournament hole two days in a row.

"No odds," said Palmer, moments after his second nearly miraculous deed in a pro-amateur tournament. "It's impossible."

For numerologists, the ace was—what else?—the thirteenth of Palmer's life.

When Palmer's shot disappeared, voices from the gallery of about a hundred began screaming, "It went in!" and two Chrysler marshals dressed in red began jumping up and down, giving the football "touchdown" sign. Everybody did something. Except Palmer, who was too stunned. No pants hitch. No smile or wink or laugh.

As people gathered around him, he talked softly, almost to himself, chuckling and shaking his head. "I can't believe that. . . . But it looked like it was going in the hole as soon as I hit it. It was right on the flag. . . . That is amazing. . . . That's a little hard to believe. . . . Aw, my goodness. . . . That's the most amazing. . . . Aw, my goodness. . . . I've had some things happen to me, but never anything close to that."

By the time he reached the green, the showman in him was awake again. "Guess I'll just have to dig this [hole] up and take it home with me," he told the Arnie's mini-Army following him on a drizzly, threatening day.

As the three amateurs in this group continued to battle the hole, Palmer waved them toward the next tee before they'd putted out and said, "Come on, pardnahs, we won't worry about this hole anymore."

Word was spreading fast. "That hole is too easy," razzed Chi Chi Rodriguez, playing in the group in front of Palmer. Then Rodriguez added, "I used to think Arnold Palmer could walk on water. Now I know it."

Lee Elder, on an adjacent hole, yelled out, "Hey, Captain Palmer, will you quit wasting those holes-in-one? Save 'em for the real tournament."

Starting today, an eight-man United States team, captained by Palmer, meets an international team for the largest total prize money on the Senior PGA Tour—$50,000 to each winning player and $25,000 to the losers. For many oldsters, very high stakes.

"He probably won't hit the green tomorrow," said Elder, laughing.

As Palmer took the long, winding walk to the fourth tee, he was almost alone. "Isn't that something?" he said. "You go for years and years and years without a hole-in-one—I went thirteen years without one once —then you make two in two days on the same hole. You know, I don't even want to play that hole again. I may skip it tomorrow."

Yesterday, one reporter and one minicam TV crew were at hole number three. If Palmer skips it today, he'll disappoint a lot of people because the crowd awaiting him won't be small.

Ironically, before this round, the Palmer group was surrounded by a sense of anticlimax, as though the previous day's hole-in-one was the allotment of excitement for the week. "I was just trying to show off for Gary Player, who was standing down by the green," said Palmer, joking on the first tee. "I assume I impressed him."

Before hitting his first drive yesterday, Palmer scanned the crowd and spotted a handicapped man. Just as he had noted a woman in a wheelchair outside of the ropes at the practice putting green and sought her out for photos, so he made a beeline for this fellow to chat and mug.

The same man followed Palmer all day. "You know what that little guy said to me just as I was walking up on the third tee?" Palmer said a few minutes after his hole-in-one. "He said, 'Now I want you to do it again today.' "

As soon as Palmer did, golf scriveners were sent to the record books. According to the Golf Digest Hole-in-One Clearing House (the best available source of such information), only five Americans have ever made consecutive holes-in-one on the same hole—the most recent in 1969.

None was a pro. Only one of the back-to-back aces came in a bona fide tournament (by Scott Porter of Ball State in the 1967 Indiana Amateur).

To grasp the rarity of Palmer's feat, it should be noted that, in all his years of golf, Palmer has played more than 40,000 par-threes. With thirteen holes-in-one. So the probability of Palmer acing a hole twice in a row is on the order of ten million to one.

Palmer refused to give his ball to a fan on Tuesday, saying he saved his hole-in-one balls for his wife Winnie. She may have to fight the Hall of Fame in Pinehurst, N.C., for yesterday's artifact.

As Palmer walked through the rain, his fans stayed with him, chatting between holes. "You know, a TV camera shot the hole-in-one, Arnie," someone said. "Maybe it'll make the national evening news."

"That would be nice," said Palmer. "I haven't made it much lately."

• • •

Two stories.

When Arnold Palmer was five years old, he'd play with a sawed-off golf club near the first tee of the Latrobe (Pa.) Country Club, where his father was a pro. One day a heavyset woman, who often had difficulty getting limbered up to hit her first shot of the day, approached little Palmer and said, "Arnie, I'll give you a nickel if you can hit my ball across that ditch."

"Whenever she asked me, I always carried the ditch," Palmer said this week, recalling those days.

Ben Hogan, in his prime, once played a practice round before the Masters with Claude Harmon. At the twelfth hole, Harmon scored a hole-in-one. The crowd went wild. Hogan, who seldom spoke to partners except to say, "You're away," said nothing to Harmon, then hit his own ball a few feet from the cup.

All the way to the green, Hogan was stone silent. Harmon retrieved his ball from the cup to more cheers as Hogan plumb-bobbed his putt, then sank it. As they headed to the next tee, Hogan put his arm around Harmon. "Here it comes," thought Harmon. "The Wee Ice Man is actually going to say, 'Nice shot.'"

"You know something, Claude," said Hogan, "I think that's the first time I've ever made a birdie on that hole."

These tales, perhaps, help draw the distinction between a folk hero, like Palmer, and a legend, like Hogan. They also help us see why the ever-helpful, dutiful Palmer is still making headlines for himself and friends for his game, while Hogan is the only great living golfer who isolates himself almost completely from his sport. The older they get, the more we see the difference between a man who is beloved more for himself than his golf and one who is primarily respected for his deeds and his isolated integrity.

When Hogan was asked to participate in "The Legends of Golf" tournament for television in the late 1970s in hopes that senior golf might be popularized, the old hawk, who's shot his age at sixty-four, said, "I will have nothing to do with it. I will not lend my name to it."

Maybe that's how a legend has to play it. All for the sake of history, for the preservation of the mystique. But when you cherish the past, you can also squander the present.

We can only wonder what the reclusive Hogan—who never grants an audience unless you fly to Fort Worth, and then only if you're lucky— thought about Palmer's headline-making, back-to-back aces on the same hole this week in Potomac.

By enduring the aggravations of age and the grinding indignity of his own diminished greatness on the Senior PGA Tour, Palmer put himself in the path of new experience. Decades from now, when all his three-putts and his back-in-the-pack finishes in obscure senior events are forgotten, Palmer's pair of aces at age fifty-six will be part of his lore. Sure, he got old, but he never lost the magic.

Hogan isn't wrong to have shunned the Senior Tour, shunned the whole contemporary world of golf, really. It's his business. However, it's a painful choice.

Pro golfers wish matters were otherwise, but respect Hogan too much to criticize him. Jack Nicklaus wanted to dedicate one of his Memorial tournaments to Hogan, but didn't because he was afraid Hogan would not even come to accept the honor.

The seniors have wished (and put out feelers for years) that Hogan would pay an occasional visit to their circus. But Bantam Ben, who still plays presentably and often with friends in Texas, has never showed up and probably never will. He won't embarrass himself with an imperfect game.

Once Hogan was asked if he had ever played a perfect round. "The perfect round of golf has never been played," he snapped. "It's eighteen holes-in-one. I almost dreamt it once, but I lipped out at eighteen.

"I was mad as hell."

Because of his rigorous standards, Hogan aces are now confined to dreams. Palmer, who has always rounded off the edges of a hard world, still makes his aces in public—though the total "Army" in attendance for his pair of ones this week wouldn't have come to 150. That's because, despite zillions in the bank and enormous business responsibilities, Palmer has been willing to flog himself back into shape and drag himself all over the country for the sake of helping the Senior Tour become established.

In seven senior seasons, Palmer has won nine tournaments. But Don

January, Miller Barber and Peter Thompson—the players Palmer thumped in his prime—have won twenty-three, nineteen and eleven times. Others, such as Gary Player and Chi Chi Rodriguez, look as if they'll rocket past Palmer's senior records. This year, Palmer is number eighteen on the money list, one notch ahead of the immortal Walt Zembriski.

Palmer surely enjoys the adulation and the adrenaline of seniors competition. He's having some fun. But he also has tons of aggravation playing sex symbol and drawing card as he approaches sixty. While everybody else has a frolic on the seniors, Palmer frankly says, "I've never worked this hard in my life. Harder than I'd like to work."

When people ask, "Why is Arnie still playing? He can't even win on the Senior Tour anymore," the easy answer is to say that he needs the limelight. That is almost certainly unfair. It's far more likely that he's hitting drives over ditches for nickels. He can't resist the chance to please.

To say that Palmer, three days shy of his fifty-seventh birthday, is pressed for time is a joke. He has his life down to micro-minute compartments. On the practice green, his caddie stands by the hole and rolls the balls back to him so Palmer won't lose the few seconds it takes to retrieve them.

When an official says breathlessly, "You're on the tee in four minutes, Arnold," Palmer laughs and says, "Plenty of time," as though four minutes were a world of relaxation in a schedule that includes golf course design, construction and development—not to mention an empire of clothes and club companies. What makes Palmer special is how he goes about being himself. He restores luster to the word "celebrity." In everything Palmer is a giver.

Chi Chi Rodriguez teases the gallery, saying, "You listen to all my jokes, then you go and follow Arnie," but he'll say to a friend, "I'm playing in front of the King today."

This week, PGA Tour Commissioner Deane Beman said, jokingly, of Palmer's two holes-in-one: "It's nice to be good at what you do, but it's better to be lucky." Of course Palmer's aces were lucky. But they were also pieces of superb accidental justice.

Palmer has not won a major title for twenty-two years or a U.S. Open for twenty-six. It has been a long time between banner headlines. No one would doubt that he has kept playing for his own pleasure and his own challenge. But it would be just as inaccurate to deny the element of sacrifice in Palmer's endurance.

When he could have lived out his life like an emperor, he has chosen to trudge through Pro-Ams with baffled amateurs, congratulating them on their least horrid shots. "Good try, Robert. Little late," Palmer said this week as a jittery partner skulked his chip to tap-in range to save his double bogey.

There's a huge chunk of Palmer that just wants to do right, to always carry the ditch. This week, he stood on the tee and noticed that one of his amateur partners had a glop of ketchup on his face. Palmer brushed his own face to let the fellow know. The amateur whiffed. Palmer looked back a minute later and saw that the man had missed. "Little lower," said Palmer softly, just helping.

Sure, Arnold Palmer is playing in events like the Chrysler Cup—now and probably for years to come—because he likes to be adored. But that's not all. Palmer earned his aces this week. And the day in the sun they brought him. Most gods don't keep paying dues. Palmer has. And if he'd made a third hole-in-one, who's to say it would have been more than he deserved.

NEW
TRICKS

PALM BEACH GARDENS, FLA., February 15, 1986–As the sky grew dark, one small man dressed all in black stayed on the practice putting green after everyone else had left. He was a rookie on the eve of his first major tournament. As one putt after another slipped exasperatingly past the hole, the player slapped his hand hard against his thigh and gritted his teeth. Nerves already.

An old fan outside the gallery ropes muttered, "Come on, make one, will ya?" Then he added, commiserating, "That'll drive a guy crazy." Finally, the golfer sank a longish one and snapped his fingers happily. "Now, *that* felt good to me," he said. The fan clapped once and actually broke into a gleeful little jog of empathy. "Soon as I make these, I'll go," murmured the rookie, methodically making three straight six-footers into the heart of the hole. "There," he sighed, confidence restored. Ready to go.

With that, fifty-year-old Gary Player, winner of 140 tournaments around the world, a man with career earnings in the millions, ended his last practice session before the 1986 PGA Senior Championship.

The loyal white-haired fan walked spryly toward the parking lot as though his spirits had been lifted, too.

By the end of the first round, Player was on the locker room phone, calling his family in South Africa. "Would you like to know who's leading?" he said, teasing like a proud little boy. "That's right. Had a 68. Let me tell you, I played a round of golf today."

As he changed spikes, Player beamed. "I feel like a young man again —injected with optimism, I'd say. Out here, I'm the youngster. Played with Sam Snead last week—the man must be the greatest athlete of all time, seventy-four years old and shooting his age—and he says to his

Gary Player happily charges toward a new career as a Senior.

caddie, 'How come this boy is outdriving me on every hole?' When I was on the regular Tour, they all called me 'Mr. Player.' "

Like most famous athletes, Player never thought his sport would still have its hooks deep into him when he was a grandfather. "Twenty years ago at the Masters, when Arnold Palmer, Jack Nicklaus and I were the 'Big Three,' we talked about when we'd retire," Player recalled. "Jack and I said we'd both be gone by thirty-five—and glad to be out of it. Arnold said, 'I'll play forever, till I can't anymore.' We laughed at him. Now, every year at the Masters, Arnold sees us and says, 'Hey, I thought you guys were going to retire.'

"Now I know what Arnold meant," said Player, who weighed 150 with a thirty-two-inch waist when he was twenty-five and now weighs 151 with a thirty-two-and-a-half-inch waist. "I tell you, this Senior Tour is a bloody joy."

These days, Player and Palmer are discovering (as Nicklaus will in 1990) that they can actually live out the athlete's most unlikely fantasy. They can hear the crowds, see their name writ large and win the gaudy prize—yes, they can play the game, really play with all their hearts— forever. It's almost like beating the house.

The saddest sight in sports is a person in his prime, probably not forty years old, realizing he's already washed up at the work for which he's prepared himself since he was a child. It is only a slight exaggeration to say that a great athlete dies twice and that, of the two deaths, retirement may seem the sharper pain. Housman's poem "To an Athlete Dying Young" often seems misnamed; in a way, how many world-class athletes *don't* die young?

All the qualities sport demands and rewards—love of competition, desire for recognition, dedication to task, ability to perform under stress— are exactly the traits most wounded and warped by a forced early retirement.

Those least suited to cope with an athlete's life are athletes. Yet nowhere, certainly not in any American sport, has any true provision been made so that great athletes can continue performing under bona fide competitive conditions before large crowds with millions of dollars at stake. Nowhere, that is, until the PGA Senior Tour began, shocking itself with success the past few years.

"It's unbelievable. If anybody had told me five years ago that I'd be playing a thirty-one tournament circuit with $7.5 million in prize money, I'd have said they were crazy," said Billy Casper, fifty-four. "We're having the time of our lives."

Perhaps the most unusual and sentimental success story in sports in the eighties has been the birth and nurturing of this rich, cheerful and booming golf tour for codgers over fifty. There's a lot of spring in the step of the geriatric set here at the PGA National course these days. Anyone who saw *Cocoon* knows how a man feels when the pleasures of youth are unexpectedly restored to him after long years of feeling (to paraphrase Yeats) that old age has been tied to him like a tin can to a dog's tail.

Player is among dozens of well-known golfers, including Palmer, who once again have a gallery at their heels and feel the delicious stress of battle. There's also the matter of big bucks, like this week's $40,000 first prize. In his best PGA Tour season, Player won $177,336; this year he expects to double that. After all, Peter Thomson won $386,724 on the 1985 Senior Tour and purses have already risen 25 percent since then. In a nation famous for worshiping youth, golfers like Palmer, Player and Casper may make gray hair and belt bulge a trend.

"When I'm coming down the last nine holes in contention in a Senior event, I feel just as wrapped up in it as I ever did in any tournament," says Palmer. "My nine wins on the Senior Tour have meant a lot to me. I'll remember 'em a long time."

"I never thought I'd wish for my fiftieth birthday to come," said Bruce Crampton, twice a Vardon Trophy winner, "but I was counting the days, chomping at the bit. I feel like I've been reborn. I'm having a ball."

Of all the eminent golfers in the last thirty years, perhaps none would have been less likely than Casper and Crampton to use such cheery phrases. "Havin' a ball," indeed. But that's part of the story too. "This isn't just a second chance for a career," said Casper. "It's a second chance for some of us to change our personalities. . . . Like who? Well, me. I used to be known as a grouch and a grump. Look at me now. Wearing knickers and [argyle] plus fours and silly hats. I never thought I'd see the day.

"But we're out here playing golf with people we've known all our lives. We get to meet some really great fans who appreciate us. We're not faced with a cut. At the end of the week, you're going to get a nice check. If that can't be pretty relaxed and a pretty good time, then there's something wrong with an individual. . . ."

For Crampton, perhaps known better for his dour demeanor than his golf, the change has been remarkable. "For some reason, turning fifty has been just a totally different psychological feeling than turning forty," said Crampton, who retired from golf nine years ago and disappeared from the scene until now. "I'm really going to enjoy myself now. The atmosphere is so different, not cutthroat, an easier existence. Then I felt like it was: 'What's this damn Australian doing, over here taking our money?' Now it's: 'God, it's good to see you back. We need you.' That warmth and respect will bring anyone out of a shell."

If the Senior Tour proves anything, it is the almost immeasurable power that the need for competition has over athletes. In retirement, Crampton was a successful independent oil and gas driller in Texas. "A real masculine occupation," he says. "When you get close to the pay zone, you know you're approaching oil that has been under the surface of the earth for 350 million years. When it comes shooting up out of the ground, it's as big a kick as winning a golf tournament."

Yet Crampton couldn't wait to get out of his drilling boots and back into cleats. "The further I got away from golf, the more it tormented me. I'd play occasionally with friends and they'd tell me how great I was hitting it. But I knew different. It was really first-class rubbish, was what it was. It just tended to tease me. I'm an all-or-nothing person. When I saw how successful the Senior Tour had become, I said, 'Now, there's something I can get my teeth stuck into again.' "

That lack of something worthy of sharp teeth is almost a nameless ache. "It fills in the void," said Palmer, perhaps accidentally meaning even more than he intended. "I've actually gotten to the point where I'm busier than I've ever been in my life—almost too busy."

While the legendary ones—the Palmers, Caspers and Players—get to listen to the cheers of their gallery armies once more, other less familiar Tour regulars from the fifties, sixties and seventies are making more money than they ever dreamed. Both Don January and Miller Barber have won more than a million dollars *as seniors.* Lee Elder, who never even reached the regular PGA Tour until he was thirty-three, has been making up for lost time, banking $307,795 last season.

"Oh, make a few putts one week, miss a few the next," said Elder, chubby and contented these days, playing out of a cart. He almost has to pinch himself. He's not the only one.

Casper watched the new name go up on the leader board *above* his own. His eyes grew hard. Competing for thirty years will do that. You don't win two million bucks with your golf sticks by being a pussycat. Then his whole face changed. "Why, it's Charlie Owens!" Casper beamed. "Isn't that wonderful?"

How wonderful? If Owens and Palmer were tied, coming down to the last hole of a senior tournament, most people in golf wouldn't know whom to root for harder.

What's most unusual about America's latest sports hero? That he celebrated his fifty-sixth birthday recently? That he limps with a stiff (fused) left leg? That he's a black in a white sport? That he wears thick dark glasses because he is, at times, almost blind from an inflammation of the iris? That he is the only successful player on earth who hits the ball cross-handed? That he uses a bizarre, fifty-inch putter to take pressure off his bad back? That he has a month-old baby daughter? Or that he's finished first and third—worth $49,000—in the last two PGA Senior Tour events? After all, that's more prize money than Owens won in his first eighteen years as a golf pro—from 1967 to 1984.

Owens epitomizes the Senior Dream that it's never too late. So let's take it from the top. Owens was raised in a shack at the Winter Haven (Fla.) Golf Club, where his father worked. "Golf clubs were my toys." Determined to achieve, the powerful six-foot-three, 215-pound Owens was a star tight end on scholarship at Florida A&M. The Chicago Bears wanted both him and teammate Willie Galimore. The Korean War was on; Owens picked Uncle Sam, instead. Joined the Army to be a paratrooper and do his duty. The NFL could wait.

Night mission. Wrong drop zone. Too low. Owens landed on a tree stump. The injury was diagnosed for six months as a pulled muscle. Four Army operations later, he had a fused knee and potential for a lawsuit. He never pursued it.

After that, Owens's luck held. All bad. An auto accident left him in a neck-to-toe cast. So he read golf magazines. Now, *there* was a sport in which he still had a chance to make some money. After an eighteen-year layoff since his boyhood rounds (some by moonlight), Owens shot 70, then 71 in his first two rounds. Out to Gaines Park he marched to hit 700 to 1,000 balls a day. And pick them up himself. By 1967, he had turned pro.

"I've only hit about ten balls conventionally in my life," he says. "I almost broke my wrist every time. . . ."

It wasn't the totally weird swing, but the walking that wore him out. In seven years on tour, he developed ankle, back and knee miseries. Ask him today how his good leg feels and he says seriously: "No no, *this* is my good leg." And he points at the stiff one. The other one's had three knee operations and not a bit of cartilage is left.

Somewhere along his arduous way, almost everything that could go wrong caught up with Owens. He had five children, but by four wives. Once, in an argument, a man stabbed him in the throat; he escaped with a long scar and his life—barely.

When the Senior Tour started, there was Owens, ready to give it one more try. A golf cart sounded good. In 1981, 1982 and 1983, he won a total of $17,000. Why would he win more? By now, he had the old-man yips. Who wouldn't? "I've got a hundred and fifty putters in my basement," Owens said. Finally, he had an idea. "A vision from God," he calls it. When you find a way to start making putts after your fifty-third birthday, that's about right.

Owens told a machinist friend that he wanted a putter that, when he bent over slightly, would come up to armpit height. How he knew that such a thing would work when no such thing existed is a fairly interesting mystery. On Christmas Day of 1983, the putter was finished. Owens headed to Rogers Park in hometown Tampa, even though the temperature was twenty-eight degrees. "That's it," he recalls saying after the first putt.

By 1985, Owens had won $78,158. Things were finally going to work out, right? Only one small problem remained. "I was going blind," said Owens. The disease is called iritis. You see the world through a fog. Eye drops at $50 a pop weren't curing the problem. Then, Owens tried pouring an herb tea into his eyes. As the leader board shows, it's working so far.

Since 1967, Owens had longed, just once, to tee it up equal with the greats of his generation—and beat the lot of 'em. Two weeks ago in Fort Pierce, Fla., Owens won the Treasure Coast Classic, shooting 65–69–68— 202 to win $33,500. "I struggled and I prayed. . . . I wanted to win an official tournament. I've been trying for nineteen years. God gave me my reward. I'm not going to ask for another one." Two people in wheelchairs followed him around the Fort Pierce course. One wanted to be his caddie; Owens laid his clubs in the man's lap for luck. Two other people on crutches shook his hand as he walked off the eighteenth green.

Owens enjoys playing the role of the star these days. He has waited long enough. Dressed all in blue after the PGA Senior, he gave TV interviews at length and signed every autograph. He knows his September song may be as short as it has been sweet, so he's not turning down any curtain calls. If his leg, his knee, his back or his eyes don't get him, then the birthdays will.

Does it bother him that the good old days may be so short after such a long delay? What a question for a man who's survived so much. Owens just gives the quiet, sober smile that so often seems to play under his graying mustache. "My heart runs from here to here," he says, putting his thumb on one side of his chest and running it all the way across to the other side. "Some guys, it's about as big as my fingernail."

How fast has the Senior Tour boomed and how high has it risen? A few numbers speak eloquently.

When Player won his first Masters in 1961, the annual purses for the PGA Tour were $1.5 million. This year, the *Senior* Tour will play for five times that much. In fact, the regular Tour didn't get its purses to $7.5 million until 1972.

All this has sprung up so quickly—almost spontaneously—that few outside the Senior Tour can grasp it. In 1978 NBC televised a nostalgia event called "The Legends of Golf." Nice, but nothing special. The 1979 "Legends of Golf," however, caught lightning in a bottle. Roberto De Vicinzo and Julius Boros won a six-hole playoff in which every extra hole had offsetting birdies. As old-timers sank one long putt after another, and

Don January was the first golfer to win a million dollars on the Senior Tour.

had fun doing it, the idea grew that these guys could still play the game. And entertain.

Pushed by PGA Tour Commissioner Deane Beman, the senior circuit started gingerly, then exploded. In 1980 there were two events, then five in 1981, eleven in 1982, eighteen in 1983, twenty-four in 1984, twenty-eight in 1985, thirty-one in 1986 and thirty-seven in 1987. Purses rose by an average of $1.5 million a season. Snead and Boros were key drawing cards in the early days, but the real luck was Palmer turning fifty at just the right moment in late 1979.

How hot are these old folks? Their tournaments are in the black before they ever tee up the first ball. The financial backbone of the seniors—the brainstorm that has made the whole shebang fly—is the two-day Pro-Am.

About 200 amateurs a week pay $1,000 to $4,500 each to play with these old heroes. Three nights of cocktail party socializing are also usually thrown in for the Pro-Am price. It is a testimony to the warmth and lie-swapping skills of the seniors that more than three-quarters of their events sell out their Pro-Ams. The seniors appreciate and cultivate their amateur partners, knowing they pay the freight.

For instance, Doug Sanders's group completed its Pro-Am round almost in the dark this week, yet (with only three spectators still in the grandstand), Sanders took an interest in each of the hackers' final putts, then headed for the nineteenth hole with them.

Companies can't line up fast enough to sponsor events. "We have thirty-five corporate sponsors waiting to start new events," said Tour official Ric Clarson. "In 1987, we'll have six new tournaments."

Despite the seniors' success, the old-folks circuit is still something of a secret. Only one senior event is carried on network television ("The Legends"), although eight tournaments are on cable TV with ESPN. Interestingly, gate attendance isn't as important economically as Pro-Am fees or corporate sponsorship. Still, some senior final rounds draw more than ten thousand people. A typical event might have five thousand for the finale and fifteen thousand for the week—with $7 to $12 tickets.

In fact, the Senior Tour has come on so strong and so fast in the last two years it has acquired the surest mark of rapid success: controversy. Anybody who's watched senior citizens play canasta knows that the older you get the more you argue about the rules. It's that way on the Senior Tour. The first casualty: Bob Toski, one of the game's most famous teachers. Early this season, Toski voluntarily withdrew from competition after fellow players claimed he had been moving his ball on the greens to avoid spike marks.

Arnold Palmer confidently strides toward the future.

"I don't think Bob Toski did anything purposely wrong," said Palmer, stating the senior consensus. "He was just a little careless. We're sorry it ever got out. On the other hand, we have to emphasize that we're the only game where you call penalties on yourself."

"Let's just say that the players had a meeting recently to remind each other that integrity was essential to the game," said Senior Tour spokesman Clarson. "Hey, nobody did anything really bad—no leather mashies [shoes] in the rough."

The best player in the brief history of the Senior Tour has been Don January, the first man to win a million dollars on the old coots' circuit. He's a tough Texan who likes to say, "I do it for the money, plain and simple. It keeps me going. I still owe the bank money. . . ."

On Friday here, January played despite having the flu. After his round, he collapsed in the locker room and had to be rushed to a hospital emergency room. As January—on a stretcher, receiving oxygen—was being wheeled out of the locker room, a worried Billy Casper looked at him and said, "It reminds you that this really is the Senior Tour."

Age, however, changes little in an athlete's heart. He looks different on the outside, but inside, everything feels so much the same. Within an hour of being released from the hospital, January was on the phone, assuring people at tournament headquarters that he was "perfect." Would he play in Saturday's round? "You bet," said January. "I may ride, though."

Why would a sick fifty-six-year-old who is fourteen shots out of the lead want to aggravate himself with two more rounds of pressurized competitive golf? After all, he couldn't really *win,* could he?

"Well," said January, "they pay more than one, don't they?"

• • •

On the seventy-first hole on Sunday, Lee Elder sank a fifty-foot uphill snake of a putt for a birdie to cut Gary Player's lead to two shots with one hole to play.

As they walked to the final tee, men who'd known each other and competed for decades, Elder's wife Rose understood that her man didn't have much chance to win. She didn't care. Lee saw Rose in the big gallery, grinned and winked, waggled his putter. Still in the hunt.

"God," said Rose Elder, "he just looks so happy."

TEMPER
FUGIT

It happened by the Marshes of Glynn, but Sidney Lanier would never understand. It was the beginning of the end for one of the great golf tempers of our time—mine.

I had gone there in part to drink the soul of the oak and put my heart at ease from men, as the poet advised, but, more particularly, to golf the old Sea Island course that lies off the Georgia coast by the wide sea marshes of Glynn.

On this April evening as I finished the eighteenth, recording my customary eighty-fourth blow, the "emerald twilights and virginal shy lights" that Lanier advertised a century ago had been replaced by the approach of a wind-swept storm. However, my last stroke had been no normal putt, but a tap-in birdie. Though the rest of my foursome knew better, I could not stop. I headed out alone to the Marshside nine.

By the third hole I was far out into the marshes, the storm apparently coming fast. I could retreat, or risk a drenching, and play one last picturesque reed-and-water-locked 475-yard par-five. Oh well.

My drive was as good as *Golf Digest* and graphite could bring out in me. My second shot—a three-wood barely flying a lake and fading toward the pin—was as perfect as the ten thousand shots that preceded it were flawed.

I faced a straight uphill four-foot putt for an eagle, a simple little darling that a hacker could play fifty years and never have again. As possessor of two sheer-luck eagles in ten years, and never a hole-in-one, I sensed this moment might not come again.

There was no one else on the course, only the wind, the smell of rain on the way, the wild, bleak marsh, the sea in the distance, and one four-foot putt for an eagle. I finally stepped up to what was going to be the

most enjoyable stroke of my life. I read it perfectly, hit it perfectly, and watched it stop dead in the center of the hole—but an inch short.

It is at such moments that I have made what reputation I have as a golfer, consigning me to the company of other famed Toms of Temper—Bolt and Weiskopf. A great black cloud crosses my mind, and unspeakable, unrealized forces that D. H. Lawrence would love rush out of the dark forest of my soul, and I do things that contradict every thread in the fabric of my life.

After just such an offending putt, I once took my mallethead putter and drove the devil ball 200 yards into the woods. My divot—nearly a foot long—was gouged not six inches from the hole.

The fellows I was playing with did not believe it then and probably do not believe it now, but I simply replaced the divot on the green and played the rest of the round without ever mentioning the incident, or apologizing. It was a very quiet foursome.

One middle-aged gentleman waited several holes, then said quietly from a safe distance, "You probably shouldn't have done that."

"Probably," I said.

I never took another such divot. But a year later I picked up another short missed putt, tossed the ball in the air like a baseball player hitting a fungo and caught it flush on the club face for another excellent drive from the green. It was a shot I'll never duplicate.

Actually, I have usually been comparatively mild-mannered on the greens. Putting never seemed to me to be worthy of a man's full attention. I may be the only golfer never to have broken a single putter—if you don't count the one I twisted into a loop and threw into a bush.

I was always harder on other clubs. That is why I have sticks from nine different sets in my fourteen-club bag. Each club has its story.

I once hit five straight balls into a water hazard. Just after the fifth splash, someone threw my five-iron into the middle of the lake. The someone was me. I don't remember how the subterranean decision—that the five-iron and I could never really be friends again—was made.

But I remember that a friend asked me why I had paused in the middle of my backswing before launching the club to its rippling grave. "I didn't want to leave it short," I answered.

Other clubs died less spectacularly: bent on trees, beaten against the earth. Once, while trying to discipline a five-wood, I broke three clubs. I threw the offending fairway wood at my Sunday bag and permanently bent the shafts of two more clubs that were in it.

Not every heave has been a disaster. I hurled a three-wood at an electric car and twisted the club head into an extreme hooded position. I hit it better that way.

A favorite driver somehow ended in the top of a tree at East Potomac

Park years ago, but I returned in winter when the leaves were gone and knocked it down with sticks.

The sand wedge is the only club that has never been thrown. I recognized early that I was a miserable wedge player. So whenever I give in to the urge ("Just once") to play the wedge and then skull it, I gently put the club back in the bag and then slap myself on the side of the head three times.

My golf temper has always been both a mystery and an amusement to friends who know me away from the game that Satan, himself, designed.

For years people who had never played golf with me were amazed to hear whatever had transpired in my latest round. It should be chiseled on my tombstone: "Tom Did That?"

Golf may not teach character, but it reveals it. Sometimes painfully. When you suddenly stop in the fairway, turn and walk two miles back to the clubhouse without bothering to retrieve your last sliced drive or bid adieu to the rest of your foursome . . . well, it is hard not to ask yourself questions during that walk.

Golf is a humbling game, but often it takes years to learn the right sort of humility. People have been trying to sort out their frayed feelings about golf for a century.

The best golf literature has little to do with Ben Hogan or instruction techniques, but is found in little volumes with titles like: *Kill It Before It Moves; How to Give Up Golf; It's the Damned Ball; 18 Holes in My Head; The Truth About Golf and Other Lies; The Dogged Victims of Inexorable Fate* and *89 Years in a Sand Trap.*

From the day I got my first set of clubs for high school graduation (what irony), I was no less perplexed than my predecessors by my own performance on the links. Every round seemed to be the same. I exploded at least once in every round. Sometimes, if the wheels came off early enough, I had time to repeat the entire Jekyll-to-Hyde cycle twice.

As every golfer knows, no one ever lost his mind over one shot. It is rather the gradual process of watching your score go to tatters shot after shot. It isn't even the big mistakes that eat at the soul. It is the great recovery shot that is undone by three putts. It is somehow playing five straight holes decently, but knowing that you have found a different way to bogey each one. So, when you finally reach the end of patience and pump one into the deep woods, and all is lost, and you know you have wasted six hours, nay, an entire day, for another 92, why, you are ready to kill—yourself.

Just as brutal is the process of watching yourself come apart. The progression was the same for me for a decade—from calm ("What a wonderful day. Great to be alive.") to annoyed resignation ("Oh well. It's just a game.") to suppressed whimpering ("Oh no. I'm going, going, gone.") to the final conflagration.

Invariably, as soon as I had my little tantrum—which nine times out of ten was not a club-throwing fit, just a complete loss of the inner control without which a golf ball becomes an unguided missile—I would relax, resign myself to fate and run off a string of pars.

But as soon as I realized I was playing well ("No no," I'd whisper to myself, "take no notice." But I had.), the tension would build again and I would go off like a toy pistol, again.

I never knew quite how to feel about my internal combustion. I knew Jack Nicklaus threw his last club at the age of eight. Nevertheless, I kidded myself that I was doing myself serious internal damage to hold the unbearable tortures of golf inside. I could feel the teeth of the gears of my soul being snapped off as I clenched my jaw.

Some infernal bon mot by one of the club-throwing philosophers—Nietzsche, Lawrence, even poor Mark Twain—would pop into my mind, and there my driver'd go, getting more airtime. "The only way to get rid of a temptation is to give in to it" must have undermined my will for the better part of a year.

So, with all this behind me, I was curious to see what I would do when the four-foot eagle putt stopped an inch short.

The world seemed to stand still. The marsh was silent. Mist hung in the air. If I had never thrown a club, this might truly have been the instant. But I had done it all. Many times. There was nothing in my repertoire of fury adequate to the moment. I either had to kill myself or shut up. I shut up. It wasn't much of a choice.

I picked up my ball and went to the next hole without so much as a "Darn it."

I played the rest of the nine in something of a daze. I remember saving par from a trap so deep that I couldn't see the top of the flag, and making a downhill fifty-foot birdie putt that some mischievous marsh sprite nudged into the hole.

The sky did not open until after I walked off the last green with the first subpar total of my life—if only for nine holes.

I still get mad, but not irrational. I occasionally flip a club, but not too far. And I still have an automatic choke on the back nine.

But now I leave the course feeling like Dr. Jekyll. Mr. Hyde drowned in the Marshes of Glynn.